THE WOUND[...]

THE FULCRUM AND THE FIRE

Other titles in the Wounded Pilgrim series
edited by Brian Thorne

THE DARK UNCERTAINTY
David and Sarah Clark

GRACE ABOUNDING
Dorin Barter

THE FULCRUM AND THE FIRE

WRESTLING WITH

FAMILY LIFE

Sue Walrond-Skinner

DARTON · LONGMAN + TODD

First published in 1993 by
Darton Longman & Todd Ltd
1 Spencer Court
140–142 Wandsworth High Street
London SW18 4JJ

ISBN 0-232-51984-6

A catalogue record for this book is available from the British Library

Phototypeset on 10½/13pt Bembo by Intype, London
Printed and bound in Great Britain
at the University Press, Cambridge

For my dearest husband,
a craftsman in every respect,
and in celebration of all the variety of
family forms in which my friends
choose to live.

CONTENTS

FOREWORD

The 'Wounded Pilgrim' series is inspired by the belief that spiritual growth demands an openness to experience and a willingness to accept the challenge of self-knowledge despite the suffering, confusion and agony of spirit which this can involve.

In different ways each book attempts to focus on the brokenness of the spiritual pilgrim and to face those areas of pain and struggle which are all too frequently swept under the carpet by the institutional churches or to which simplistic or dogmatic answers are given. The hope is that such books, written by those who do not flinch from the exploration of personal suffering and who acknowledge the complexity of social and psychological reality, will touch the hearts and minds of those who yearn for nourishment on their spiritual pilgrimage but who find the life of the Churches hard to bear, or who have long since abandoned the practice of institutional religion. The series is also a passionate response to the Churches' call for a decade of evangelism or evangelization. It reflects, however, a deep antipathy to the spirit of crusading and triumphalism and to the tone of theological and moral certitude which not infrequently characterize evangelistic campaigns.

The authors in this series write from the perspective of those who have no glib answers. Often, however, they bring a wealth of experience from their personal and professional lives and this is particularly true of Sue Walrond-Skinner's volume on family life. Sue is a family therapist of great distinction as well as a deacon in the Church of England and her book will be of compelling interest to those who have a special interest in counselling and pastoral work. Her contribution to the series reminds us, too, that those who dedicate much of their lives to the care of those in psychological and emotional difficulties are themselves committed to a pilgrimage which is often perilous and painfully demanding. The professional helper is a vulnerable human being like the rest of us and the suffering which comes from bearing the wounds of others frequently has about it something of the shadow of Calvary. The expertise which shines out from the pages of this book should not obscure the deep anguish from which no amount of professionalism can protect the helper who seeks to live his or her life in accordance with Kingdom values.

Chapter 11 provides moving accounts, in their own words, from those who have been caught up in the eye of the storm and their experiences leave the reader in no doubt about the agony which can result from family conflict and disintegration as well as the fragile joy which comes with the gradual rebirth of hope. We do well to remember, however, that those who are bold enough to embrace the roles of counsellor and pastor and to accompany those who suffer are as much in need of love and understanding as their clients. We are members one of another and perhaps that is the inescapable and ultimately redeeming truth about our joint inheritance as sons and daughters of the same God.

BRIAN THORNE

INTRODUCTION

'When you hear a reference to "the family" from a politician or a preacher, beware!' Many of us are beginning to regard such a maxim as an essential precaution against manipulation. We know we are about to be presented with some doubtful arguments, or that an otherwise unattractive programme is being sold to us on the basis that it will promote the well-being of 'the family' – and who is going to be against that?

Yet such a suspicious response, while entirely justified on the basis of our experience, needs to be balanced by some reflection on why such a manipulative use of 'the family' is so often successful. An appeal is being made to an ideal, and the ideal in turn appeals to the need of human beings for an area of intimacy grounded in early childhood. As is the case with ideals, it contains elements of truth, and at the same time enables us to escape from the ambivalence of our early years, and certainly to avoid facing the fact that for many 'the family' may be filled with destructive power.

What is needed is a careful evaluation of what 'the family' is, which means considering what kinds of families there are. We need to look both at representative examples and at the wealth of research that has been done. That will enable us to look at the reality alongside the ideal, and to stop using 'the family' as a way of manipulating people, and in the process responding with insensitivity to those whose experience of 'the family' may be very different from our own.

There is a further need, especially for those who link their Christian faith with their experience of and beliefs about family life. That is to examine afresh what is believed to be the content of the ideal. The

Bible, and the tradition of interpreting its message, has to be looked at carefully, so that the range of its examples and teaching can be perceived.

Out of that fresh examination of the realities of the range of family groupings in which people find themselves, and of the tradition of teaching about the family within the Church, there can emerge a new sensitivity to the needs of families. Then both politicians and preachers can make the message they proclaim and the programmes they offer more responsive. And in the process all of us in our different experiences of life in families can be supported as well as sharing that support with others, not least those whose life-styles appear so threatening to the supposed ideal of 'the family'.

Sue Walrond-Skinner has looked at the research evidence and at the theological tradition, and has brought to her study the sensitivity of her own therapeutic work. I am grateful to her for meeting the needs of the present time in relation to our experience of life in family with such a wide-ranging study.

PETER SELBY
William Leech Professorial Fellow in Applied Christian Theology in the University of Durham

PREFACE

In the beginning of the book of Genesis we are given a picture of God as fellowship, creating by means of the Creator Word within the embrace of the Holy Spirit. Even the myth of our beginnings suggests the 'familiness' of God, creating, brooding over and seeing that what he had made was good. The imagery is reinforced by the incarnation. Familiness and homeliness become the context of the Word's humanity. And family experience is a continuing part of Jesus' incarnate life – Cana, the home at Bethany, Peter's family home, Jesus' own home, the many occasions when he ate in other people's homes, the frequent references to weddings, the preparation for home, in the parables of the kingdom.

But family is shown to us as means and not as goal. Family is a means by which we gain the nurturance and security we need to live out our Christian calling. It is a means by which we learn by analogy about God's own trustworthiness and love. The wholeness and holiness to which all God's people are beckoned, are to be discovered through our relationships with one another in their many and various forms. This is the good news that the gospel is about – that God's love is to be discovered, in part, through loving relationships with our fellow human beings.

But for this good news to be heard during this final decade of the century, we have to let go of the outer form in order to cling more strongly to the inner meaning. If people are to be able to *hear* the good news, we have to be able to discover it *with them*, within the relationships that are *already conveying* to them love and faithfulness and grace. We have to learn from these relationships and hear the good news in them as well as helping them to expand their possibilities for mediating God's love to those who live within them. Most of all we need to affirm that it is out of the depths of failed and imperfect relationships that God's new miracle of healing grace is brought to birth. It is against the fulcrum and out of the fire that new life leaps into being.

This is, I believe, one of the essential lessons of Pentecost, when everyone heard in *their own tongue* the wonderful works of God. The marvel of Pentecost was that there was no requirement laid upon anyone to learn a new linguistic form — each heard the message in the tongue that he or she was already using, and with which he or she was familiar. In the same way, we are given the gift of the good news within the way of life that is natural and familiar to us — and within the form of family life in which we have chosen to live.

This book is a small contribution towards encouraging the good news to be heard during this Decade of Evangelism. I write as a Christian, as a family therapist and as a feminist woman. I am influenced by each of these and probably in that order, so the book reflects a specific point of view. I write in particular as someone who is mainly involved with counselling families in terms of their day to day difficulties and this is obviously a different perspective from that of the policy maker, the educator or the campaigner. However, a Christian who is interested in and concerned about family life needs to be aware of the importance of these perspectives too and I hope that this book reflects that fact. It goes for publication as the General Synod's new Working Party on the Family continues its work, trying to perceive the will of God for the human family within contemporary English society.

In the first paper produced by the Working Party, 'Towards a Theology of the Family', Stephen Barton (1993) comments:

> If God's desire is for human beings to grow to mature personhood as embodied, historical and interdependent, according to the pattern of Christ, then the domestic group — understood in a pluralistic and inclusive way — has an important role to play. Theologically, it can be a relationship and an institution where God's grace is experienced and where people can find nurture and healing, and thereby grow as persons in their individuality, in their social relations and in their relations with God. (p. 11)

I hope that the work of others that I have tried to summarize in this book as well as some thoughts of my own may also serve to forward the search for God within the joy and pain of family life.

In acknowledging the many people who have helped me during the last few months, I would like to thank first my dearest husband Graeme for all his love and care; even more than usual, he has kept the home running, as well as doing his own demanding job as a parish priest. I am grateful to Brian Thorne for all his help and patience; and I owe special thanks to Jane Wallworth for typing the manuscript with such care. My thanks also to Paul Pengelly from the Tavistock Institute of Marital Studies for helping me to create space for regular reflection in the midst of a busy job; to the Revd Clare Herbert for reading and helpfully commenting on Chapter 3; to John Carpenter and Bebe Speed, editors of the *Journal of Family Therapy*, for permission to use (in adapted form) some case material previously published in the Spring 1989 edition of the Journal; to Margaret Walker, librarian at the Tavistock Joint Library for her help and kindness; to Duncan Dormer at One-plus-One, Alison Webster at the Lesbian and Gay Christian Movement office and the staff of the Family Policy Studies Unit for their help and advice; to Pam Ware of the Lay Fraternity of Charles de Foucauld for her beautiful insight into the roof problem in Mark 2:4; to my new colleagues and friends in the Southwark Diocese who have shared their wisdom and knowledge with me during the past year; to those families and individuals who have struggled with so much difficulty and pain and who have taught me so much; and to all my friends who rejoice in their different forms of family and who enfold me in their love.

SUE WALROND-SKINNER
1 January 1993

1

❧

PRELUDE

More lies are spoken and written about family life than
any other subject.

FERDINAND MOUNT, *The Subversive Family*

The premise from which every idea in this book begins and on
which every development of thought is predicated is that *relationships*
are the crucial, central concern of every human being. Just because
this premise is basic, it can seem banal and commonplace, too obvious
to notice; my hope is that it can be heard again as the revolutionary,
mind-blowing discovery that it really is, so that what follows in these
pages will be usable in the tasks of being human, being Christian and
enabling others to hear the good news of the gospel during the last
decade of the twentieth century.

A few vignettes may serve to nudge the exploration of this over-
worked word, relationship, into life. In 1978 I spent four months in
India working at a home for people who were dying of various stages
of malnutrition, compounded by accidental injury and infectious
disease. Four months was too short a period to eradicate my western
prejudice, derived from common-sense and psychological theory, that
there exists a hierarchy of need – moving from the basic physiological
need for food and shelter to the higher levels of need for love,
self-esteem and self-actualization and on again to the meta-need for
unity, truth, justice, creativity and spiritual experience. Two memories
stand out for me. The first was the refusal of a dying woman to eat
a morsel of food, though she had been severely deprived of food
for months. The reason she gave was that her son, her only son, had
not come to her. Though fed, she still starved; though cared for,

1

she nevertheless experienced herself as abandoned. She died of her abandonment.

The second memory is similar but the experience was more widespread. Because of the difficulties of organizing food supplies in this disorganized part of the city, we frequently ran out of either rice or bread. On almost every occasion, those patients who traditionally ate rice but not bread refused the bread and those who ate bread but not rice refused the rice. Each group carried within itself an understanding of what was suitable and acceptable as food, based upon the customs and values of their family, caste and religious grouping. Such an extreme circumstance as starvation does not automatically or even generally overrule the need to remain loyal to deeply experienced relationships, nor, in the first example, did the satisfaction of the immediate need for food take away the profound pain of abandonment by a loved one to the point where life could have become worth living again. Even in other extreme circumstances, such as the concentration camps of the Second World War or the crash landing of an aeroplane in a remote mountain area, when the eating of strange or forbidden foods became essential to life, many were unable to overcome their taboos when these infringed a deeper sense of relatedness to others.

These two memories reflect two different kinds of relationship. The first is the close-in, intimate personal relationship of mother and son; the second is the extended, non face to face relationship with a wider circle of family members, friends, compatriots, or even just other human beings, to whom one feels connected and with whom one experiences relationship. The first kind of relationship may be expressed as personally and intimately as the passing of milk from mother to child or the passing of semen from man to woman. The second may be as distant and diffuse as 'the family of humanity', where the object of the sense of relatedness is neither seen nor touched but is nevertheless experienced in a compelling and powerful way by the subject who feels she or he 'belongs' to it. These two kinds of relationship differ in type rather than in degree and the disturbance in or exclusion from both is usually experienced by all human beings as profoundly distressing.

I am stating nothing new at all. We have known since Harry Harlow's experiments with monkeys in the 1940s and the detailed observations of John Bowlby in the 1950s that young monkeys and young human beings alike suffer severe emotional pain when they are deprived of attachment to one or more close survival figures. We know too, from the many studies completed on the effects of war and sudden disaster, that communities and individuals associated with them suffer severe dislocation and alienation through the upheavals that result from these disasters. But I need to underline the crucial *importance* of this knowledge and if possible invite you, the reader, to recall to your mind an *experience* of this knowledge which either involved you personally as a subject or, as in my experience in India, as an observer at first hand.

Let me offer another set of examples from my own experience of relationship. When I was four I behaved so badly one evening that the unthinkable occurred. My mother got so fed up with me that she walked out. I can picture the scene precisely. She said nothing at all. She simply walked into the hall, put on her coat and a snug fitting felt hat, opened the front door, walked down the path to the gate – and then – even more unbelievably, went through the gate and down the lane to the bus stop. I was stupified. I watched her walk as far as the gate and then I began to run after her as fast as my tiny legs could carry me. 'Mummy, mummy,' I cried, 'don't leave me, don't leave me.' Even as I write the words, the tears come back into my eyes. The sobs that convulsed every inch of my body then, still lurk somewhere close in my chest and in my throat. *'Don't leave me'*, that terrible cry of dereliction, echoed on the cross, that existential dread of abandonment by our closest most dearly beloved, our most profoundly needed human other – be they parent or child or partner or lover or friend – this dreadful pain of threatened or actual loss is what tells us more clearly than anything else what relatedness is all about. This is the first type of relationship – the close-in intimate relationship of kiss and care and touch.

But the second is not different in degree, only in kind. During the first three months of 1991, I, alongside the rest of humanity, experienced the shocking, dislocating and alienating experience of being part of a war waged by a huge and powerful block of nations against Iraq, ostensibly in order to liberate Kuwait from Iraq's control. Before the war began I wrote to the bishop of the diocese where I then lived and asked him who was going to help us to bear the pain and

3

the anguish, the guilt and the grief which would be contingent upon us declaring war against Iraq, however just and reasonable the immediate cause. I do not think he understood the question – at least I have no evidence that he did – and the fact is that we were all asked to experience the pain of our relationships being dislocated and fractured, as we watched the sanitized images of war projected to us hourly on our television screens. With the minimum of psychological help, other than what, through mutual support, we were able to provide for ourselves, we had to cope with the experience of participating in our own, because of the other's destruction. During 1992 the experience has again been different in kind though not in degree. With less immediate guilt but perhaps even greater helplessness, we have watched Somalia starve and the former republic of Yugoslavia tear itself to bits.

I am part of a network of relationships which unite me ultimately with all my human sisters and brothers in a way which is profoundly important to my sense of emotional well-being. I belong to this family of humanity most of which I cannot see or touch, as really and actually as I belong to my close-in family of immediate significant others. And I am damaged and diminished by my part in their destruction as really and actually as if they were close family members because I have two overwhelming types of relational need. I need to belong to a close, intimate network and I need to know that the world I belong to out there is OK. I need to belong to a family and I need to belong to a Family and both have crucial significance for my experience of life and the living of it.

Why should this be the case? There are several ways we might answer. The family is a fulcrum which brings its influence to bear on our most powerful experiences of life. The family provides for us a hearth, whose fire warms, kindles, purges and sears all our human experience with the heat and brightness of its flames. Each of us carries within us an array of family experiences, many repressed into our unconscious, and acquired from the earliest moments of our existence. We begin our life within the body of another human being and we are forced to live our lives, whether we choose to or not, in an awareness of and participation in family relationships. Thus we carry within our internal world and live out in our external lives a knowledge of family that determines how we respond to every other

4

attempt to structure our lives meaningfully and purposefully. Our experience of family influences the way in which we understand our lives and it influences the way in which we respond to the theories and constructs that aid our understanding. In a major way therefore it determines how we respond to the gospel and to its central constructs of love, death and resurrection, and it influences both the way the gospel is heard and the way it is preached.

Some of our most ubiquitous experiences of family include our experience of closeness and fusion with others; our alienation and separation from them; our sense of being inside and outside simultaneously (either of these being felt to be positive or negative), our experience of transition, and our repeated attempts to reconcile our lived reality with a utopian concept of family life. Depending upon the quality of these experiences in our lives we shall hear the gospel in a radically different way, and because *every one* of us is deeply affected by our experiences of family life, both the preacher and the hearer of the Good News engage with the gospel through the medium of the internal and external family experience of each of them. No one can claim to have better or more experiences of family life – the validity of each person's experience is the same. But the experience of each of us is different and it may be a hard struggle for the preacher and the hearer of the good news to identify with the experience and perception of the other. Expertise in family belongs to us all, but we may be worlds apart in the kind of family experience we have had.

It may be hard therefore to understand the pain of being outside a set of family relationships and wanting to come in if one has spent one's life being inside and struggling to get out. It may be impossible to understand the violence and abusiveness of someone else's family, if one's own experience has been of conflict lived through and worked with well, or with conflict repressed and denied behind a conforming mask of respectability. A parent's abandonment of a child or a wife's abandonment of her husband may be outrageous to the person who has struggled for many years to remain within an unfulfilling and debilitating relationship. A third party's wresting away of the partner of another may be a matter of total condemnation to the person who has never longed in vain for the deep comfort and security of a committed sexual partnership.

Our own experience of family makes us experts in the phenomenon of family but ignoramuses in terms of its particularity for others. This means that we need to follow two apparently contradictory courses. We need to be reticent in applying our own experience to that of others and judging our own to be the norm of what ought to be. But we need also to be creative in seeking from within ourselves the resources for understanding the other's pain and joy. Family life is likely to have wounded us as well as moulded us into the shape that we are and it is our wounds which create the beginnings of solidarity. They are our most reliable tools for constructing a shared meaning with others and the door through which we may walk with a hand outstretched to pastor and proclaim.

This leads me to a third important assumption which undergirds this book. Much of our experience of family, whether we are Christians or not, is hell. In fact Christians who are faced with the ordinary sufferings of family life that everyone must face to some degree are often further assaulted by guilt and shame at their inability to rise to what they perceive to be the requirements of discipleship in their situation. It may be, and usually is, impossible to experience the hope and certainty of resurrection whilst one is being crucified on the cross of unaffirmed identity, poverty, sickness or a sterile or violent sexual relationship. The disappointed hopes for a teenage child whose life choices appear to be death-dealing to themselves and their parents alike, may produce only shame and guilt and a feeling that God is clearly dead. The breakdown of a marriage relationship always brings an experience of death, which will be carried, hidden deep in the centre of the self, until the grave. Whatever subsequent experiences of fulfilment come to that person through new and functional relationships, the past will be part of that new present. The pain of these situations deserves the deeply creative understanding which only the unjudging eye of Christ can bring. It certainly does not need the destructive assault of Christian moralizing however well disguised.

By now another assumption at the root of this book may be becoming clear. Family needs to be interpreted in a broad and inclusive sense if it is to do justice to people's real life experience; and the issues involved in wrestling with family life concern all those human issues which have to be addressed by small, intimate, face to face groups in their daily life, as well as in the relationship of these groups with the wider community. The term family is not of course coterminous with the term relationship or even 'important' relationship. We may have important relationships with the milkman, the bank manager, our work colleagues, our school friends or the people we meet each week or fortnight in the dole queue. We may have long-term relationships with friends and spiritual directors and people we meet each week in the pub or in church or at the bowls club – but none of these would probably rate in our minds as family. To equate 'family' with 'relationship' will not do. Such a definition would be so inclusive as to be meaningless. Yet we need to be clear that the term 'family' cannot be restricted either to what are sometimes described as 'normative' or conventional family situations. Such a definition would be so exclusive as to bear no relationship to real life. This problem of definition is an experiential one as well as a problem of theory, as the Rapoports (1982) point out:

> When people speak of their families, they may mean a rather vague collection of people extending outward in space and backward in time. It may never be necessary for them to give an accounting of who is included and who is not, though some occasions require the drawing of boundary lines e.g. who should be invited to a party, or wedding reception or who should get what by way of inheritance. (p. 486)

We will return to the issue of definition in chapter 5.

Moreover we must not lose sight of that other area of relatedness and sense of belonging that is as emotionally real to us as the near-in relationships of our intimate network. Our sense of belongingness to the family of humanity, to a race, a nation or a religion is different from the casual or ongoing or important relationships we have with many of the people to whom we have referred – it is, as we have noted, family-like and family-related, different in kind but not different in degree of emotional and psychological importance.

During the week before Christmas 1991, the BBC showed a series of short films describing family situations which the editor entitled *Not the Nuclear Family* and these were followed by a longer film which examined social trends and some of the influences that were shaping the form of family life today. During the same week, the *Guardian* published a leader which analysed several important indices of family life and drew some important conclusions. In speaking to at least a dozen groups of Christians in the two or three months that followed, I found hardly a single person who had seen any of these programmes or had read the newspaper article which followed. This may of course simply be a reflection upon the preoccupations of Church members during the week before Christmas, which do not include much television viewing! However, considering that all of these groups were convened in order to discuss with me some aspect of family life, I found it strange that so few people had wanted to acquaint themselves with some easily accessible data about the status of family life in Britain today.

I suspect that the pre-Christmas rush was not the whole reason why a series entitled *Not the Nuclear Family* received such scant attention from these various groups of Christians. The present state of the nuclear family is unpalatable, incomprehensible and unbeliev-able to a significant portion of the Church. Part of the reason for this lies in the generalized ambivalence that all of us experience in some measure towards the family. 'The family is the cradle of ambiv-alence' remarked Ackerman (1966) in an important early book, and the family does indeed evoke deeply ambivalent feelings in us because of our early experiences in it of dependency, frustration, fear and control, intermingled in varying measure with the love, support and hope we may also have gained from it. But because the experience of family evokes such ambivalence, we are faced with particular problems at its threatened demise. Like all objects about which we are ambivalent we defend them forcefully, because we have to defend them not only from the destructiveness of the outside world but also from the destructiveness that lies within ourselves. The prospect of a disintegrating family writ large within society awakens in us guilt as well as fear because of what we have contributed to the demise of a structure that haunts us with the continual but elusive hope that our dependency needs can be satisfied.

But these threats to the structure of family life are profoundly disturbing to the Christian for additional reasons too. The break up of the family, of the familiar, creates an experience of unease in Christians because it resonates with other areas of unease evoked by questions of ministry, membership and faith. The debate about the resurrection, the controversy over the ordination of women to the priesthood in the Anglican Church and falling rolls and church attendance all contribute to an atmosphere of uncertainty which accentuates the need to hold fast to traditional values. Paradoxically therefore, the family, as well as being an area of intense anxiety, simultaneously holds a magnetic appeal for the Church. Working parties, reports, motions passed in General Synod, television and radio programmes involving churchmen all proliferate, as do the numbers of books and articles being produced on the subject.

For the family signifies more to the Christian than simply the institution itself or even the emotional connectedness with one's own roots and early experiences which are significant for us all. For many Christians, the family, both as a concept and as an emotional experience, has come to hold together something of profound significance at the central core of their Christian faith. If the family is in danger, then faith is endangered, so the family must be defended in order that the Christian faith itself can be sustained.

How have we arrived at this point? By colluding too easily I believe in the proffered alliance between emotional need and the invitations of faith; by exploiting each person's profound emotional need to belong and subsuming this within the core beliefs of Christianity. The family, like other structures of society, has provided a useful vehicle for conveying, preserving and transmitting the faith, and just as the state has needed the family in order to sustain itself, so too has the Church. Thus the Church, alongside other institutions and individuals, is struggling to understand the changes that are happening to the family, to keep pace with them and maybe to influence them a little too.

Considering the complexity of the subject and the extreme rapidity with which the family and its environment changes, it is hard for anyone to wholly avoid the criticisms of Ferdinand Mount.

> Soaring divorce and tumbling marriage rates, more old people and violent swings in the number of school leavers, more than a quarter of babies born outside marriage, either to women on their own or to 'cohabiting' couples: these are just some of the moving pieces in the kaleidoscope which family and living patterns have recently become. (Roll (1991), p. 11)

Policy makers, government planners, sociologists, family theorists, marital and family clinicians and the many other professionals who offer care and support to families all struggle to keep up with the movement of shape and colour and form in the kaleidoscope. The task is formidable and the speed of change phenomenal. Yet however slippery a concept it is and however chameleon-like the family may appear to us to be, we have to do our best to ground ourselves in some of the fundamental actualities of family life as it is today. We have to consider the very real pressures upon the family that are being exerted and the way in which it is having to develop and adapt to a changing social, political and global environment. We have to understand that change and development are the only means by which something new can be born. Theories, myths, romanticized notions derived from our own pasts or our own hopes and fears for the future do not constitute a sound basis from which to study the family or to consider the ways in which we, as Christians, might be able to be of service to it and its members. In chapters 4 and 5 we will therefore look at some basic facts and figures from which we can begin to develop some relevant definition of the contemporary family. But first we will examine some different approaches that have been taken recently to the family as a unit of study and research.

2

GATEWAYS

Of course the first thing to do was to make a grand
survey of the country she was going to travel through.
'It's something like learning geography' thought Alice,
as she stood on tiptoe in hopes of being able to see a
little farther.

LEWIS CARROLL, *Through the Looking Glass*

The changing ways in which the family has been regarded by those
who are professionally involved in its study, influences and shapes our
views of the way in which we feel family life should be lived. In
trying to understand these different approaches we cannot be quite
as ambitious as Alice or make a 'grand survey', but we might stand
on tiptoe for a moment in the hopes of being able to see a little
farther. Theory builders in sociology, psychology, therapy and philosophy have all focused attention upon the family and have drawn
various conclusions about the core relationships between women and
men, between parents and children, and about the way in which
gender and human sexuality can best be managed and understood.
What often becomes clear with hindsight is the way in which each
new emphasis, each new ideology, has its period of ascendency and
is then overtaken by something else. What is often less clear is the
way in which the theorist is himself profoundly influenced by his
own family experiences. Even when we are considering so-called
objective theories about the family, we are caught up in a hidden
reflexive process where the family is itself a key influence upon the
theory of family that is being explained. Studies of people making
studies of families and studies of these studies make fascinating

11

reading!* The point to be emphasized here is that none of us, not even the most scientific theoretician, comes to the notion of family value free. We are all deeply influenced by our own experiences and beliefs and it is difficult to avoid creating models of the family which do not simply yield the answers that we wish them to give.

We need now to consider some different theoretical approaches that have been taken to the family. Between them they help us to understand some different ways the family can be viewed. The family as a meeting place between the personal and the political, between the public and the private, can be approached from both a sociological and a psychological point of view. It can also helpfully be studied in terms of its history as a social institution and criticized as such from the perspective of radical political thought. We will examine some representative views of each of these approaches.

Functionalism

The functionalist approach is particularly associated with the name of Talcott Parsons. A giant amongst sociologists, Parsons dominated American social science in the post-war years. His great contribution at the time was to describe the functions which marriage and the family fulfil for the wider social system of society. The family is a prime agent of socialization, transmitting values and norms to the next generation.

Parsons provides a general theory of the family based on an analysis of its structure, roles and functions. The most important of these are the organization of sexual relationships, the procreation, rearing and socialization of children, the structuring of role-related behaviour between men and women, parents and children and the creation of a haven of physical and emotional support for individuals from the alienating experiences of society.

This approach tends to view families which can serve all these

* See for example Schatzman's (1973) commentary on Freud's (1911) commentary on Schreber's (1903) account of his relationship with his father, and Rycroft's (1985) commentary on Schatzman! The various studies of Freud's family too are informative: for example, McGoldrik's (1989) genogram. Autobiographies also help us to understand subjective influences upon theory building. See for example R. D. Laing's (1985) autobiography, *The Making of a Psychiatrist.*

functions as normative and therefore views the conventional nuclear family as being best equipped to produce a happy, secure and lasting environment for its members. Thus although apparently supporting a wide range of possible family structures, this approach to the family tends in practice to reduce all families to the conventional type of nuclear family. In particular, it isolates two features as essential – a hierarchy of generations and a differentiation between the genders, whereby the man provides the instrumental and the woman the expressive functions within the family group.

In Parsonian logic, the family is essentially structured around the marital relationship. The husband is economic provider and the wife nurturer of both the children and the emotional life and needs of the family group as a whole. Parsons identified a transition that has occurred over time from the wider kin grouping to the modern nuclear family and he links this transition to the developing economic and social order of western society as it moved to a capitalist industrial society.

At a subliminal level, Parsons' functionalist approach still remains influential in our current thinking about family – it still normalizes the nuclear family as a social unit that has emerged over time, and presents it as the structure which best harmonizes the needs of the individual and those of society. It is an approach to the family which has been largely absorbed in an uncritical way by many who seem oblivious of its recent theoretical roots. But more recently, critics have pointed out its many weaknesses – its static nature; its inadequacy when faced with opposing anthropological analysis, demonstrating the fluid occupation of roles and functions between men and women in a variety of cultures and societies; and its inability to explain or assist the inevitable tensions and conflicts which emerge within the nuclear family structure. In particular, the functionalist approach makes assumptions about the history of the modern family unit which are difficult to sustain in the light of recent empirical research.

History

Our historical roots provide a unique perspective on our contemporary dilemmas: history is the key which so often unlocks the meaning of the present within both our personal and social consciousness. By the same token, a defective knowledge of history leads to many erroneous assumptions being made both about our present situation and the future of our social institutions. For Christians in their effort to understand the contemporary family it may also be the case, as Dowell (1990) points out, that 'defective history leads to defective theology' (p. xi), and to defective theological assumptions about the nature and purpose of the type of family we call the modern nuclear family. In addition, Casey (1989) points out that our modern preoccupation with the family as a unit of study, by which we make sense of the past, gives the nuclear family a spurious identity. To study the family in isolation narrows the field of enquiry because it blots out its interconnections with other social institutions and other aspects of life that provide its essential context. We can do no more here than consider one or two important themes to be found in this historical perspective on the modern nuclear family.

It used to be thought that the Industrial Revolution heralded many changes in the structures of domestic life because of the changed economic demands upon individuals. However, a considerable amount of recent research has succeeded in exploding several myths about the family. First, the work of Laslett (1972) and others on family size suggests that there is no clear distinction between the extended family household of the period before the Industrial Revolution and the isolated nuclear unit of contemporary society. Examining records from between 1564 and 1821, he found that only about 10% of households contained kin beyond the nuclear family. This is the same percentage as in 1966. He discovered that the average actual size of family households remains remarkably constant although there were wide regional and class variations within that broad similarity. Even if the modern family unit has fewer kin living in the immediate neighbourhood on whom it can call in a crisis, there are obviously vastly more sophisticated means of remaining in close communication with kith and kin now, through fast transport, reliable postal services and the telephone.

This means that the supporters of the conventional family cannot argue that the absence of extended family members introduces a different and sharper pressure on current family life nor that the nuclear family has any unique position within the wide configuration of different family forms. Likewise its opponents cannot argue that the small nuclear family unit is anything particularly new or malignant.

The truth appears to be that there has always been a multiplicity of family forms ranging from large extended households to smaller units, where a marriage relationship is often but not always the central relationship. Flandrin (1979), for example, argues that very different family patterns have always existed between different social classes so that neither uniformity of structure nor a progressive development from one family type to another can at all be discerned from a reading of history. Second, there is no easy comparison to be made around the idea of the stability of family life. The argument that families had a greater degree of stability prior to the late nineteenth and twentieth centuries when the divorce rate began to rise to its present level of around 165,000 a year (OPCS, 1992) cannot be sustained. A high mortality rate meant that families were regularly ruptured by death and that the experience of step-parenting was as common before the nineteenth century as it is today.

Third, the idea that women used to stay at home and fulfil domestic and child-rearing functions more continuously than they do today is clearly erroneous. In pre-modern societies throughout the world, the great majority of women have always been 'working wives and mothers'. Only a minority of affluent and privileged social groupings have been able to avoid the need for women to contribute to the family income either within a home-based industry or in factories or on the land. This fact allows for no simple causal connections to be made between, for example, current problems of social disorder and the absence of mothers from the home. The *cri-de-coeur* of many of the contributors to the symposium on the family 'Families for Tomorrow' held in Brighton in 1990 regretting women's involvement in full-time work, is in fact only the wistful memory of a small minority social grouping.

Psychoanalysis

Psychoanalytic approaches to the family have provided a rich arena of study. Freud's interest remained almost entirely concerned with the internal world of the individual but nevertheless his work is deeply embedded in the study of the family through the eyes of his patients and through his own direct observations. His theory of human development presupposes a conventional two-parent nuclear family, derived from researches conducted within the narrow field of the Austrian middle-class society of his time, from which his patients came. These are obviously limiting factors, but nevertheless the depth and significance of Freud's insights remain extremely important. Because his primary, almost exclusive focus was on the childhood experience of his patients, he was deeply interested in the way in which the structure of the very young child's mental and emotional life developed through his or her earliest experience of parental figures. The family therefore assumes an importance in the earliest psychoanalytic writings that was rare in psychological or other scientific work before Freud.

However, Freud's emphasis on the family was always as a means to discovering the deeply repressed origins of his patients' neurotic disorders. He failed to develop any theory of the family as a group or to focus attention on the way in which the behaviour and experiences of one family member directly affect and are affected by all the others. Even so, in uncovering the process of development of the human psyche and the way in which it copes with traumatic experiences, he also highlighted the seminal importance of family relationships, putting them 'on the scientific map', so to speak, albeit in an oblique way.

Three very different developments of psychoanalytic thought which emerge later have all been highly influential in shaping our understanding of the family. The object relations school of psychoanalysis has been particularly important in this respect, developing through the work of several different figures, including Melanie Klein and W. R. D. Fairbairn. Two particular expressions of it were Winnicott's work with mothers and their babies and the enormously influential work of John Bowlby, on the theory of human attachment and loss.

Winnicott's great contribution was to accelerate the process whereby the *environment* (and especially the family environment) of the baby and hence of other individual family members was understood to be as important as the individual's internal world. In a very real sense Winnicott bridges the gap between the intra-psychic focus of Freud and Klein and the wider systems focus of Parsons. For

Winnicott, mother and baby and the relationship between them are all equally important. The individual's psychological development consists in making a transition from her internal experiences to the world of external reality. She does this first through her experience of her mother's breast and then through the fantasy world of play and by means of a variety of 'transitional objects' (toys, dummies, rags, etc.), which represent security and attachment for the child, and which help her to move towards making full 'object' relationships with people. In so far as the child is provided with a 'facilitating environment' primarily by her mother, she will be able to develop towards maturity.

There are various problems in Winnicott's analysis, as there are in Freud's. He has, for example, as Rycroft (1985) puts it, a 'blindness to things masculine and sexual' (p. 142). Fathers are viewed as a kind of auxiliary mother rather than as people who hold influence and create relationships in their own right. Second, his thinking can be misused to burden mothers with full responsibility for their child's functional development. Rather in the same way as Bowlby's early work on maternal deprivation was to set the scene after the Second World War for the recall of women to the work of full-time motherhood, so Winnicott's emphasis on the facilitating environment was easily recruited into an ideological stance against women's choice to work both inside and outside the home as and when they saw fit.

Bowlby's later work on attachment and loss clarified his own theoretical position. All human infants, like those of other species, require a mother-figure (though not necessarily the biological mother) with whom they can form their first and earliest attachment, and the quality and reliability of this earliest attachment will affect the way in which the individual is able to develop trusting and confident relationships during adulthood. All human beings experience separation anxiety when the object of their attachment is withdrawn and it is extremely important, in the early months and years of the child's life, that bonding with the primary carer is interrupted as little as possible. Nevertheless, the child and the adult can be helped to manage separation and loss if they are provided with other loving and trustworthy relationships and if they are allowed the opportunity to regress into a needful dependency.

Bowlby and others have helped us understand much more clearly the ongoing need of the individual to become functionally dependent throughout his or her adult life. Far from being pathological, adults need to learn how to accept being dependent again when a situation demands it. Admission to hospital for example or the normal processes of grieving, and any occasion when the individual needs to ask for help, all require a person to become temporarily dependent again. Bowlby's work was also capable of springing the deterministic trap of earlier psychoanalytic formulations, so that early family experiences, whilst being important, were not seen as being the sole determinant of later health and happiness. New opportunities provided by later relationships were all potentially capable of healing early wounds and the possibility of growth and development for the individual's personality could continue through the many relational experiences of later life.

The second strand of psychoanalytic thought useful to us in our wrestle to understand the family is that of ego psychology. Eric Erikson amongst others divested Freudian theory of much of its more mystical elements and its preoccupation with the least conscious and most irrational part of the personality, and grounded it instead in the workings of the more conscious part, the ego. He viewed the ego as the centre of the person's sense of identity and as central to one's sense of 'being one's self, of being all right and of being on the way to becoming what other people, at their kindest, take one to be' (Erikson (1950), p. 35).

Erikson approached the human psyche from a broad background of art, anthropology and child psychology as well as from the viewpoint of psychoanalysis. This enabled him to consider the role of culture in determining differences in child-rearing practices which in turn influenced the ways in which patterns of family life developed. The social environment of the family, society and the wider culture all become important in Erikson's work as do a longitudinal view of human development. The fact that Erikson views the whole of life as a process of development towards maturity means that the individual's intimate relationships, not only in the early years with parents, but throughout life with partners, children, friends, colleagues and mentors of every kind provide a complex relational field within which development takes place.

One of Erikson's major contributions was therefore to set the scene for important developments in family theorizing based on his well known description of the life cycle and the progressive stages of development through which the individual will typically pass. Each of the eight stages marks a point of developmental crisis, an opportunity for the individual to expand his or her personality and move on to the next stage, or 'to get stuck', or to regress for a while until a new impetus for growth can be discovered. Each stage presupposes the importance of family experiences and of the connection between family and the wider social system. An important step forward is therefore taken in understanding the influence of family.

But there are still problems. Erikson's work is still essentially focused on the individual rather than upon the family group as a set of relationships that interacts both ways amongst its individual members. More importantly, Erikson's life cycle theory still 'irons out' cultural differences and conflict. As Poster (1978) puts it,

> The main difficulty for a theory of the family with this focus on synthesis is that it shifts the field away from conflicts, from discontinuity, from antagonisms and allows one only to see society as a harmonious unity, as a self-regulating mechanism, always re-adjusting itself, never needing to be challenged fundamentally or to be over-turned, never really oppressive. All family structures are adequate, to Erikson, as long as they provide for values that will fit the individual in to society armed with his 'schedule of virtues'. (p. 71)

The third strand of thinking that stems from psychoanalytic thought is one which certainly confronts the potentially oppressive nature of the family as an institution. It is associated with the names of R. D. Laing, David Cooper, Aeron Esterson and their colleagues. In contrast to the extremely focused, narrow field of attention engaged by Freud, Laing relates the family and the many problems he sees associated with it to a range of social structures, to existential philosophy, eastern mysticism and to radical political thought. He examines the way in which family members construct a social reality around the shared understanding and meaning attributed to the self-images and identities of its members. These shared meanings, which are constructed from the shared experience of living together, create a common understanding of the experience of 'being-in-the-world'.

He suggests that everyone possesses an 'internalized' family of relationships which has been introjected from the past. These relationships influence and help to create an understanding of the current family relationships of which the individual is a part. Each family member superimposes on to the current family an understanding of relationships derived from the past, from which a shared understanding of roles, ritual and behaviour is constructed. This shared meaning is reinforced by being lived out in the present and becomes powerful over its individual participants to the extent to which there is a conjunction between past and present. Thus, individuals may get caught into this shared construction of meaning and unable to break free. A sick member for example is unable to shake off the attribution or 'label' of sickness because of the power of the shared understanding, derived from the past and enacted in the present, which is constructed around this label by all the members of the family. Laing concentrates particularly on the parent–child relationship and exposes the many ways in which the various dyadic relationships within the family enable each member (but particularly parents in their relationship with children) to manipulate and mystify each other. This approach to the family views the individual and the family group as involved in a struggle, whereby the individual needs to break away in order to gain self-fulfilment and fully to achieve identity.

'Families are bloody training camps' says one of the characters in the Laingian film *Family Life*. Thus Laing and his associates view the conventional nuclear family with suspicion and as intrinsically harmful to people's psychological and emotional well being. Cooper (1972), in his book *The Death of the Family*, regarded alternative family structures such as communes, with their open and detached relationships, as better milieux for the rearing of children and for developing healthy individual identities.

Radical politics

Likewise, radical political approaches to the family view the conventional nuclear unit as responsible for the repression of both women and children. Marxists hold the nuclear family responsible for creating the psychological conditions which encourage its members to conform to dominant social structures. Engels (1884), for example, saw monogamy as marking a new stage in human evolution and creating a conflict which had been entirely unknown in prehistoric times.

It was the first form of the family based not on nature but on economic conditions, namely, on the victory of private property over original, naturally developed common ownership. The rule of the man in the family, the procreation of children who could only be his, destined to be the heirs of his wealth – these alone were frankly avowed by the Greeks as the exclusive aim of monogamy. For the rest it was a burden, a duty to the gods, to the state and to their ancestors, which just had to be fulfilled. (p. 233)

The development of the conjugal nuclear family is seen as inextricably entwined with the development of capitalism and thus the family is seen as holding an ideological importance for capitalist society and for the whole retention and operation of the capitalist political and economic system. Families are inherently conservative in their relationship to social structures and therefore make it difficult for individuals who are oppressed economically, sexually or by other power imbalances to change the *status quo*. Likewise, feminists argue that the family, seen in the narrow sense of the conventional nuclear family, retains men's dominance over women and engenders expectations and behaviour in men and women that militate against more healthful gender relationships. They also criticize the family and the institution of marriage for preventing women from having full control over their own fertility through contraception and abortion. Feminism will be considered in more detail in chapter 4.

Others who approach the family from the radical political point of view are concerned to assert the rights of homosexuals to enter a form of legally recognized committed relationship analogous to marriage, together with their right to adopt and rear children. All of these groups are concerned to reform radically the traditional nuclear family as well as gain greater validation for other forms of family experience. Poster (1978), in summarizing the aspirations of those who approach the family from a radical political perspective, suggests that

the isolation of the family from other families and from the work structure needs to be reformed. A democratic community is called for in which family relationships can find wide sources of support. Relations between husband and wife and parent and child must be rid of their possessive and devouring character. Multiple patterns of marital relations must be recognised, so that feelings of affection can expand throughout the community . . . love, domesticity and empathic child care are in themselves unobjectionable. When restricted to the contemporary family they work to undermine sociability and distort relations within the family. A democratic community must avoid the terrifying choice confronting people today of commitment to the family or complete loneliness. (p. 204)

Pro-family

The 1980s saw the development of vigorous pro-family movements in the United States and in Europe. Arising out of what were perceived to be the threats from feminism and the radical political approaches, from the soaring divorce rate and from huge increases in extra-marital pregnancies, several strands, often fired by widely different motivations, have coalesced under the pro-family banner. The International Congress on the family held in Brighton in 1990 provided a forum for many of the British promoters of family values to come together, although other pro-family groups would not have wanted to be represented there (Bogle, 1991).

This in fact is one of the difficulties. As Elliot (1986) points out: 'The counter-movement in favour of the family is a complex phenomenon containing diverse and mutually antagonistic elements' (p. 205). It is often difficult for people working from very different perspectives to join together with others with whom, on many other issues, they find themselves to be diametrically opposed.

The movement has been spearheaded by the political Right and, both in the United States and Britain, the Republican and Conservative parties have claimed to be 'the party of the family'. It was one of the major ironies of the 1980s that in Britain the most pro-family party presided over by the most pro-family leader witnessed the most significant increase in the rates of divorce and extra-marital pregnancy this century. From the point of view of the political Right, the family is an agent both of social care and control, enabling the state to divest itself of a range of direct responsibilities for the care and welfare of various vulnerable groups. Community care policies for the sick, the elderly, the disabled and the mentally infirm are highly dependent upon the family as an institution being both strong and morally responsive. A closely related argument is the economic one, which urges the return to clearly differentiated gender roles. The return of women from market-place to home is seen as having the multiple benefits of relieving unemployment, reducing the need for child care facilities, reducing the numbers of children involved in crime and providing for the care of elderly and disabled dependent family members 'at a stroke' as it were!

However restrictive such policies obviously are to women in general it is unsurprising that for some women, the threat that they perceive in feminism creates strong motivation to support the nuclear family. As Weeks (1985) points out: 'In a culture where it is still relatively difficult for many women to become economically independent, and where status depends on the position of the male, women may see their very survival as dependent upon family life' (p. 37).

In both the United States and in Britain, those motivated by political and economic ideologies have made strenuous efforts to create links with those who are concerned with the erosion, as they see it, of moral and spiritual values. Politicians have been quick to capitalize on what are often quite other preoccupations of the pro-family movement. For example, in the United States in particular, the pro-life lobby which is, for many, deeply rooted in the Christian belief in the sanctity of life, has been adopted by the political Right. For both groups, the alliance serves a complex web of interwoven needs. Others, concerned for the needs of children, re-argue the case for close and ongoing care by the mother. Most advocates who put forward this point of view today would, however, argue for strong *parental* involvement rather than simply restating the earlier more exclusive emphasis on sustained maternal care (Berger & Berger, 1983). The Mothers' Union within the Anglican Church would approach the family from this perspective as well as from the point of view of the unique sanctity of the marriage relationship. They and others are concerned with the increasing pluralism within sexual relationships and believe that moral and religious imperatives preclude the developing variety in relational patterns. Some too would oppose all forms of artificial contraception as well as abortion, others would not.

The Church in general has adopted a conservative stance to the family. It is therefore continually in danger of being seen to have its back to the wall, in a vain attempt to stem an unstemmable tide. The Roman Catholic Church's positions on contraception, abortion and (stated more recently) on homosexuality, only appear to indicate its inability to engage authentically with the complex issues of world population, gender and sexual politics. At the same time, there is a remarkable absence of Christian outrage at the phenomenal level of physical violence perpetrated against women and children within what appear to be impeccable conventional nuclear family units.

No one doubts the strong desire to support, protect and rescue the family that exists in all branches of the Christian Church. The inauguration of the Family Life and Marriage Education initiative in the Anglican Church; the bishops' report on *Issues in Human Sexuality* and parallel reports by the Methodist and URC Churches, the setting up of a new Working Party on the Family by the General Synod of the Church of England, all indicate the Church's real concern. But is the Church really willing and properly qualified to undertake this task? Does it understand the full implications of what is required? Is it capable of displaying the comprehensive and all-embracing love which those who would bring abundant life to others are called upon to show?

Some feminists, whilst remaining clearly identified with the arguments in favour of real equality between women and men, argue cogently in support of the family (cf. Barret and McIntosh, 1982). Many Christians feminists too (I count myself one) who set a high value on marriage and family life, believe passionately in the need to reform the interior of marriage and the family and the relationship between the sexes. They believe also in the validity and necessity of other kinds of committed relationship lived out within different forms of family life.

Many of those who espouse this position would want to attend to the importance of symbolism and the written word in helping to reform and liberate the family. Whilst pornography and organized prostitution are defences against dealing with profoundly dysfunctional relationships between women and men, and need to be acknowledged as such, opportunities for introducing the use of more functional language and imagery in schools, in churches and through the mass media need simultaneously to be vigorously encouraged. Christian feminists acknowledge the potential of marriage and the family as institutions, but they also acknowledge the need to eradicate the structural violence, the injustice and the inequalities that still abound in both (Furlong (1988), Borrowdale (1991), Dowell (1990)). This 'pro-family' stance does not disqualify the needs and aspirations of those who wish to create other relational patterns or deny that they too, if they so wish, may legitimately claim to be included under the name of 'family'.

The deconstruction and reconstruction of marriage and the family

This leads us to consider the ways in which we might approach the deconstruction of some of the problematic features of the old forms of family and the reconstitution of some new ones. Collard and Mansfield (1991) usefully summarize some of the recent research that has looked at the way in which the personal and the public experience of living in relationship can be understood. There is a need for some overarching concepts and definitions which take account of the fact that people are creating new and different ways of living in partnerships and in family groups, and which would therefore more accurately reflect what they describe as 'the present evolving reality' (p. 28). The search is also for greater clarity as to what constitute the essential ingredients of all committed relationships. Fidelity and altruism, freedom and trust, intimacy and separateness, congruence and difference, loyalty and love, equality and respect are, I submit, the fundamental ingredients required in varying degrees within all committed relationships whatever their outward shape or form. Thus, whilst there is a continuing need to deconstruct the old institutions, there is also a parallel need to reconstruct some alternative means of providing social recognition for the interior identity and experience of the couple or family group so that the essential qualities of a committed relationship can be given the maximum encouragement and support. Both the conservative thrust of post-war family ideologies and the destructive iconoclasm of the sixties need to give way to a search for the means by which committed relationships can be fostered and fed and appropriate structures be developed for their support, so that friendship can flourish and thrive; couples of either gender can experience the life-giving mutual release of each through the other, and children can enable parents and parents their children to become the unique and different people that they are, within a society of others to whom they feel bound and committed in freedom and hope for the future of us all.

Social recognition and the acceptance of relational structures different from our own is of the utmost importance in enabling the development of these core ingredients of all committed relationships. Collard and Mansfield (1991) comment, 'The social recognition of a couple may actually assist them in preserving their identity, at the same time as it is helping them to become interdependent with and committed to each other' (p. 32).

Cohabiting heterosexual couples, homosexual couples, single people living within a network of friendships, lone parent households, single people with dependent parents as well as married couples redefining the roles and structure of their relationship are all claiming the right to receive recognition, social support *and* the freedom to create and recreate relationships that have meaning and identity for them. The essential value of both personal relationships and social institutions is being recognized and an increasing number of people are refusing to acquiesce in the kinds of 'either or' choice between the two to which we have until recently become accustomed. Hence many cohabiting couples express the wish to be accepted 'as if ' they were married, and gay and lesbian people are expressing the need to have their partnerships publicly affirmed. In 1989, Denmark introduced a register of partnerships for homosexual couples and in this country many gay and lesbian people are claiming the right to have their partnerships accepted and acknowledged by Church and state (John, 1993). It seems obvious that the fundamental relational needs of commitment and interdependence are hard to sustain without any system of social support. Collard and Mansfield (1991) comment:

> The way in which reality has to be continually created is an endless process of deconstruction and reconstruction . . . for we

are in transition as a society, moving away from marriage in the sense of kinship and obligation, to another form of close relationship which is socially recognised and fortified. (p. 34)

And yet it is hard it seems for us to reach out towards an expression of this broader vision of relational realities which would help us be more effective in promoting the loving, trusting, faithful and forgiving experiences for which all human beings yearn and for which the gospel provides such relevant and explicit tools.

3

ༀ

KINGDOM

'I will . . . make you clean from all your idols.'

Ezekiel 36:25

How does all this relate to a biblical perspective upon the family? For it is with the biblical and religious perspective we must now engage. The foregoing discussion of the many other approaches that are taken to the family locates the biblical and religious perspective as one amongst many. As our understanding of the psychological and social forces which shape the family has become greater, so we are now forced to consider the roots of the biblical approach to the family in a new way. There is a kind of double difficulty about the biblical approach to the family. It is both imperialist (family life is 'Christian in its essence'; marriage is a 'Christian institution'; 'Christians should set a standard, God's standard, for everyone else to follow';) and exclusive as though there cannot and could never have been any other social institutions that fill the essential requirements of human aspiration within the will of God. It purports to hold up to us what Furlong (1982) has described as the 'tyranny of an ideal', though as we shall see, it is unclear as to whether there *is* such an ideal described in the Bible to which many people would really wish to adhere.

This is a book about the family, not about sexuality as such. Thus the Bible's attitude to sexuality, to gender and to the relationship between women and men can only be noted in passing, and very inadequately, in this short chapter. Nor is it possible to trace the development of later attitudes towards family, marriage and sexuality through the history of the Christian Church. This is a huge area of scholarship which has recently been tackled in a detailed study by Brown (1989). In this chapter we will explore the way in which

28

family is understood in the Old Testament and the way in which the Gospels and Paul understand family in its relation to the imperatives of the kingdom.

The need for relationship

But first, some anthropology. The traditional Christian approach to the family is predicated upon a central, monogamous pair-bond, yet such a monogamous pair-bond is neither an exclusively human arrangement nor the only way in which human family life has been organized. Oppenheimer (1990) introduces a delightful piece of palaeontological evidence for the fundamental nature of the pair-bond in human experience by citing Johanson's 1974 discovery in Ethiopia of a female skeleton, dating from over three and a half million years ago. Johanson called her Lucy, and in one chapter of his book, he develops a complex argument that Lucy's way of life was family life: in other words, that the family lies further back in our origins than our brain power. Oppenheimer goes on to comment: 'It is an attractive thought that the spouse is older than the technician; even that our distinctive humanity has something to do with relationships not just with cleverness' (p. 10).

Thus she argues against what she calls the 'monopolizing take-over bid which believers are too apt to feel that they ought to try to make' (p. 8). She claims that there are no grounds for believing that either the family or marriage are particularly Christian institutions nor is there any argument for imagining that pair-bonding is exclusive to humans or even to pre-human hominids like Lucy.

The need to establish committed relationships is intrinsic to the human experience and to its earliest beginnings as it is to the existence of many of the higher mammals, to some birds and to a whole range of animal life. Many animals and birds form monogamous relationships and the pair-bond is an integral part of their social organization. Many however do not and, equally, the evidence yielded by historians and anthropologists studying a variety of primitive human societies, including those described in the Bible, show patterns of social life that are quite diverse. Polygamy, polyandry, concubinage and, in Israelite society, the Levirite marriage were all practised as viable means of organizing social life. One of these arrangements was monogamy which became a prevalent and, in some societies, a predominant framework for organizing sexual and family relationships. Consanguineous rather than conjugal relationships remain however central in many societies and the bond between the mother and her young has, in all species, remained a more fundamental relationship than that created by sexual partnership.

Because the Bible is appealed to by many Christians as providing a yardstick and model for family life and because we are frequently urged 'to return to biblical values' about the family, we must now examine the Bible's views in a bit more detail. Some of the hard questions that have to be asked include: Is there one biblical pattern of family life? If so, is it relevant to our twentieth-century needs and difficulties? If not, does the Bible have anything to say to us at all about family life?

The patriarchal family

Since the concept of family essentially concerns the relationship between women and men, a fundamental question has to be investigated regarding the patriarchal nature of the family as it is described in the Bible. Thus, in any effort to wrestle with family life in the 1990s, we have also to consider the way in which the whole Christian tradition and the Bible in particular is shot through with an understanding of the relationship between the sexes derived from a particular theological stance. Feminists criticize this stance and some have concluded that it is not possible to remain committed to feminist values and at the same time subscribe to an understanding of God which enables such damaging conclusions to be drawn about the way in which men and women must relate in marriage, within the family and in every aspect of social life. Other Christians, as we noted in chapter 1, believe that any criticism of the Bible's view of family can only lead to the destruction of the faith. Oppenheimer (1990) puts the point sharply:

> For Christians concerned with the relations between men and women, among all the slogans and stereotypes a question has to be faced. Is it possible both to believe in the God of the Bible and also to take feminist concern seriously? Because we call God

Father, does it follow that men really are more god-like than women and that Christian family life should somehow reflect this idea? (p. 100)

A third group are those Christian feminists who believe that the insights of Christianity and feminism can be brought to bear upon each other, to the mutual enrichment of both. It is to these writers that I now wish to turn. Dowell (1990) and others have done important contextual work on unearthing the essentially patriarchal nature of the Old Testament's view of the family. But the world of the Old Testament is not co-terminous with the world as a whole. As Dowell (1990) points out:

> If we look beneath and outside the text, we discern the power of earlier female-dominated symbols and beliefs that were denied and repressed by biblical patriarchy. In other words the question of the inevitability of patriarchy was a live issue in the ancient world not just a pre-occupation of late twentieth century feminists. (p. xiv)

Other feminist writers such as Ruether (1983), as Dowell (1990) points out, 'chose to lay some restorative stress' (p. 14) upon understanding the context of the beginnings of Hebrew religious and social customs and the influence of the host communities of Canaan after Israel's exodus from Egypt. Those who turn to the Bible for a model of faithful monogamous family life are in some difficulties. There is nothing to suggest that the first patriarchs – Abraham and Jacob – understood God as requiring monogamy. Quite the reverse. Abraham maintained a wife and a concubine. Jacob had two wives and two concubines. Esau had several wives and Solomon had a thousand! Polygamy was of course commonly practised amongst the Israelites and neither polygamy nor the equally common practice of concubinage is condemned anywhere in the Old Testament. Thus it is hard to know what to make of the statement: 'Marriage (meaning monogamous marriage) was ordained of God in the beginning . . . [it] was established for everyone everywhere' (Phypers (1985), p. 154).

Family life in Israel was patriarchal, with wives and daughters expendable in order to achieve a variety of important goals. Sarah for example was passed off by Abraham as his sister, so that the

Egyptians would not be forced to kill him in order to acquire Sarah for the king (Genesis 12:10ff). Lot's daughter was offered to the late night callers from Sodom for gang rape, in order to protect his male visitors from a similar fate. Dinah's rape was regretted – not because of any injury done to her, but because through it, the people of Israel had been insulted. It was nevertheless put to good use in providing a reason for the Israelites to kill all the men of Shechem's clan in revenge!

The husband was his wife's lord and he had the absolute right to rule over her (Genesis 3:16). A husband could divorce his wife simply by writing her a note informing her of his intention but there was no reciprocal possibility for the woman. A father could sell his son or daughter into slavery (Exodus 21:7; Nehemiah 5:5) and in early Israelite society, child sacrifice seems to have been practised, although later on it was repudiated as a pagan custom (Leviticus 18:21; 20:2–5; 2 Kings 23:10; Jeremiah 32:35). On the other hand family customs which all Christians so far as I am aware would find wholly acceptable today, such as the adoption of children, were not practised in Israelite society or commended in the Bible, although adoption was a common practice amongst Israel's neighbours. Instead, the essential purpose of the family, the continuity of the male line, was achieved when necessary through temporary cohabitation with alternative wives, relatives or slaves. The basic social unit of society was indeed the family, but it was a type of family which consisted of a large network of wives, concubines, slaves and children, together with all of *their* wives and children as well. This group of related kin and dependants lived in a compact social group, tending their flocks, moving around together and bound one to the other by carefully constructed codes and practices which enabled their corporate life to be regulated and contained.

The emergence of monogamy

In one particular respect, the Israelite model of family life was markedly different from that of earlier more primitive societies because the link between sexual intercourse and pregnancy had now been firmly established. It was only when the male partner was understood to have an active and essential role in the creation of new life that his greater equality and gradual superiority over the female emerged. From the little we know of the earliest human societies, the first deity to be worshipped was a Goddess. The Earth Mother, so obviously fecund and life-giving, was both an object of veneration and a pattern of human productiveness. The two were wholly interrelated – so that it was understood to be the woman and not the man who was the source of human life. Rich (1977) points out that this understanding of human reproduction 'worked to endow all women with respect, even with awe, and to give women some say in the life of a people or clan' (p. 93). By the same token, when the male's active part in the reproductive process became gradually understood, so his status in relation to his female partner changed. Gradually came the realization that 'the child she carries and gives birth to is *his child* who can make *him* immortal' (p. 60).

In the ancient and primitive societies living in the fertile crescent of the near east around 2000 BCE, these new shifts of understanding were percolating into the cultural consciousness of the different tribal peoples of that area. The Goddess Earth Mother acquired a male counterpart in the Sky Father who gradually began to supplant her so that the scene was set, as it were, for Yahweh's appearance as the male god-figure of the Hebrew people, called into being around 1800 BCE by *their* father figure Abraham. Yahweh had a long battle to establish himself as the uncontested God of the Israelites. This battle is recorded in the pages of the Old Testament in the children of Israel's many lapses into cultic practices, the purges of their foreign deities and the punishments that they must undergo before they were able to assimilate the new religious order.

And as the Earth Mother waned and the God of their fathers gained his primacy, so the balance of power and influence between man and woman changed and the patriarchal family was born. There was a parallel swing in understanding the process of paternity. The male now began to be viewed as the *sole* source of life, responsible for planting new life into the passive womb of the female, whose only task was to nurture and give birth to the male partner's offspring. The contribution of the male had become pre-eminent but produced a new set of problems – experienced by the male in all species – how to ensure the female's offspring is in fact his own. If his heritage and line were to be safely secured, he must, like males of other species, 'see off' others who might compete for his female and extinguish his seed with their own. What better mechanism for safeguarding the integrity of his issue than a morally bound monogamous union of one male with one female?

Gradually, monogamy began to emerge as the normal pattern of family life within Israelite culture but only after generations of diversity. The family, polygamous and diverse and later monogamous, became the primary social institution of Israelite society, a community of kith and kin, a vehicle for preserving past tradition and passing on customs, precepts and religious values and beliefs for the next generation. Barrenness was considered to be a disastrous affliction, as witnessed by the pain and shame expressed by Sarah and Hannah. The task of the family was to perpetuate itself and to hand on the law and traditions of the community from one generation to the next. Thus, family and religious belief became inextricably intertwined. Gradually a new moral code was established to support and undergird this monogamous pattern and to ensure it fulfilled its primary task of safeguarding the male's issue and his line of inheritance. As property rights and laws became more developed, the rights of inheritance became in further need of safeguarding so that a woman's adultery was an evil to be eradicated by all possible means, and thus carried with it the death penalty. And since a woman was herself her husband's property, adultery was doubly to be condemned as Spong (1990) points out.

> If someone other than a woman's husband took from her the sexual pleasures she had to give, then that man was both robbing her husband of something that belonged to him alone and tampering with his line of succession. (p. 131)

Unsurprisingly, despite the heroic efforts of some feminist theologians to redeem some of the biblical texts (Ruether (1983), Fiorenza (1983), Moltmann-Wendel (1980), Moltmann-Wendel and Moltmann (1991)), the repeated message that emerges is that of the subjugation and exploitation of women, to the spiritual as well as the physical detriment of everyone.

A new vision

However, as Dowell (1990) argues very fully, the story of God's revelation to his people described in the Old Testament brings other messages too. Otherwise it would hardly be possible to accept the models of family or relationship portrayed in these books as a source of nourishment at all, let alone as an idealized model 'of biblical family' to which many Christian writers would apparently bid us return. But the Old Testament also holds out the promise of redemption and grace to all people. The prophets' denunciation of injustice and oppression and their vision of a time when relationships between nations, between humanity and the natural world order, and between individuals will be healed offers a framework for the way things might be in the future – a goal to be worked towards as well as a gift to be received. The core relationship of the sexes is not part of this picture in any direct way except by analogy nor is the family identified as an institution which might require regeneration, which is curious considering the central place that the family came to hold within Judaism. However, as Dowell (1990) concedes:

> The covenantal theology of the Old Testament is potentially affirmative of this gift relationship between the sexes. The metaphor of God's marriage to his people, which became foundational to later Pauline ecclesiology, militates against male-dominated, highly individualistic concepts of family, particularly the modern nuclear unit of today. (p. 33)

However depressing the general picture given by much of the Old Testament, glimpses of a different order are clearly to be seen, providing some fertile soil for the reception of Jesus' own redemptive, transforming approach. We are given pictures of loving relationships which allow us to see beyond their structures and form. Jacob worked seven years for Rachel, his bride to be, 'and the time seemed like only a few days to him, because he loved her' (Genesis 29:20). Hannah is comforted by her husband Elkanah in the extreme pain of her childlessness in a way which indicates the strength of the emotional relationship between them and of his care for her. 'Don't I mean more to you than ten sons?' (1 Samuel 1:8). The mutual love and self-sacrifice of Naomi and Ruth, each insistent upon the welfare of the other above their own; the intimate love of David and Jonathan and David's terrible grief at Jonathan's death; the love poetry of the Song of Songs and the tender passages in many of the Psalms, where God's love is compared with that of mother and child: all of these give us glimpses of the content and the variety of loving and life-giving relationships that existed within and alongside the norm of the large hierarchical, patriarchal extended group of close and quite distant relatives, servants, concubines and sojourners which comprise the key social structure in Israelite society.

Whilst its strong boundaries are exclusive they are also sufficiently flexible to include aliens and foreigners who may become temporarily or permanently a part. The roles and tasks of family members are developed and identified over generations to become clearly defined. The duties and functions of father, mother, sons and daughters were defined by custom and religious practice and were enforced to some extent by codes of law (cf. Leviticus and Deuteronomy) but within and perhaps in part because of the security afforded by these structures, the family's internal relationships are understood as a mirror of the overriding relationship of God with his people. 'Israel is my first-born Son. I have told you to let my Son go so that he might worship me' (Exodus 4:22).

Considering the overriding importance of family in Jewish society and in religious practices, Jesus' own approach was startlingly different. Even though much of his teaching and action was built upon what already existed, it is hard to overestimate his revolutionary approach to personal and familiar relationships. In much of what he said and even more in what he did, his approach created discontinuous change with the past. The family as a central social and religious unit of Israelite society is now radically redefined. This is not to deny that as Dowell (1992) argues, 'Jesus himself explicitly refused to pronounce a 'new' sex ethic or to add to or dilute the old' (p. 10), but his urgent engagement with the imperative needs of the kingdom created quite other priorities. Indeed, it is hard to understand how 'the family' as a structure has ever become so inordinately preoccupying for Christians from the way in which it is treated in the Gospels themselves. Whilst it is easy to see how the Jewish religion is indeed 'the religion of the family' (Sachs, 1991), how has the family come to hold so central a position for Christians? How is it that for the Church, the family has become 'the one salvific symbol in a naughty world' (Furlong, 1982)? So far as we know, Jesus neither married nor founded a family himself and much of what he says about family and marriage severely challenges the *status quo* of a lineally descended conjugal, consanguineous household. On the contrary, the new command is to become a beloved community of equals brought into being not by the blood of parenthood nor the legality of marriage but by the grace of adoption. No one will be excluded by virtue of not belonging to a tribe or clan or family group, for all are called equally to belong, having no *claim* to membership other than the invitation that is proffered.

The priority of the kingdom

The new order of belonging is worked out in detail by Paul, but it is demonstrated for all to see in the actions and words of Jesus. At the age of twelve he confronts his parents with an order of priorities radically different from their own. 'Didn't you know that *I had to be* in my father's house?' (Luke 2:49, italics mine). He denies his own family's special claim upon him.

> 'Look, your mother and your brothers and your sisters are outside and they want you.' Jesus answered 'Who is my mother? Who are my brothers?' He looked at the people sitting round him and said 'Look! Here are my mother and my brothers! Whoever does what God wants him to do is my brother, my sister, my mother.' (Mark 3:32–6)

Jesus calls his disciples away from the familiar – their ordinary jobs and their family commitments – to follow him. Joanna had to leave her husband Chuza, an officer in Herod's court, at least on a daily basis, in order to accompany Jesus (Luke 8:1). Susannah and Mary and all the other many women were called away from family to participate in the proclamation of the good news (Luke 8:1). Likewise, Peter and Andrew, Matthew, John and James and the others are called, commissioned and sent out (Luke 9:1) away from family and out to preach the kingdom of God. The seventy-two men and women (Luke 10:1) were again called to leave their families and were sent out in twos to heal the sick and proclaim the kingdom. To those who argued the prior claim of family duties, Jesus was unequivocal: 'Let the dead bury their own dead. You go and proclaim the kingdom of God' (Luke 9:60). Even their request to be allowed to say goodbye to their families first is met with a rebuke: 'Anyone who starts to plough and then keeps looking back is of no use to the kingdom of God' (Luke 9:62).

Jesus points out that there is something inevitably divisive about the challenges of the gospel and that this divisiveness will get worked out, not only between the claims of the kingdom and of family obligations but within family relationships themselves.

> 'Do you suppose that I came to bring peace to the world? No, not peace but division. From now on a family of five will be divided, three against two and two against three. Fathers will be against their sons, and sons against their fathers; mothers will be against their daughters, and daughters against their mothers; mothers-in-law will be against their daughters-in-law, and daughters-in-law against their mothers-in-law.' (Luke 12:51–3)

Many of these hard sayings get conveniently forgotten by Christian writers on the family. They become embarrassing to those who try to uphold the pre-eminence of the structure and form of family to which Jesus sat so lightly. Perhaps most striking of all is Jesus' summary of the cost of discipleship.

> 'Whoever comes to me cannot be my disciple unless he loves me more than he loves his father and his mother, his wife and his children, his brothers and his sisters and himself as well. Whoever does not carry his own cross and come after me cannot be my disciple.' (Luke 14:25–7)

And the rewards for getting these priorities the right way round are many:

> 'Every one who has left houses or brothers or sisters or father or mother or children or fields for my sake will receive one hundred times more and will be given eternal life.' (Matthew 19:29)

This does not mean that Jesus did not recognize that family

relationships *have a part to play* in promoting the work of the kingdom. When Jesus healed Jairus' daughter, he did so in the context of her family.

> When he arrived at the house, he would not let anyone go in with him except Peter, John and James and the child's father and mother . . . Her life returned and she got up at once and Jesus ordered them to give her something to eat. (Luke 8:51 and 55)

When Jesus raised Lazarus from the dead, he did so with the help of his sisters, who summoned him in the first place, remained closely involved throughout and, like Jairus and the child's parents, took over after the miracle had been performed. 'Untie him,' Jesus told them, 'and let him go' (John 11:44).

When Jesus hung on the cross, he commended his mother to John and John to his mother, creating a relationship between them by adoption, of mother and son (John 19:26–7). Jesus takes the ordinariness of family relationships and uses them in the service of the kingdom. His attitude to his own home is instructive too. In the Gospel of John we are told of the curiosity of Andrew and his companion about where Jesus lived. 'Come and see' says Jesus. 'So they went with him and saw where he lived and spent the rest of the day with him' (John 1:39). His home is at their disposal, to welcome them, offer them time and space and presence. The story of the healing of the paralyzed man in Mark 2:1–12 is particularly costly in its demands on Jesus' home. After everyone leaves, Jesus is presumably left with a roof to repair!

Jesus' teaching on marriage

Jesus' teaching on marriage too redefines its purpose within the new perspective of the kingdom. In heaven there will be no marriage (Matthew 19:12). So marriage is a temporal institution, providing a framework for supporting a potentially kingdom-oriented relationship. Marriage is dissolved by death (Matthew 22:23–30), but in Paul's redaction of Jesus' teaching, the harvest that has been built up by each partner helping the other towards full maturity, according to the measure of the stature of Christ, will endure forever. Some will be called to forego marriage altogether 'for the sake of the kingdom' (Matthew 19:12), a teaching that is left for 'those to whom God has given it' fully to understand. But it is a teaching that is presumably to be understood in general terms as the necessary relativizing of all that is not itself the kingdom, along with home, possessions, personal ambition and security of all kinds – so natural and needful in their own way to human well-being.

Jesus proclaims that marriage can be used or abused in terms of kingdom values – faithfulness, self-abnegation, humility, obedience, poverty, purity, forgiveness and love. These values were denied by the frequent resort to divorce by men who were prepared to 'put away' their wives on the smallest pretext. Divorce was of course a one-way street in Mosaic law – enabling the full force of men's control and ownership of women to be experienced. The divorced wife was cut off from her family, her security, her inheritance, her livelihood, her sources of protection in a world where to be excluded from family meant enduring a life-threatening abandonment. When the Pharisees asked Jesus whether their law allowed a man to divorce his wife for whatever reason he wished (Matthew 19:3), Jesus does not reply directly. Instead, he uses the opportunity afforded by the trick question to restate God's original intention – the fundamental equality and unity of female and male: 'The two will become one. So they are no longer two, but one' (Matthew 19:5). The unity and equality of all people is heralded in this analogy of all human relationships, and marriage becomes therefore a primary image of the essence of the kingdom itself and a sign and a symbol of the spiritual destiny of humanity.

This 'oneing' with another human being, in order to bring about the 'oneing' of all human beings, is itself contingent upon leaving home. 'For this reason a man will leave his father and mother and unite with his wife and the two will become one' (Matthew 19:5). The demands of the kingdom involve taking the risk of leaving the original family behind and dissolving the self in a relationship which becomes more than the sum of either part. The relationship becomes a school of charity in which each partner is helped to leave self behind and to grow in kingdom values so that these may be disseminated throughout the earth. The old order will then be changed and justice, righteousness, truth and peace will be created throughout the land.

The divorce of a wife, allowed by Moses because men had been 'so hard to teach' (Matthew 19:8), interrupts this process. It is like the man who sets his hand to the plough but turns back (Luke 9:62). It is a turning aside from faithfulness, love and self-abnegation and was not what was intended at the time of creation. It is a means by which half the human race is placed at the mercy of the other. As Dowell (1990) points out, Jesus 'clearly recognised the overall patriarchal context in which the Law had developed and when asked his trick question specifically condemned the masculine bias' (p. 38). He exposed 'the ubiquitous double standard in women's status as property at the disposal of fathers, brothers and husbands' (p. 39). It is important to grasp this context of what divorce actually meant in Jesus' time in order to avoid falling into the trap of applying his words in their absolute sense to the form rather than the meaning of the marital relationship. Jesus' words can be understood as having as much to do with his compassion for the abused, the outcast and the poor (of which women in his day were prime qualifiers) as they were to do with marriage *per se*. They rebuke the cruelty and abuse heaped upon the innocent, whilst recognizing that *both* parties may create the conditions for the divorce law to be appropriately applied (the 'Matthean exception' 19:9). Later in the book we will consider ways in which the interruption of divorce can be helped to become the means by which the partners can take new steps forward in their growth towards emotional and spiritual maturity.

The Samaritan woman

Jesus' teaching on the family has to be deduced from his approach to people in all sorts of different situations. The richly nuanced discourse between Jesus and the Samaritan woman (John 4:1–41) and Martha's dialogue with Jesus before the raising of Lazarus both provide important contextual corroboration for the understanding of the relationship of family and kingdom outlined above and for the relative emphasis placed by Jesus upon them. Leaving aside whether or not the point of the first story is really an allegorical comment on the imperfect religion of the Samaritans, the meeting with the Samaritan woman was an extraordinary event, as many commentators have pointed out. Jesus, a Jewish rabbi, talking with a Samaritan woman was an unheard of breach of convention. The disciples in the story were 'greatly surprised' (John 4:27). But it was made more extraordinary still because of the depth of the dialogue and the delicacy of the verbal dance which took place between them. After his initial request for refreshment, Jesus immediately moves into a theological discussion to which the woman eagerly responds. There is a quality of cut and thrust about the quick moving interchange, an equality (in human terms) between their contributions, and an enjoyment which seems evident in both participants. At the point when the woman takes a step forward in her understanding (John 4:15) Jesus suddenly introduces an entirely new issue. 'Go and call your husband,' says Jesus, and he adds 'and come back.'

How are we to understand this request? As a trap? As a tease perhaps? Obviously it is not a straightforward open-ended question, arising from ignorance, because Jesus knows the answer already (John 4:17). 'I haven't got a husband', the woman answers. She does not sound defensive or trapped. She clearly wants to continue the conversation – but this must have been a moment when she held her breath, waiting for Jesus' response – for his judgement perhaps. However, there is only approval. 'You are right when you say you haven't got a husband. You have been married to five men and the man you live with now is not really your husband. You have told me the truth' (John 4:17–18). Jesus does not comment at all on the fact that she is currently cohabiting with a man, having already had five husbands – he simply shows his pleasure in her transparent straightforwardness. Of course we have no way of knowing whether her previous five marital relationships ended in death or divorce. However, we might perhaps be permitted to hazard a guess that *for all five* marriages to end in death is beyond all reasonable odds, even given the considerably poorer standard of health and hygiene in first-century Palestine! However that may be, Jesus seems to be not at all interested in the form of her personal relationships either past or present. Rather, he responds to this woman in her capacity to be transparently truthful herself; to be fully engaged with *his truth* and to be openly eager to hear the good news he has to give. He has found someone who is prepared to leave her water jar (i.e. her domestic family preoccupations), go into the town and tell people about the Messiah she has just found. She is so effective in her apostolic work that 'many of the Samaritans in that town believed in Jesus because the woman had said "He told me everything I have ever done" '! Isn't that wonderful! That the story should have this delicate, delicious denouement! Not only is she not asked to repent or amend her living arrangements, *it is the fact that they have been revealed and accepted by Jesus*, that enables her to believe and to tell others about her belief. She is accepted by Jesus just as she is and his acceptance kindles her apostolic zeal. Jesus' eye is on the kingdom, not on the outward form of things. What really *matters* is that people receive from him the Water of Life which will bring them to eternal life in him and, having received, will bring others to receive that life for themselves.

Martha's prophecy

The second story seems at first quite unrelated to this exploration of the relationship between family and kingdom values. It is the story of Martha recorded in John 11. Lazarus has died and his sisters are beside themselves with grief. They are deeply immersed in their family troubles. The sisters send a message to Jesus. 'Lord, your dear friend is ill' (John 11:3). We are then given the sharp juxtaposition of Jesus' love for these people who had provided a kind of substitute family of friends for him and his strange delay in coming to their aid. 'Jesus loved Martha and her sister and Lazarus. Yet when he received the news that Lazarus was ill, he stayed where he was for two more days' (John 11:5–6). Instead of responding immediately to his own human need and the needs of his friends, he acts instead according to a quite different set of imperatives. His actions are governed entirely by the needs and requirements of his obedience to God; he waits upon the possibilities of the kingdom. But the struggle is real. Verse 35 makes it clear that Jesus experiences the pain of his own emotional relationship with Lazarus and the sisters. *This* family is *his* family. And Martha too is involved in the same struggle. Angry maybe at the Lord's delay, she struggles to see through her own and others' surface needs to the deep place in the relationship where eternal life is to be found. Martha who, at another point in her story (Luke's version) was trapped by her family and domestic responsibilities, now rises to the supreme challenge of perceiving and proclaiming who Jesus really was. In her confession of faith, fuller and more detailed than the comparable one made by Peter (Matthew 6:16), she acknowledges him for who he is. 'Yes Lord, I do believe that you are the Messiah, the Son of God who was to come into the world' (John 11:27). Moltmann-Wendel and Moltmann (1991) makes the point that

> Martha makes this statement when she has experienced Jesus as the one who is light in the darkness, who gives life in death and the pains of death: warmth, nearness, hope. She does not make this statement when everything is back to normal and her brother is alive again. (p. 48–9)

This story is interesting for our present purposes for two reasons. First it occurs within the context of Jesus' own network of personal relationships. He was intimately involved in the events. We are told that when he was taken to the grave he wept. It was clear too to the onlookers how much Jesus loved Lazarus and was moved by his death and by the grief of his friends. (John 11:33–5). Second, the story is about a woman who has become an icon of domesticity for the Church throughout the ages. Martha is 'the good, diligent housewife, seeing to the welfare of the guest' (Moltmann-Wendel and Moltmann (1991), p. 46).

Since becoming more aware of this stereotype of Martha myself, through reading the work of the Moltmanns and others, I have been fascinated at how pervasive is her imprisonment in the Luke account of who she was. I frequently ask groups what image comes to mind when Martha's name is mentioned and I have *never once* found that anyone, either clergy or lay (nor even when I once tried it among a group of bishops!), refers to the story in John! Martha is perceived as the sort of person a woman ought to be, running a home for her brother and sister. Maybe she is a widow, maybe she is unmarried, but either way that is the sum total of what Martha is all about – her home-making. But this interpretation is completely contradictory to the actual biblical picture. In John we find the 'forgotten Martha' (Moltmann-Wendel, 1980). John 11:20–7 describes a complex interchange between Martha and Jesus about the ultimate concerns for which Jesus came into the world. Jesus has come as the resurrection and the life to overcome death for all people and for all time. He has come to reveal God and all other considerations are to be subordinated to this end. So we are told: 'Jesus told them plainly, "Lazarus is dead, but for your sake *I am glad that I was not with him, so that you will believe*" ' (John 11:14–15, italics mine). The requirements of the kingdom come first over and above all natural claims of duty or affection whatever the cost. And so it is for Martha. She complains to Jesus that he was not there to prevent Lazarus' death but her preoccupation with her family's need, even in these extreme circumstances, does not override the pre-eminent importance of Jesus' claims upon her. She is prepared to put his claims first, for her attention, for her confession of faith, for her prophetic witness to his true identity. It is, as the Moltmanns point out, *only after* Martha's confession and witness to the Lord, that her natural, entirely legitimate and understandable but nevertheless secondary family concerns come to the fore and receive attention.

The family and the kingdom

Anderson and Guernsey (1985) in their illuminating analysis of the family, point out that Jesus 'did not dissolve the natural order of family, though he qualifies it as an absolute and brings it into the service of the New Order, which is itself the original order' (p. 140). They quote Barth in showing how Jesus questions 'the impulsive intensity with which [the disciple] allows himself to be enfolded by, and thinks that he himself should enfold, those who stand to him in these relationships' (Barth (1969), p. 550). Instead, people are liberated from the tyranny of structures and are invited to live the kingdom's values of justice, faithfulness and love. For those who have been most oppressed – women, especially the barren, the unmarried, the divorced, the ritually unclean – there are special reasons to rejoice. But as Barth points out, one wonders how far the Church (he speaks specifically of the Protestant Church) has actually taken on board any of these freedoms for her children:

> To a very large extent it has acted as though Jesus had done the very opposite and proclaimed this attachment – the absolute of

family. Can we really imagine a single one of the prophets or apostles in the role of the happy father, or grandfather, or even uncle, as it has found self-evident sanctification in the famous Evangelical parsonage or manse? (Barth (1969), p. 551)

It appears to have been extraordinarily difficult to hold together both the primary claims of the kingdom and the subordinate claims of social and familial relationships throughout the Church's history. Always there is a tension to be worked out. Sometimes the balance moves towards the denial of all claims made by natural relationships and is accompanied by a denigration of sexuality, marriage and family life. Sometimes the Church swings towards a denial of kingdom imperatives with an idolatrous position being claimed for the family. The Church is more prone to hold this latter position when as is the case today the surrounding culture has broken loose from traditional family structures or when particular threats such as war or disease are experienced in the outside world.

In Paul, we see the attempt being made to hold the two positions together within the complexities of trying to establish the new faith within a wide range of different cultures. That marriage and family and other personal relationships can be used as a *means* of living and proclaiming kingdom values, whilst being always subordinate to them, is clearly uppermost in much of Paul's thought. Some of what he teaches portrays the difficulties of trying to avoid subverting too destructively the host culture into which the fragile new Church is being planted. Sometimes the belief that the parousia is imminent affects the emphasis that he gives to his teaching. Much of what he teaches is good news, as West (1987) has pointed out: the equality of marriage partners; the mutuality of marriage; the freedom of choice between marriage and celibacy; the acceptance that divorce is sometimes the right and necessary course to take; the valuing of the contributions of each person within the organic whole of the Body of Christ. And always his emphasis on the wider concerns and commitment to the community of Christ and to the primary claims made by membership of his Body and to the call of the kingdom. Moreover, Paul is always clear that the letter (or outer form) brings death and only the Spirit (or inner meaning) gives life.

It remains however extraordinarily difficult to gain a proper perspective on the past or to make history usable to us, even our own sacred history of Scripture and tradition. Brown (1989) highlights the difficulties in trying to understand the relationship of past and present. He warns about the 'irreducible particularity' of every situation and at the beginning of his book comments: 'We shall be dealing with a Christianity whose back is firmly turned toward us, untroubled by our own most urgent, and legitimate, questions' (p. xvii). In other words, some of the issues which confront the family today have no precedent and therefore for some of its contemporary problems there can be no obvious appeal to the past. Moreover, we need to be reminded of the recent origins of our faith story and of our Christian belief and traditions. Spong (1990) puts this point sharply:

> When one considers the present astrophysical estimate that our planet is between four and five billion years old and the current anthropological conviction that recognisable if primitive, human life has been on this planet for between one and two million years, then a faith story born in one thousand eight hundred BCE is not ancient but relatively new and modern. If that faith story is literalized and claimed as the exclusive bearer of God's inerrant and infallible plan of salvation, one must wonder why a gracious God would leave human beings in both ignorance and sin for 99.9 percent of the time that they have inhabited the earth. (p. 98)

This kind of comment helps us to let go of our 'absolutes' and relax some of our strictures on what is right for all people, in all cultures, for all time. It helps us recognize that God, who was the God of his creation long before either the Bible or the Church made their appearance, holds all things in his loving embrace and breathes his life-giving Spirit into the great diversity of structures and models that human beings have used and will continue to develop anew, in organizing their intimate, personal and social life. One thing we can be quite sure of is that the created order, as Anderson and Guernsey (1985) point out, 'does not yield any law of the family that is not superseded by the Lord of the family' (p. 143). And since the Lord is eternally creating all things new, we should expect to be continually surprised by the new forms and structures into which God is calling human beings to bear witness to his life and love.

4

CONTEXT

*There is no creature whose inward being is so strong
that it is not greatly determined by what lies outside it.*

GEORGE ELIOT, *Middlemarch*

Neither families nor individuals exist in a vacuum. Both are highly influenced by and are dependent upon their social, political and cultural context. The developing discipline of family theory over the last forty years has helped us understand that the behaviour and experience of the individual is essentially related to the context provided by the family system. In the same way, family systems themselves can only be understood by considering some of the important features of their contemporary environment. Thus, to wrestle with the family means that we must wrestle too with some of constituents of the family's environment.

In any society, values lie at the deepest level of experience. They operate at a level somewhere below that of full consciousness and strongly influence the way in which the institutions of society develop. We struggle in our post-modernist world between a dominant culture which emphasizes an instrumental stance and is bound up with the pursuit of freedom, independence, self-reliance and conquest. In contrast, the increasingly influential rising culture emphasizes wholism, ecology and subjective experience (Capra, 1982). For the present, our society is governed by the dominant culture and it is one which lays great stress on the development and fulfilment of individual aspiration; it places great importance upon the material – on the acquisition and ownership of goods – and it prizes consumerism as a process which enables daily life to be continuously transacted.

Ambition, hard work and competition are rewarded by personal

48

achievement and considerable financial rewards, by high status in the community and by the opportunity for the enjoyment of leisure pursuits. Other values operate too as a foil to this system of dominant values. These include generosity, charity, participation in the political and social processes of the community, investment in and provision for the future and the protection and enhancement of life. It is, however, the dominant values of individualism, materialism and consumerism that most powerfully influence our day to day experience of how life is in our society. It is these values that most critically influence what people actually do and how they behave.

Rushton (1992), for example, has observed that outside the daily experience of work, for those who are employed, the great majority of people spend most of their time shopping, travelling and watching television. Shopping enables consumerism to proceed; travelling provides the reward of leisure and an escape from the pressure and demands of the competition to achieve and television provides a spur to shop (consume) and a means of escape from it.

Take two snapshots of family life.* One picture is of a family group, sitting around the television set, eating the meal provided for them on a tray by mother and silently focused in on the same central image projected to them on the screen from the outside world. The second is of a moving 'dance' of family members coming and going around the central focus of a refrigerator. Each person helps themselves to a 'meal', and then retreats to their own room, switching on their own television and watching one of a number of different images projected to them from outside.

The first snapshot used to be held up as evidence of the loss of much that was previously held to be important about the family – the shared meal around the family table, the conversational engagement with one another as people, and the involvement in the real experience of each member's different worlds. But the second snapshot highlights what the first in fact retained. Now each person provides food for himself, comes and goes without sight of or contact with others and creates and participates in a separate world of meaning through his own individually selected television programme.

---

* I am indebted to Elaine Storkey for this telling comparison (at Southwark Diocesan Conference, Telling the Difference, April 1992).

These snapshots, a little caricatured perhaps, may convey something that is of general significance about family life in the 1990s. But they need earthing in some of the environmental influences that impinge upon families in different ways. We will look at several of these influences in some detail.

Poverty

The number of families with children on supplementary benefit doubled, from half a million in 1979 to about one million by 1986. This means that about one in six of all children in Britain are being brought up in families where their income is that of supplementary benefit alone. Commenting on the consequences for these families and their children Kiernan and Wicks (1990) write:

> The essential picture is one of drabness, a life that is mean and meagre. One analysis of the inadequacy of benefit levels sought to examine what kind of living standards were experienced. It drew up the kinds of budgets that could be achieved. The conclusion was clear: 'By the standards of living of most families today, the evidence reveals that most families on supplementary benefit can only afford an extremely restricted and drab lifestyle'. The study also noted that: 'The average weekly expenditure of all families with two children is two and a half times that of families on supplementary benefit. They spend fifty percent more on food, four times more on alcohol, five times more on clothing and footwear, six times more on services and durable household goods and seven times more on transport.' (p. 40)

Moreover there have been real changes in the *differential* between the income of families during the 1980s. On the one hand there has been a significant rise in the wealth of a great many families. As Kiernan and Wicks (1990) point out, 'The average family at the end of the 1980s was a far more affluent one than at the start of the decade. Rising real incomes and more two pay-packet families ensured this' (p. 39). But rising levels of unemployment and increasing numbers of lone-parent families also increased the numbers of families experiencing real poverty and produced sharper inequality. Roll (1988) points out that while the top 20% of two-parent families saw their income increase by an average of 9%, those among the bottom 20% saw a real decline of 6%.

All families who are in receipt of income support are more likely to have to borrow money in order to purchase essential items of clothing or household goods. The need to borrow to provide for essential items has been accentuated by the advent of the Social Fund (which became operational in 1988) whereby grants were mainly replaced by loans. The fact that a family's capacity to repay a loan is part of the assessment for eligibility means that the poorest and most disabled families are most likely to be refused. The rate of successful applications for grants fell to 25% in 1991/2, from 40% the year before, whereas the rate of successful applications for budgeting loans fell from 56% to 53% and that for crisis loans from 90% to 88%. 6.6% and 7.5% of these loan applications were refused during these two years because of the applicants' 'inability to repay'.

Loans are often experienced as being inadequate as well as difficult to come by: 'Calculations have shown that a two child family receiving supplementary benefit (now income support) could buy a woman's coat only once every fifteen years. A fridge would need to last fifteen years and an iron twelve' (Family Policy Study Centre, Fact Sheet 4). It should not take much imagination to conclude how difficult it must be to manage a budget that is geared to provide for only the minimum needs of family life and yet to allow some scope for repayment of debt, either to the government, the pawn shop or the money lender.

Other changes in benefit arrangements have had complex effects on family life. The withdrawal of the automatic right to benefit for sixteen- and seventeen-year-olds has meant that young people who are unable to find work, and can therefore make no contribution at all to the family budget, are at much greater risk of being required to leave an already struggling family unit. This has meant a dramatic increase in the numbers of homeless and destitute children living rough in the cities and the premature rupture of family relationships. The Child Support Act of 1991, whilst appearing to tackle the reasonable expectation that fathers should be required to maintain their children, is likely to have an adverse effect upon the income of single-household families and thus upon the well-being of mothers and children. Mothers who refuse 'unreasonably' to identify their children's fathers may face reductions in benefit. It does not take a great deal of imagination to see how mothers may often find themselves caught between the competing threats of violence from a previous partner or even more severe financial hardship than they are already experiencing. The consequences of either for the well-being of these families should be a matter of crucial concern. The freezing of child benefit in the late eighties at £7.25p with an increase of only £1.00 in 1991 and 1992 (but for the first child only) has further reduced the standards of the poorest families. In the early 1970s, Wyn (1972) argued for the 'redistribution of national wealth and income in favour of children, or, in other words, the transfer of resources to investment in future generations' (p. 281). Not only have child benefits failed to reach a level where they might begin to approach this task, but in 1984, the government undertook a fundamental review of all welfare benefits. There were sharp reductions in rent rebates and housing benefit, and free school meals were abolished. The measures were condemned by a range of critics including the Bishop of Durham, who described them as 'verging on the wicked'.

Poverty, unemployment and homelessness are the experience of families of various different types. However, some are more at risk than others. Lone parents for example are more likely than other families with children to be dependent upon income support and are less likely to be in receipt of earnings from employment as their main source of income. This means that they are automatically poorer to a dramatic degree since the Family Expenditure Survey of 1988 showed that the gross average weekly income of unemployed households is half that of employed households (HMSO, 1992). The fact that 42% of all families originating in the West Indies/Guayana and 24% of all African families are lone-parent families is likely to mean that poverty is disproportionately experienced by those ethnic minority groups in Britain.

Poverty is also used as a means of promoting one form of family life to the detriment of others. Government legislation in recent years continues to favour the traditional nuclear family as the Social Services Policy Forum (1992) points out:

> Families which do not fit this narrow and distorted perception of family (single parents, gay and lesbian parents, large extended

families) are controlled and if not brought 'into line', attacked in a variety of ways. The state enacts this control through such forces as the Child Support Act, immigration legislation, 'Clause 28', social security regulations and so on. This is the context within which 'family and community responsibility' is being promoted. (p. 40)

The calculation of poverty is of course notoriously complex and open to differing interpretations. Nevertheless, using a variety of different measures, the gap between the majority and the minority can be seen to be profoundly greater and the plight of many of these families so affected is severe. Successive government reports have built up a consistent picture, showing that both absolute and relative poverty have increased. In July 1992, official government figures showed that the poorest families had suffered a 6% cut in real income. Using below half of the average level of income as the nearest available measure for identifying a poverty line, the data showed that in 1988/9, twelve million people were living below this line compared with only five million in 1979. Similarly 25% of all children were living below this line in 1988/9 compared with 10% in 1979. These figures were worse still than those produced for the year before which showed a mean 30% rise in income for the population as a whole and a 2% rise in real income for the bottom 10% (HMSO, 1992). Thus, data produced in 1992 by the analysis of households living below the average income between 1979 and 1988/9 clearly show that the gap between rich and poor has grown profoundly greater.

Poverty in all these forms is a major deterrent to the quality of a family's life together. For poverty is not, as the Church's Report, *Faith in the City*, pointed out in 1985, only about a shortage of money: 'It is about rights and relationships, about how people are treated and how they regard themselves; about powerlessness, exclusion and loss of dignity' (p. 195). Members of poor families are prevented from full participation in the mainstream experience of life which the majority take for granted. Choices and options are extremely limited, because most of their small income must be spent on food and other basic necessities. Physical space within the home may be very restricted and recreational opportunities in the immediate area very limited. The intrusiveness of noise, smell, litter and violence from one's immediate surroundings creates an inhospitable environment for family life.

The conditions of poverty may produce tension, apathy, anger or depression; they certainly make it far more difficult for adults and children to believe themselves to be worthwhile, uniquely precious individuals, or to treat each other as such. In its annual review of its work for 1991–2, Relate commented repeatedly on the relationship between poverty, unemployment, redundancy and debt and the increased demand for marital counselling. The report draws attention to the toll which all those factors take on family relationships. The limitations on space and the daily grind of trying to make ends meet uses up emotional energy fast, increasing the pressure on people who are often already vulnerable in terms of their ability to contain and manage frustration. Moreover there is often a clustering together of factors which become cumulative in their effects. For example, black women who are employed and heading single-parent households experience powerlessness in the form of being poor, isolated and badly housed as well as being the recipients of sexism, racism and violence.

The fact that almost every family in the land owns a television set means that there is an acute awareness of the increasing differential between different sections of the population. An idealized norm of what life can aspire to be for the many is portrayed through advertisements and soaps to the progressively disadvantaged 'few'. In many cities rich and poor live cheek by jowl so that even within one street, there may be elegant single family occupancy accommodation next to deteriorating middle- and high-rise housing stock. (In the area where I now live, I can walk within thirty yards in any direction and encounter high- and low-rise flats in an extremely dilapidated condition, several large squats, a group of permanently parked travellers, large multi-occupancy nineteenth-century houses and a range of elegant, beautifully maintained early Victorian houses accommodating one family apiece.)

Walking along that part of the street at night where lighted rooms reveal all that money can buy, and comparing these circumstances with one's own cramped and unappealing high-rise flat is likely to increase acutely one's sense of being 'outside' the mainstream of what most families can expect to enjoy. Such impressions may be based somewhat on the fantasy of what one assumes to be the experience of the 'other' but there is enough reality within the economic divisions in our society for there to be a sound basis for such judgements being made. In 1989, the Audit Commission for Local Authorities in England and Wales' Report could comment:

> Although the U.K. economy continues to grow rapidly, urban problems remain. They differ from place to place in character and intensity. Sometimes whole cities are affected, in other places there are deep pockets of deprivation alongside prospering communities, elsewhere the problem is located in urban fringe estates.

How much more severe an experience this final decade of the twentieth century is proving, now that the economy is *not* continuing to grow rapidly for those already marginalized and deprived families.

In 1990, a follow-up report to *Faith in the City* commented:

> Our conclusion must be that for a considerable number of poor people the picture looks bleaker than it did in 1985. For some at least this is because, in real terms they have *actually less cash* in their pocket now than then. For many it is because their *relative* position is so much weaker. It is they who are most affected by the cuts in social services provision, in declining patient care in the health service, in day nurseries for young children, in affordable decent housing for themselves and their children. (p. 88)

The argument being advanced is that the structure and process of the family's continuing life is considerably influenced by economic circumstances and that poverty is one of several environmental influences that has been shown repeatedly to have a deleterious effect upon the functioning of family life.

Housing and homelessness

Perhaps nowhere is this made more visible than in the area of housing and homelessness. The degree to which family life can reasonably be expected to flourish is highly dependent upon the quality of its housing. Although a 'house' is not the same as a 'home' it is nevertheless hard to create anything remotely resembling a 'home' below a certain level of material provision.

Three major pieces of legislation, the Housing Acts of 1980 and 1988 and the Local Government and Housing Act of 1989 provide the framework for current government housing policy. Central to this policy has been the encouragement of increasing home ownership which rose from 57.4% in 1980 to 66.8% in 1988. As is well known, there have been several disastrous side effects to this policy. The first is the consequent severe drop in local authority rented accommodation which has in no way been compensated for by the increases in private sector rented accommodation; and the second, a huge increase in homelessness arising both from the drop in local authority rented housing and from the high rate of housing repossessions contingent upon mortgage foreclosures.

The Local Government and Housing Act restricts the ability of local authorities to replenish their stock of rented accommodation as it gets sold off and also the extent to which it can renovate existing housing. As a result there has been a sharp decrease in the amount of affordable housing available and a decline in the condition of old stock. The follow-up report (1990) to *Faith in the City* comments: 'There has been a continuing fall in the number of dwellings lacking basic amenities, and over three million families still live in homes which are unfit or in need of repair' (p. 94).

The increase in property repossessions, contingent upon the failure of families to keep up their mortgage repayments, climbed steadily throughout the 1980s from 3,480 in 1980 to 43,890 in 1990, to a staggering 75,540 in 1991 and 68,540 in 1992.* Each of these repossessions represents the dashed hopes of one family, the inevitable disruption of their relationships with neighbours and with their local community, the certain stress of major internal upheaval, often with severe consequences for the well-being of marital and parental relationships. Some of these families find temporary lodgings with relatives, some are able to return 'down the ladder' of home ownership aspirations to rented accommodation once more. Some join the ranks of the truly homeless.

Homelessness is a profoundly disturbing fact of our national com-

* Source: Council of Mortgage Lenders.

munity life in the 1990s. And homelessness must be a matter of the gravest significance to anyone concerned with the well-being of families. Nowhere does the phrase 'wrestling with family life' have greater impact than when we consider the plight of parents endeavouring to care for children in bed and breakfast accommodation, in hostels or in temporary squats. Again, the rise in the numbers of people affected during the 1980s has been staggering. In 1980 there were 1,380 people in bed and breakfast accommodation and 3,380 in hostels, whilst in 1990 there were 11,130 in bed and breakfast and 9,010 in hostels.* There was therefore not only an enormous rise in the absolute figures of people having to be provided with these types of accommodation but a shift in favour of the less controlled and therefore highly variable bed and breakfast type. Whilst many hoteliers struggle to do their best for families, and some families may benefit from the 'community life' which develops in the hotel, the lack of space for children to play, the communal sleeping arrangements for parents and children, the large numbers sharing few facilities and the frequent necessity for the family to walk the streets and eat out during the day creates an appalling environment for both parents and children and for the growth and well-being of relationships between them.

In addition to these, around 25,030 were listed as living in other types of accommodation or in none (compared with 4,200 in 1982). Many of these are the single homeless who have lost all connection with their families and who live in squats or on the streets, in doorways or in the 'cardboard cities'. Some are the young people who have run away or been ejected from their homes, and some too are young parents trying to keep together and prevent their children being taken into care. All of these are disqualified from regular benefits by their homelessness. They are lost from most normal agencies of help and must beg or steal to keep going at all.

---

* Figures from written answer of Timothy Yeo, Junior Environment Minister, to Jeremy Corbyn, 17 April 1991.

The pressure to succeed

Poverty is only one aspect of a cluster of economic influences that crucially affect family life in the 1990s in Britain. The pressure to compete, to achieve paid employment or to hold on to it, to gain promotion, to achieve financial and material success has become fiercer and more desperate in a climate of contraction and uncertainty. Moreover, the 1980s significantly if subtly altered the value system which undergirds such activities. The increasing tendency to value all activity in terms of its economic worth and the pre-eminence of wealth creation as an all-encompassing goal of human aspiration is pervasive in its effects. People become worthwhile in proportion to their material success rather than as persons in their own right. Education, health care and other social provisions are evaluated against a yardstick of what they will enable the recipient to achieve in terms of these economic goals.

The pressure to succeed inevitably affects every aspect of family life. The very long hours and total, exclusive commitment demanded by many companies of their highly paid executives in middle and top management are as stressful on family relationships as the pressures of poverty. Husbands and wives are often both caught into what may be parallel and competing areas of professional or commercial activity, with little time available for one another and a progressively widening gap in their commitment to the relationship between them. Children spend longer hours with other carers and become inducted at a very young age into a depersonalized culture where they take their place (and often necessarily a lower place) in their parents' order of priorities, competing with the need to succeed in the market-place. All this comes additionally and on top of the 'normal' pressures on family life. As Harries (1992) points out:

> The rich are people too, and so they share many of the ills to which flesh is heir. These include sickness, handicapped children, problems of relationships, divorce, death and all the pressures of striving to compete in a competitive world. Children of a wealthy home who are emotionally rejected by their parents and who grow up to become drug addicts are indeed to be pitied. It is of course true, as the cynic has often observed, that if one is going to be unhappy it is far better to be unhappy on a

comfortable income. Nevertheless, the unhappiness of the rich is still unhappiness. (p. 8)

The pursuit of excellence, untempered by other values, carries with it the burdens of continual performance anxiety, stemming from one's own self-scrutiny in response to accountability required by those in charge. A chaplain at a major public school told me recently how everything in the school must necessarily be geared to giving parents value for money. They sent their children to the school in order to achieve spectacular academic results, in order that the children in their turn might compete successfully for jobs and rise quickly in their chosen area of occupation. Everything at the school (including the teaching of R.E.) was evaluated in the light of this requirement, so that the levels of stress on both the students and staff were very high. He commented on the important role of the sanatorium and the way in which his own ministry and that of the san. provided the only 'softening' of this unrelentingly competitive atmosphere.

Now that we live in a more sharply divided society, the pressure on those that do *not* belong to the bottom 10%, to avoid doing so has increased. Few families can make choices between whether or not both parents work – if work is available for both – and few can argue with their employer about the number of hours demanded of them. The requirement of the job comes first and, if the family's material needs are to be met, their emotional needs may have to take second place.

This atmosphere of pressure and strain is not the experience of an isolated few. The rewards of success are very high but the price of failure is disastrous. The vast majority of people who occupy the middle ground between these two poles are affected by the magnetic pull of the one and the aversive push of the other. The vignette of family members weaving in and out of one another around the refrigerator before disappearing to watch their private television or to work on their computer console emerges out of the social and economic pressures facing the family today. Whatever dislocation of relationships occurs as a result, stems as much from these social pressures as from the motivation and behaviour of the individual members of the family themselves. When we are trying to understand the causes of family difficulties in the 1990s we have therefore to

examine a complex, multi-causal model which includes both individual and social factors and the transactional needs of the system
itself.

The political context

None of this of course is new but it is subtly more influential upon
us all now than it was. Not only do we know more about what is
going on in the world and therefore of the escalating pressures upon
people in many different walks of life, but we are much more conscious of living in a world hedged around by its own limitations.
Resources are now known to be finite and limited. Non-renewable
energy resources are expendable, the rain forests are being depleted
at a colossal rate and even the availability of such basic commodities
as water and air seem threatened by changes in rainfall levels and the
ozone layer. For those living on the margins of society and used to
receiving little of what it can offer, the depletion of the world's
natural resources may feel less immediately critical to them than it
does to those involved in wealth creation on a large scale. But
everyone is susceptible to the pervasive anxiety engendered by the
threat of global warming and to the generalized uncertainty of life
on the planet in the final decade of the twentieth century (cf., Baker,
1992).

Uncertainty and anxiety pervade the political context of our lives.
Whilst the nuclear threat appears to have diminished, new uncertainties are emerging as old empires fragment into tiny tribal pieces. The
euphoria which greeted the dismemberment of the Berlin Wall has
given way to a realignment of forces that seem less predictable because
less known. These uncertainties and anxieties hold related consequences for the experience of family life.

> Many people's experience of powerlessness in the face of external
> threats and pressures tends to drive them back into the family
> for sanctuary, protection and peace. Such a retreat from the
> outside world necessarily increases the pressure and the demands
> on the family. Inevitably, the experience of important things
> happening 'out there' which are controlled by the computer,
> the government or maybe the state of international relations,

none of which the individual feels able to control, increases his or her expectation that it is the family which must supply all his or her needs and allay all anxieties. (Walrond-Skinner in Furlong (1988), p. 65)

The AIDS epidemic

Since writing those comments in the mid eighties, a threat of devastating proportions has become more apparent. This time it is no vague, faraway threat from 'out there' but the close 'in here' threat of the AIDS epidemic. Whilst the events and consequences of a Chernobyl disaster provide only a distant, albeit significant context for all but the individual families who were directly affected, the threat of AIDS hovers at the very centre of our personal and intimate network of relationships. Invasive and invisible, the virus erupts unpredictably within the most central places of family life, affecting partners and parents and children either directly or as they grieve for the premature death of those they love.

The advent of AIDS at the end of the seventies has created several highly significant shifts in the social environment. This new and at present incurable disease has further disrupted our sense of security. In July 1992, the World Health Organization reported that one person is affected with the AIDS virus every fifteen to twenty seconds across the world. In some parts of Africa and Asia, the effects of the death rate from AIDS of men, women and children is such that whole families have disintegrated and the village and rural economy has broken down. AIDS has the psychological effect of decreasing our assurance that the world is a safe environment and that life 'out there' is OK. On the contrary, we have had to face the fact that we are 'out of control' of the world around us. We approach the end of the twentieth century knowing that despite so much achievement and so many scientific and technological advances, unprecedented in any other era, we nevertheless sit beneath multiple, mysterious threats to our existence.

In August 1983, *The Sunday Times* reported that 'Fear of catching the mysterious killer disease, AIDS, is causing more harm in Britain than the disease itself, with one London hospital reporting 'hundreds of patients suffering from AIDS-related anxiety – some to the point of considering suicide' (*The Sunday Times*, 14 August 1983). In its close association with sex, AIDS has had particular effects upon our approach to relationships and to the family. Although AIDS is now prevalent amongst heterosexuals of all races, and is raging on every continent, its early association with homosexuality has had the effect of further marginalizing the gay community, and, in so far as AIDS was originally viewed as an 'African illness', it has lent vigour to both anti-gay and anti-black sentiments.

Second, as AIDS has been gradually understood to be a western, heterosexual disease as well, it has faced us with new dilemmas and posed some sharp questions. Should church youth club leaders dispense condoms? Should the state provide brothels, housing 'clean', registered prostitutes? Should clean needles be provided to heroine addicts to enable them to inject without risking contamination? Indeed should drugs be legally prescribed in order to stifle the market and protect the health of addicts by reducing the sale of adulterated substances on the streets?

A third major effect of the AIDS epidemic has been to create a strong lobby amongst some Christians and others for a return to 'traditional values' in family life. AIDS has been seen as the 'finger of God' upon us, pronouncing punishment for our sexual misdemeanours. The perceived association between AIDS, homosexuality and promiscuity has created a powerful impetus in producing the 'pro-family' movement with its religious and political affiliations. It has concentrated our minds powerfully on the crisis of sexuality and on how we might understand its meaning. The crisis of sexuality is of course a far bigger phenomenon than the crisis of AIDS and although sexuality is rightly receiving the attention of a book of its own in this series, it would be impossible not to comment on some further features of the sexual revolution that provide part of the background and the context for our understanding of family life.

The women's movement

Chief amongst these is the women's movement with its far-reaching influence on every other kind of cultural transformation in which our society is currently engaged. The feminist critique of social institutions and the family in particular has highlighted a host of interlocking issues that profoundly affect the way in which family life is conceived and lived. The right to an abortion, the availability of adequate contraception and the valuing of feminine experience as equally valid though different, and new techniques of reproductive technology have all radically altered the degree to which women can claim some control over their lives. In the therapeutic sphere, psychoanalysis (Chodorow (1978) and Miller (1976)), psychotherapy (Brodsky, 1980), and family therapy (Hare-Mustin (1978), Osborne (1983), Golder (1985)) have been significantly influenced by a feminist critique of their traditional values and assumptions. In the field of family theory, the Parsonian analysis of gender roles and the tasks properly allotted to each has been severely challenged, so that family therapists, who in the seventies were still advocating clear divisions of function along gender lines between parents and spouses, have had to undertake a thoroughgoing revision of their therapeutic approach.

Women's claims to equal treatment before the law, to equal opportunities in the labour market and to equal remuneration for the work they do have created a shift in their status and experience. Feminism has a long history but the partial advances made in all of these areas of social and economic life have come partly as a result of the progressively influential work of a variety of recent feminist writers. But feminism is by no means a homogeneous entity, and feminist writers disagree in some important areas. Stanley and Wise (1983) have summarized the only three themes which they believe are common to all feminist approaches: the acknowledgement that women are oppressed; the assumptions that the personal experiences of individual women have social and political sources and solutions; and the recognition that women's different perceptions, values and beliefs are an equally valid way of interpreting and constructing the world around them. Beyond these three generally agreed positions, feminists are divided in terms of the degree to which they link feminism with a political ideology, the ways in which they perceive the causes of women's oppression, whether or not this oppression seems to have consequences for the oppression of men as well and how far certain groups (such as ethnic minority groups and working-class women) are identified as experiencing particular levels of oppression.

The ways in which these difficulties should be addressed are also the subject of disagreement.

Feminists also hold different perspectives on the family. The radical feminist critique of the family in the late 1960s and 70s had associations with the radical psychiatry movement of Laing and Cooper referred to in chapter 2. Whilst Laing and his associates highlighted the oppressive nature of the parent–child relationship, feminists concentrated their attention on the relationships between the spouses. Both groups have been concerned not so much with identifying the family's 'problems' but with arguing that the family itself is 'the problem'. It is the family that both requires and maintains gender divisions in terms of role and status and is therefore the source of patriarchal power – the domination of women by men. This analysis led to the abandonment of both family and of heterosexuality as appropriate means for developing intimate relationships and some radical feminists created instead communal and lesbian relationships in which to share and exchange support and mutual care. Alternatives to the segregated heterosexual unit have allowed radical feminists to create a more benign environment in which to develop interdependent relationships and to share the care of children and to conduct 'field experiments' in destroying the roots of patriarchal oppression.

Firestone (1970) offers a thoroughgoing assault on the roots of patriarchy and the way in which the fundamental inequalities which it produces should be addressed. She views the roots of all gender inequality as lying in the unequal burdens of procreation that are borne by women. These make her economically dependent upon men, confine her to the home and prevent her from participating equally in the job market. Millett (1970) on the other hand locates the roots of patriarchy in a deeply imbued ideology which makes men both 'preferred' and pre-eminent. These attitudes and values are developed through socialization, particularly within the family, and are internalized by women and men at an early age, to be reproduced in all other male–female relationships in society. In their earliest family experiences, males are given a 'birthright priority' which is subtly reinforced by parental attitudes. Thus women can only be liberated from their inferior position by attacking the process of socialization which imprisons them in a subordinate role.

Others have linked women's oppression with the economic

relationship that is established between men and women within marriage. Women's unwaged labour in the home is provided free in exchange for protection and control by her husband. Even when women work outside the home for wages, they continue to perform their unwaged labour at home in addition. 'So women remain disadvantaged in waged work and still shoulder vastly unequal burdens of domestic work. Working or not, women do 80% of domestic chores' (comments Segal (1983), p. 21). In many respects therefore, the main effect of marriage for women is as an agent and means of their oppression. It provides a legal endorsement of men's control of women for in the marriage service, the woman vows to obey her husband, she makes available her body for his sexual pleasure, and she is inducted into the all-consuming roles of housewife and mother.

Oakley (1981) and Barrett and McIntosh (1982) both identify the alienating and oppressive nature of the woman's domestic role. Others have pointed out the equally oppressive and monotonous nature of many men's repetitive manual jobs and the equally alienating experience of unemployment. But such arguments are countered by the linkage of woman's domestic imprisonment with the unequal burden of child-bearing, child-rearing and economic dependence, which, even allowing for the exceptional arrangements of job-sharing and paternity leave, make the domestic roles of women within marriage particularly problematic. Other feminists have highlighted the psychological distinctions and inequalities in the developmental processes of women, a matter to which we will return in chapter 7.

Violence in families

The 1980s saw the progressive acknowledgement of the reality and scale of domestic violence. A recent paper in the *Journal of Marital and Family Therapy* (Avis, 1992) summarized some North American statistics on family violence. One out of six women in the United States is abused every year by the man she lives with and one out of ten women in Canada. There is severe repeated violence in one in fourteen marriages. During the period from 1967 to 1973, the United States lost 39,000 in the Vietnam War. During the same period, *17,500 American women and children were killed by family members.* In other words, a staggering near half as many women and children were killed within families during this period as the deaths of men caused by the casualties of war.

95% of all marital violence is perpetrated by men against women and 95% of all incest is perpetrated by men, with the majority of victims being female. We have therefore to confront the severe power imbalances that exist between women and men in families and become much more aware of both the causes and the consequences of violence in families. Various studies show that high levels of marital conflict and low socioeconomic status emerge as the primary predictors of an increased likelihood of wife assault. Avis (1992) remarks that sexual abuse too of female children by male relatives has reached 'epidemic proportions' in North America (p. 227). She suggests four reasons for the very high incidence of the physical and sexual abuse perpetrated by men: violence is a normal response to the attitudes engendered within a partriarchal society, not the action of a sick few; male violence is explicitly sanctioned by a patriarchal culture; there is a global reactionary backlash against women as they move into non-traditional roles and are perceived as threatening; and there is a family pattern of transmission with 75% of men who abuse their wives having observed their fathers abuse their mothers.

In Britain, the number and rate of children registered on the NSPCC Child Protection Register doubled between 1983 and 1987. There was a rise of 50% in the rate per 1,000 registered for physical abuse and the sexual abuse rate increased from 0.08 to 0.65 per 1,000 (Creighton and Noyes, 1989). Creighton and Noyes acknowledge that these increases may be due in part to increased vigilance and to better monitoring but they suggest that the incidence of both physical and sexual abuse against children is likely to be increasing in absolute terms and also in terms of the seriousness of the injuries being inflicted. Their research undertaken for the NSPCC shows that abused children are likely to come from larger families and to be the eldest child. Slightly more boys than girls are physically injured, neglected or fail to thrive but the overwhelming number of cases of sexual abuse (80%) involve girls. Husbands and cohabitees are about equally likely to be implicated in the abuse of their children, but step-fathers are significantly more likely to abuse their step-children. The overwhelming number of people who abuse their children are male and of white European background. They tend to be unemployed or in semi- or unskilled manual occupations. Other environmental factors included the fact that over half of the families on the At Risk register were on supplementary benefit. Marital problems were the most frequently recorded factor of importance within the family dynamics and an inability to respond to the child's maturational needs or to deal with normal child behaviour were found to be significant factors.

Glaser and Frosh (1988) in their study of child sexual abuse investigated the patterns of transmission. They found the rather puzzling fact that 'the statistical link passes down a maternal chain (girls who are abused have daughters who are abused) and yet it is men who actually do the abusing' (p. 47). They suggest that the experience of abuse as children increases a woman's vulnerability in adult life to sexually exploitative behaviour in men and reduces her ability to protect either herself or her children. There is much more work now being done with adult survivors of sexual abuse who are progressively becoming more able to talk about their experiences and this is revealing the scale of the problem. Glaser and Frosh remark: 'Sexual abuse is no fiction nor a bandwagon which will roll away when the next interesting problem appears on the scene; it is a real phenomenon and its magnitude is only beginning to be recognised' (p. 12).

The re-valuing of masculinity

The effects on men of the women's movement have been complex. Some researchers, as we have already noted, suggest that the possible increase in the level of violence perpetrated by men against women and children reflect a backlash against the altered role and status of women. It is a prolonged crescendo leading perhaps to the death throes of patriarchy.

Other effects are witnessed by those of us who counsel couples and families. These include the uncertainty and anxiety of men in relation to the fundamental question of how to be a man. Tatham (1992) in an important new study comments:

Until about thirty years ago, the nature of a man and his masculinity was little questioned. Generally speaking, it was assumed that a man would inevitably wish to be strong, powerful, and decisive, and that he would concern himself more with what went on outside the home than with domestic details. Since this ideal was assumed to arise in some way from his actual biological nature, it was therefore inescapable. (p. xv)

If the old certainties about masculinity and maleness are now so severely questioned, what should be put in their place? How should male sexuality now be expressed? How is a man supposed to relate to his children and to his partner in ways which are divested of dominance and control and yet are other than a feminized version of maleness? The development of men's groups – some specifically targeted at a self-examination of male violence, others looking at broad questions of gender identity – offers a small but important arena for this debate to take place. Increasing numbers of colleges and universities too are offering courses in men's studies and there is a small but growing literature on the subject. We move through the final decade of a century that has witnessed perhaps the most severe manifestations of glorified masculine violence as well as a fundamental assault on the old certainties of gender identity. This confusion and uncertainty, created by a vacuum in understanding and expressing the creative potential of the male psyche, provides part of the context of contemporary family life. But the family is also the place where the struggle and the dilemma is most painfully witnessed and felt.

Tatham (1992) has made an important and original contribution to this debate from a Jungian perspective. He sets out the concepts of the archetypal nature of maleness and the ways in which a reformulation of these might be attempted. He suggests that the dominant male 'hero' archetype might be replaced by that of 'craftsman' and he makes the crucial point that 'the absence of the generative father from our minds and souls contributes I believe to the distortion of maleness in our society that has been called patriarchy'. He goes on to suggest that 'what is not experienced within is projected out upon the world. The metal-worker [or craftsman] however whose raw materials are from the earth, partakes I suggest of this divine ground, now reimagined as male' (p. xxiii).

It is plain to many of us how fully the Church has participated in

men's need to compensate for a deeply experienced vacuum of biological generativity and their desire to lay hold of and incorporate
this longed for creativity whilst cleaving simultaneously and fearfully
to the archetype of 'hero'. The all-male priesthood has precisely
answered this dual need and has so far prevented the search for a
new, more mature inclusive maleness emerging through the medium
of the Church's liturgy, symbolism and mode of ministry. For the
same reason, the Church will most powerfully symbolize the letting
go of this defensive need when women are admitted to priesthood.
The Church will then be able to address with authenticity the pain
and the promise of the death and re-birth of masculinity, with all
that that will have to offer, in both the personal and societal
spheres.

Multi-cultural influences

Another area of crucial significance to touch upon here is the family's
multi-cultural environment. The fact that families from different racial
and cultural origins often now live side by side means that the analysis
of customs, attitudes and ideologies concerning family life has become
even more complex. There are some obvious linkages between the
experience of being black and being female in our society and there
have been some parallels drawn between black and feminist writing
on the structure and effects of the family. The feminist critique of
the family has been adopted by some black feminist writers but they
have also pointed out that the experiences of black women have
often not been sufficiently recognized as being different from those
of their white sisters. 'We struggle together with black men against
racism while we also struggle with black men about sexism,' point
out Moraga and Anzaldma (1981).

Black women may view their families as sources of strength and
security in a way in which white women may not. Black women
may have much more in common with black men in their common
experiences of slavery, colonialism and racism and this is likely to
produce a different attitude to family life. Family is where one can
retreat from the alienation of being a minority in a hostile culture to
being in a place where one can create in microcosm the world 'like
me'. On the other hand various politicized self-help groups have

highlighted the ease with which erroneous conclusions about family life can be drawn by apparently 'enlightened' writers. In a collection of papers published by the Southall Black Sisters (1990) for example, Hannana Siddiqui writes:

> Women are being forced into arranged marriages, homelessness and denial of education. The multi-culturalist has failed to intervene and support these women. For them it is all part of a culture and religion which must be tolerated. And the anti-racists allow this to continue because they see the fight against racism as the central struggle. (p. 62)

Likewise, Ahmed et al. (1986) have drawn attention to the way in which social workers draw erroneous conclusions about their clients and show how cultural explanations of the facts of a client's situation are often misunderstood or misused because of profound misunderstandings about culture.

Many black families living in Britain today display a remarkable and tenacious hold upon the concept and experience of family and if it were not for the pervasive and persistent racism that infects our white response to family life amongst black people, we could undoubtedly be helped and enlightened by the insights and experiences that are on offer to us who belong to the dominant white culture. The forces that handicap us in doing so are the same forces that work so negatively within the daily environment of black families. First and fundamentally, this involves the concept of their being one black family, a stereotype which, as Dominelli (1988) says, 'acts as the norm whereby all black families are gauged' (p. 95); and, as she goes on to point out, 'except that "the black family" exists in the perceptions of and is reinforced through the practices of white people, there is in reality, *not the black family, but a rich and diverse variety of black family forms*' (p. 95).

This failure to recognize the varieties of family life amongst ethnic minority groups in general and amongst black families in particular is partly due to the extraordinary inability of white British people to see the world other than from the perspective of Britain being at its centre. The sheer scale of other countries compared with our own seems lost on most of us most of the time. The crude lumping together of people originating from the Caribbean Islands for example fails to recognize that a thousand miles or so separates some of these islands from one another and that each island has its own distinctive culture and way of life. People originating from different parts of Africa will be distinguished also not only by national but also by tribal identity, each having a bearing on the way that the family is viewed. Part of the environmental influences on the family include the tendency to conflate the distinction that exists within each social and racial grouping. This conflation leads to stereotyping and stereotyping in turn leads to pathologizing, so that black families are disproportionately drawn into the controlling functions of social work agencies (the criminal justice system and the psychiatric services), whilst being included less often for therapeutic services and practical help (Dominelli, 1988). In the London Borough of Lambeth where I now live, a report by the Social Services Committee revealed that black children were more likely to end up in care than white children, not because they or their parents were more disturbed but because white social workers were making inappropriate judgements upon the way black families live. Black children coming into care were found to come from families which were 'very representative of black families in the borough, covering a wide range of income, employment and housing situations' (Lambeth (1981), p. 7). In other words, the intervention of white social workers working from an internalized model of what was felt to be normal family life and a stereotypical pattern of 'the black family' were creating a situation whereby black families were more likely than white families to be broken apart. This being so, there is obviously a particular need to address the factors which create this situation, in particular, the ignorance and stereotyping taking place amongst professionals, as well as offering quality care to those children from black families that are taken into care. There is as yet not much evidence as Ahmed et al. (1986) point out, that the identity confusion of black children revealed by some researchers has been sufficiently addressed. Much work has been done to ensure the more appropriate placement of children with families from their own cultural origin but even this policy has its problems because, adhered to too rigidly, it can become a way of depriving black children of all family experience.

In the second place, history, for black families as for white, is part of the continuing environment, internalized within the family group and re-experienced through the perceptions of others. For Afro-Caribbean families, this history involves the uniquely devastating experience of having been slaves. This history is extraordinarily recent – only three or four generations, or two or three lifetimes stood end to end separate slaves and slave owners from us, their descendants. We, the descendants of those slaves and those slave owners, are profoundly influenced by our shared history. It is a history that is largely ignored and seldom mentioned. It is the unnamed and unnameable 'secret' that binds together the children of those that were so deeply and irredeemably oppressed and those who oppressed them. But at deep levels within our collective psyche, the humiliation, shame, guilt and anger of that shared experience remain. For black families originating in Africa or in the Indian subcontinent, history involves the different but still problematic experience of occupation and colonization.

Third, and in some measure created by the historical relationship between black and white, the contemporary experience of racism in all its forms, personal, institutional and cultural, continues to be a major environmental influence upon all family life – black and white. The under-representation, exclusion and marginalization of black people in the job market, within education and in areas of political and economic influence, creates special conditions for the experience of family life for black people. Racism also helps to ensure that black families are over-represented in terms of their poverty and powerlessness.

Fourth, the way in which some current legislation militates against and actively destroys family life for many black people should not be underestimated. As Dominelli (1988) points out: 'White people ignore the fact that black people do not have a right to family life. Immigration controls since 1962 have made it virtually impossible for black family units to exist in their totality in Britain' (p. 96). The Asylum Bill will have the effect of making this situation worse in specific cases, but more importantly, it will further strengthen the general sense of exclusion and hostility experienced by the black community as a whole.

Stereotyping, heritage and racism form part of the environment for all families, experienced differently depending on whether the family is perceived to be part of an ethnic minority or majority grouping. In overcoming some of the great weight of these influences, both groups need to experience their commonality *and* their differences. Each can be used negatively, and it is not surprising therefore that it is hard to track a path through all the self-help initiatives, professional approaches, political positions and community efforts that interact upon each other to try to alter the worst consequences of these influences on British family life. Both assuming that there are no differences between the experiences of black families and white, or assuming that the differences are greater than they are, prevent us from advancing in knowledge and understanding of the family and of the most effective means of helping families experiencing difficulties.

Moving forward in this area is a highly complex process because it involves members of the dominant ethnic culture hearing, understanding and repenting of the negative aspects of their heritage which has created our contemporary racist society. It involves members of ethnic minority groups discovering ways of becoming sufficiently confident in the identity and value of their culture and in themselves to assert their claim to be accepted as equal members of society with the right to participate equally in its economic, political and social life. It also involves the members of each group forgiving and being forgiven.

Religion as context

The Church is also part of the context of family life and, alongside other faith communities, impinges upon its experience. The ringing of the church bell, the muezzin's regular call to the faithful to pray, the sight of turbans and saffron robes and halal butchers' shops, all in their different ways proclaim the existence of a religious dimension to the family's environment. But are these influences beneficial or malevolent? Is religion part of the solution to some of the family's difficulties or is it part of the problem? Take for example the experience of an Asian woman. Is she oppressed by her Muslim faith, which subjugates her to her parents' choice of a husband and thereafter to her husband's protection and rule? As a feminist I must, along with black and Asian feminists, say obviously yes. But I have also to listen to Muslim women convicting me of the cultural stereotypes that inform my judgement. For them, Islam can nurture their individuality and also interpret their family unit's passage through its own formation and development. For them, a marriage arranged by loving parents who hold their daughter's welfare as a precious trust may hold out the promise of a secure union between two extended networks who pledge their support and continuous care of the young couple.

Take for example, the Christian Church. Its emphasis upon the importance and priority of the nuclear family unit has, as we explored a little in chapter 3, become at times little short of idolatry. Does this emphasis serve to support the structures of marriage and family life, as it intends, or does it serve to exclude all those who do not perceive themselves as belonging to this particular form of family structure? Even those who do indeed belong to nuclear family units, may find the Church's position ambiguous. For many women for example, the Church's almost exclusively male ministry, calendar of Saints, and liturgical language is a reflection of the excluding and oppressive structures and attitudes to be found in secular society.

Christian feminist writers (Maitland (1983), Morley (1988), Holloway (1992)) have endorsed much of the work of secular feminists but have offered critiques of their work as well as new insights. They pick up the same theme as their secular counterparts and expand it to show how the Church too has been deaf or complicit in the woman's plight. Bussert (1986) points out, in relation to the Church's covert acceptance of domestic violence, 'If submission continues to be the "theory" then battering will inevitably continue to be the practice' (quoted in Borrowdale (1991), p. 104). Borrowdale goes on to point out how 'Christian writers in this country have made little attempt to tackle the issue of male aggression and violence towards women' (p. 109). The physical and sexual abuse of children within the family has also been a subdued theme for Christian writers and the even more unpalatable fact that the Church, in terms of both its clerical and lay members, is statistically over-represented amongst the perpetrators of abuse is still hard to come to terms with. Dowell and Hurcombe (1981), Hebblethwaite (1984) and others have worked on an integration of the social and political themes of secular feminism with the work of feminist theologians (Ruether (1983), Fiorenza (1983), Moltmann-Wendel and Moltmann (1991) and have helped to expand the new awareness of what the women's movement has to say about family, gender, language, symbolism, sex roles, ministry, oppression and power within the arena of the Church.

The Church's sexism is matched only by its racism. The non-racial inclusive character of the gospel, good news for the whole of humanity, has suffered serious distortions throughout the Church's history with consequences for families from ethnic minority cultures and for every other family. Leech (1988) gives a thoroughgoing account of the way in which the Church has persistently ignored, colluded in and actively augmented the racist attitudes and policies of secular society. Indeed, Christianity has nourished and lent support to perhaps the most extreme forms of racism this century that our world has ever witnessed. Nazism, apartheid, the Klu Klux Klan, can all claim to have been fostered within the bowels of Christian belief. In a powerful synthesis of some of these themes, Selby (1991) reflects upon the tribal nature of the Church and concludes that 'it has not been hard to see the sources of the defensiveness and possessiveness which participation in the life of the Christian community can bring' (p. 75).

In chapter 5 we will consider how the family, shaped by some of these many influences within its environment, has developed a range of different patterns and forms.

5

❦

PATTERNS

'Behold, I make all things new.'

Revelation 21:5

We now need to turn our attention to the various patterns of family life being lived within our society during the last decade of the twentieth century. Both continuity and change are features of the family's evolutionary life. Some trends stand out very clearly as indicating significant change. Others suggest an unclear pattern and some features suggest a considerable degree of continuity.

Marriage

There has been a marked decrease in the numbers of marriages being contracted. In 1990 there were 318,000 marriages contracted in England and Wales compared with 404,000 nearly twenty years earlier in 1971. In 1989 there were 347,000 marriages in England and Wales and of these, 219,000 were first marriages for both husband and wife. Taking the figures for 1989 and looking at them in some detail, only 63% of marriages were first marriages for both husband and wife compared with 79% in 1971 and likewise the proportion of all marriages that were second marriages had risen from 12% in 1971 to 20% in 1989.

Age at first marriage has increased steadily being 22.6 for women and 24.6 for men in 1971 and rising to 24.8 for women and 26.9 for men in 1989. There has been a steady decline in teenage marriage since 1970 with a consequent widening of the gap between the onset of puberty and the age of first marriage. Although by far the greater majority of people still marry at some time during their lives, the proportion is declining to around 77% of men and 78% of women compared with 96% and 93% respectively in 1971.

Dormor (1992), in a useful analysis of contemporary relationships in Europe, poses three questions: Will marriage become obsolete? Will serial monogamy become the norm? And will Europe become a matrilineal society in the next millennium?

With the perspective of the 1990s, it is now much easier to understand the declining popularity of marriage within a developing trend that has shown marked changes during the twentieth century. We are able to discern an increasing trend during the first half of the twentieth century towards younger and more universal marriage throughout Europe, rather than, as before, in the southern part of Europe alone. In each generation, a greater proportion of people married and at a younger age until what has been called the 'Golden Age' of marriage was reached during the 1960s and 1970s when the popularity of marriage was at its height. A variety of reasons for this golden age have been advanced, including the buoyant hopefulness of the post-war era and its increasing prosperity. 'Rarely have marriage, sex and child bearing been so tightly bound together', comments Dormor (1992), and pre-marital sexual activity, extra-marital child-bearing and cohabitation fell to very low levels. But this golden age was the exception rather than the norm and it is important to register that fact in considering how future trends might be evaluated. After 1975 marriage rates began to fall dramatically. This was linked with a longer time spent by the young on their own, or with parents, or in living with their peers. But the fall is also significantly paralleled by a steep rise in the level of cohabitation.

Cohabitation

The rise in the incidence of cohabitation marks one of the most significant changes in the way the family is now structured. Some cohabitation is undertaken as a *substitute* for marriage and some as *preliminary* or as a preparation for it. In 1987 just under half of all women marrying for the first time had lived with their husbands prior to marriage compared with only 7% of those marrying in 1971, and by far the majority of couples who remarry cohabit first.

The sharp increase seems to reflect not only the influence of a range of economic and material variables but also a fundamental change in *belief* – namely that many feel that the chances of making a successful and durable marriage are improved by a prior period of cohabitation. A variety of attitudinal surveys conducted in different parts of Europe indicate that a significant number of people believe that premarital cohabitation is beneficial to their subsequent marriage. For example, Scott (1990) found that in Britain and the Netherlands, 43% and 45% of respondents respectively supported the idea of living together before getting married and likewise, in Hungary and Ireland, where actual cohabitation is still uncommon, 40% and 32% recommended a pattern of cohabitation followed by marriage. These findings are extremely interesting because a considerable number of studies are suggestive of an association between premarital cohabitation and subsequent marital disruption, although as we shall see in a moment, a causal link is neither proven, nor, where it is presumed, is it fully understood. It is clear however that significant numbers of people in different European cultures *believe* that premarital cohabitation, far from being detrimental to marriage is in fact beneficial.

Thus, the rising numbers of premarital cohabitations do not represent a disregard for marriage as an institution, still less an attack upon it. Rather, it seems that an increasing number of people regard marriage as being important enough to take a significant step in preparing the ground thoroughly and well, in the hope that it will meet their expectations. This is further borne out by the virtually universal practice of cohabitating prior to a second and subsequent marriage. Couples who have experienced a divorce are, it seems, at pains to try to prevent its recurrence.

Both the complexity of the facts and the heat which they generate in the Church serves to make cohabitation an interesting topic on which to dwell for a moment. 'If you want to make your marriage likely to fail, then cohabit first.' This arresting headline of a *Church Times*' article (12 June 1992) betrays an appealing but simplistic approach. Changes in this particular pattern of family life are too recent to allow such accurate interpretation of the evidence, so that such dogmatic statements of cause and effect should be treated with a good deal of caution.

On the other hand, cohabitation, or unofficial marriage, is not at all new. As Dormor (1992) points out:

We don't have to dig too deeply into history to find evidence of unofficial marriage. For example, in this country, the Hardwicke Act of 1753 was introduced to protect against bigamy and led to the civil registration of marriage. Prior to such registration, the practice of betrothal displayed similar characteristics to modern cohabitation, allowing sexual activity between those who were to be married, but also permitting separation. (p. 12)

Thus in some ways, this recent rise in the practice of cohabitation as a form of preparation for marriage represents both continuity and change in the pattern of family life, depending on the time perspective which is being adopted.

An important recent research preoccupation has been the examination of the relationship between cohabitation and subsequent marital instability, measured both in terms of marital satisfaction and the incidence of subsequent separation and/or divorce.* A great deal of this research is being conducted in the United States and much of it has used rather specialized populations (e.g. university students) but work has also been done in Sweden and Canada and a small amount in Britain.

Demaris and Vaninadha (1992), Thomson and Colella (1992) and Haskey (1992) all show a clear association between marital dissolution and premarital cohabitation. The amount of recent cumulative evidence of this association is impressive and Haskey (1992) goes so far as to say:

> The results are clear-cut; by every duration of marriage the accumulative proportions of marriages which had broken down are higher amongst marriages in which there was pre-marital cohabitation than amongst marriages in which there was no pre-marital cohabitation ... couples who pre-maritally cohabited were about 40% more likely to have divorced within 15 years of marriage ... and if marital breakdown is taken as either divorce or separation, the marriages of those who

---

* Balakrishnan et al. (1987), Bennett et al. (1988), Bumpass and Sweet (1989), Teachman and Polonko (1990), Hoem and Hoem (1992), Trusgell et al. (1992), Thomson and Colella (1992), Haskey (1992).

pre-maritally cohabited were 60% more likely to end in break-down. (pp. 15–16)

The results are very consistent and it is tempting for those who hold an ideological position which is opposed to cohabitation (for example, Pratt (1992), Jenkins (1992)) to see them as confirmation that pre-marital cohabitation is causally linked with the increased likelihood of a breakdown of that marriage. By this argument the equation can be neatly drawn, namely, that cohabitation is intrinsically wrong because it 'falls short of God's intention' (Jenkins (1992), p. 19), and it is also wrong because it causes the further wrong of divorce.

However what we are examining here is an *association* between two variables, those of cohabitation and divorce, not a *causal link*. The material is highly complex and much further research is needed before any causal link could be inferred. Moreover, some studies do not confirm this association at all between cohabitation and marital break-down. For example, White (1987), using a very large sample of Canadian couples (10,472) showed that premarital cohabitation had a positive effect on staying married subsequently. Bennett et al. (1988) showed no relationship between the two after eight years of marriage and Teachman and Polonko (1990) found that there was no corre-lation if the total length of the cohabitors' unions was compared with the total length of the marriage relationship. Schoen (1992) found that the differentials were either much smaller or the association between cohabitation and marital breakdown was reversed.

But it is obviously important to consider seriously those studies which do show an association between the two. The consequences of marital breakdown, separation and divorce are so damaging and distressing for both the couple concerned and for the whole family that it is important to try to understand what it is about cohabi-tation that may be associated with an increased risk of marriage breakdown.

There are a variety of reasons which may be significant in linking the two sets of circumstances. First, Thornton (1991) has shown that those who experience the breakdown of their parents' marriage are more likely to cohabit. However there is also evidence to show that couples whose own parents have divorced experience a greater risk of marital breakdown themselves. Thus, for those couples within this group who cohabit prior to marriage, the causal link may be confined to the effect of their parents' marriage and be unrelated to any specific effects contingent upon their own decision to cohabit or to the experience of cohabitation itself.

Second, the incidence of cohabitation prior to a second or subsequent marriage is now very high indeed, whereas the rate of breakdown of second and subsequent marriages is also higher than for first. Here, the causal link is as likely to be the unresolved malignant components of the first or prior marital relationship(s) rather than the experience of cohabitation itself. (This factor will be considered further in the discussion of marriage preparation in chapter 8.) Several authors suggest that the decision to cohabit reflects an intrinsically weaker commitment to marriage as an institution and that the higher rates of breakdown stem from this weaker commitment. Alternatively as Teachman and Polonko (1990) suggest, it may reflect a weaker commitment to this particular union rather than a weaker commitment to marriage generally. In other words, the couple makes a rational assessment of the degree of commitment that they wish to make to one another and make the more limited commitment to cohabitation rather than the lifelong commitment of marriage.

There are other characteristics which have been shown to distinguish the two groups, any or all of which may be causally related to a higher risk of marital breakdown. For example, cohabitors have tended to be more unconventional in their beliefs and life-style, hold higher expectations (perhaps unrealistic ones) of what marriage can offer and have poorer relationships with their families of origin. In other words, until recently, cohabiting unions may have been intrinsically more divorce-prone on a number of related indices. However, it may be that, with the continuing dramatic rise in the incidence of pre-marital cohabitation and its consequent normalization, the characteristics of cohabitors and non-cohabitors will become much more convergent. This is likely to erode significantly the current association between cohabitation and marital disruption.

Cohabitation is a way of creating family and is increasingly chosen as an alternative to marriage. Many couples consider their relationship to be fully committed, monogamous and permanent, whilst others regard it as permanent within certain defined parameters, i.e., 'whilst the children are dependent upon us' or 'whilst our relationship

81

remains vital and life-giving'. As with marriage, the reasons for the choice of partner and of cohabitation rather than marriage may not be fully understood by the partners. These may include fears and anxieties, as well as hopes and ideals for a relationship that forgoes the security of the marriage vows in favour of accepting that the commitment always depends upon its daily re-creation. Issues that are particular to the cohabiting couple are well summarized by Goldenberg and Goldenberg (1990) and include social stigma; the difficulty of finding an appropriate term to describe the partner; expectations about the future and the possible unequal commitment of the partners.

Divorce

Britain now has one of the highest divorce rates in Western Europe and although the majority of marriages are still terminated by death, divorce rates more than doubled during the 1970s. The divorce rate remained roughly constant at 150,000 throughout the 1980s with an increase at the beginning of the 1990s to 165,000. Estimates suggest that if divorce rates continue at the same level, then just under four in ten or 37% of marriages contracted in the mid 1980s are likely to end in divorce (Haskey 1989). Moreover, second and serial divorces are becoming increasingly common. Since the early 1970s, the proportion of divorces involving a second or subsequent marriage for one partner more than doubled from 7% in 1971 to 16% in 1989.

These figures lend themselves to differing interpretations. Some attribute the increased incidence in divorce to the peculiar instability of marriages in the late twentieth century. Others suggest a range of general explanations including longevity; increased (and perhaps unrealistic) expectations of marriage; decreased support of friends and extended family, because of increased mobility and the transience of modern industrialized society; increased expectations and reduced tolerance level of women; and greater opportunity for divorce because of better legal aid and benefit facilities as well as a more liberal divorce law.

Some groups are less divorce-prone than others. For example, those who profess a religious commitment; people in the top of their social or occupational class groupings according to the Registrar General's stratification, and people in social class 1. By contrast, people in social class 5, people who are unemployed or who are in certain occupations (for example long-distance lorry drivers, the armed forces) show a considerably higher incidence of divorce.

The effects of divorce on the men, women and children involved have been repeatedly shown to be highly traumatic. Couples experiencing divorce are six times more at risk of being hospitalized for mental disorders. Even after the divorce process has been completed, divorced people have more car accidents, more serious physical illness and a higher instance of alcoholism and substance abuse. They are twice as likely to commit suicide as members of the general population. Divorce, like marriage, is a 'family affair' and affects the family system as a whole. (In chapter 7 we will examine divorce as a phase within the family life cycle. Ways in which couples can be helped during this process will be discussed in chapter 10.)

The effect of the increased incidence of divorce on the institutions of marriage and the family are harder to access. Most divorced people re-marry so that as Fletcher (1973) points out, divorce does not necessarily reduce the possibility of marriage. However more recently, there has, as we noted earlier, been a drop in the marriage rate, which may have some association with the wish to avoid the well documented damaging consequences of divorce. The experience of divorce (actually experienced, or witnessed at one remove) may therefore have some aversive effect on the desire to enter marriage, and divorce may therefore increase the diversity of family forms, not only through the direct effect of creating lone parents and remarried families, but also because people are avoiding marriage altogether and are cohabiting instead. For this reason, divorce may also be an important factor in reducing the numbers of people who subsequently experience divorce, though not the numbers who experience the breakdown of a committed relationship, since cohabiting relationships are as prone to breakdown as marriage.

Lone-parent families

During the 1980s, the proportion of families with dependent children headed by a lone parent increased from 8% in 1971 to 19% in 1990. This increase was created by the doubling of the number of lone mothers bringing up dependent children. The proportion headed by a lone father has remained almost unchanged at 2% over the last two decades. Of these lone parents in 1989, divorced mothers made up the largest single group (33%) and single mothers the next largest (31%). The rest were made up of separated mothers, widows and lone fathers.

The growth in the proportion of single mothers reflects the growth in extra-marital child-bearing. Most European countries have shown substantial increases in the numbers of births occurring outside marriage with fewer people moving from cohabitation to marriage because of pregnancy. In 1990 28.3% of all live births were outside marriage and the provisional figure for 1991 is 30.2% (OPCS, 1992). Some of these trends can be seen throughout Europe and are not specific to Britain although Britain with Denmark has one of the highest proportions of lone-parent families.

But there are also geographical variations whereby some areas within Britain produce much higher numbers of lone-parent families. In 1981, for example, compared to the national average of 14%, inner urban areas had far higher concentrations. Inner London had 26.6% of all its families headed by one parent and in Lambeth it was 32%.

More lone parents are likely to experience the stress of poverty and of poorer housing and poorer schools for their children than two-parent families. If they become a one-parent family as a result of divorce, they usually have to adjust to a far lower standard of living as well as coping with the stress and aftermath of the divorce experience. Some families which are technically 'intact' nuclear families function 'as if' they were lone-household families for much of the time – for example where one partner is in prison or in an occupation which takes him away from the family for prolonged periods. The small number of lone fathers bringing up children are an important group to keep in mind. They may well experience problems additional to those of lone mothers. Hipgrave (1982) suggests that 'the attitude of the community at large can often serve to isolate one-parent families – and fathers in particular' (p. 183). Again we are faced with the fact that it is often the community's response to a different family form that creates many of those families' problems.

Remarriage

A substantial proportion of divorced people, including lone parents, eventually do remarry. Men are more likely than women to remarry after divorce and to do so more quickly. Remarriage is not a new phenomenon. Laslett (1971) shows that about a quarter of all marriages in the seventeenth century were remarriages. However the essential difference is that those remarriages followed death and not divorce. Despite Gittins' (1985) sanguine interpretation that death 'was an arbitrary breaker of marriages in a way that divorce is not', most research suggests that both step-parents and step-children find the forming of a remarried family more difficult after divorce than after death.

Although remarriage rates like first marriage rates have fallen continuously since 1971, reflecting the growing popularity of cohabitation, the proportion of all marriages that are remarriages has risen sharply during the last two decades. In 1971 about 10% of marriages involved the first marriage of one partner to a divorced partner and 4% the remarriage of two divorcees. By 1989 these had risen to 19% and 13% respectively.

Remarriages are at greater risk than first marriages and it is likely that the greater the complexity of the reconstituted family, the greater the risk. Those marriages where both partners are remarrying for the second or subsequent time and where both have children from previous marriages, with previous partners involved in access arrangements, have the highest risk of all.

A variety of terms have been used to describe this type of family, including step-families, reconstituted families, blended families, restructured families, and remarried families. Each has its difficulties – some implying the intrinsic oddness or difference of this family form. Because more mothers than fathers are given custody of their children, it is usually step-fathers that become part of creating a reconstituted family. There are in fact four times as many step-father families than step-mother families. Step-mothers are more likely to bring children with them to the new relationship so that these families are more likely to have to cope with relationships with new siblings.

Children

Because of these increased trends towards cohabitation, divorce, remarriage and lone-parenthood, children are increasingly being brought up outside the conventional nuclear family and are experiencing a variety of family forms. Approximately 30% of children are now born out of wedlock in Britain and around $2\frac{1}{2}$ million children live in reconstituted families with a step-parent. It is estimated that by the year 2000, only about half of all children will be experiencing a conventional childhood in a nuclear family with two natural parents. However another important change in family pattern is the decrease in the number of children born within each family. Parenthood is postponed until later, and women born in the late 1940s and early 1950s are more likely to remain childless than in previous generations. Although more couples exercise the option to remain childless, Phoenix et al. (1992) found that childlessness, whether chosen or not, is still viewed negatively, as an indication of personal or social inadequacy. This may particularly apply amongst those who belong to a faith community where there may be deeply held beliefs about children being 'a blessing from the Lord'.

There are some differences in fertility rates amongst ethnic minority groups, with Afro-Caribbean mothers being slightly lower and mothers born in India, Pakistan and Bangladesh having a somewhat higher fertility rate than white mothers.

A relatively small number of children join families through adoption. Figures for 1988 indicate that compared with 780,000 born in Britain and Northern Ireland combined, 1,000 babies and 4,000 older children were adopted. Many adoptive parents are unable to conceive children themselves and the stress that many experience in having to come to terms with their own infertility may increase their commitment to parenthood. Raynor (1980) suggests that adoption is frequently successful and the chances of parents and children being satisfied with their family life is increased if there are major similarities between them. Children who are adopted early on in their lives do better on a variety of measures – socially, intellectually and emotionally – than children who are adopted when older. But this may simply reflect the fact that older children have often had extremely traumatic experiences in their pre-adoption life.

Haimes and Timms (1985) suggest that adoption is a marginal status and that, because of the way society considers adoption – as a somewhat different and exceptional experience – adopted children may think of themselves as different or deviant. However, considerable changes have taken place in the last twenty years in the way that adoption is viewed. First, a high priority is placed upon helping a child to gain and hold knowledge of his earliest weeks, months and years of life, through photographs and scrap-books prepared by social workers and/or the natural parents. Adoptive parents receive considerably more help in creating continuity with their adopted children's past, and the right of adopted children to explore their origins when they become adult is respected.

Second, the range of children considered 'available' for adoption is much wider than used to be the case – older children as well as children with learning difficulties, Down's syndrome and multiple physical disabilities. Specialist agencies such as Barnardo's New Families Projects take immense trouble in finding, preparing and supporting adoptive parents in the care of these children. Third, more people such as gay and lesbian couples and single people living with relatives or alone are now being allowed to adopt children, and there is more flexibility in the age range of prospective adopters. Fourth, trans-racial adoption policy has undergone considerable change. In the late 1960s a number of agencies experimented with the placement of black and mixed race children with white families. Gill and Jackson (1983) reported that, viewed from the perspective of adopted children in general, these adoptions were in many respects successful. However it was clear that the child's racial identity was often being denied and assimilated instead of affirmed, and it was certainly not being established strongly enough for him or her to withstand the racism he or she was likely to encounter later on in society.

There is now a much sharper awareness of the needs of black and mixed-race children to be affirmed positively in their black identity and to retain strong links with their cultural roots, as well as forming new relationships with children and adults from their own racial group. This has resulted in the concerted effort to recruit more adopters from amongst black families and to place as many black and mixed-race children as possible with them. However the fundamental necessity must be to combat the racism which interferes with the needs of children from ethnic minority groups at all levels, preventing them from growing up affirmed and valued in their own unique identity as black, Asian or mixed-race children. We are challenged to overcome our colour-blindness and our stereotypes in such a way that more black social workers are available to help more black families *and* more white families fulfil these fundamental tasks.

Rapid developments in reproductive technology have meant that families can now be formed through artificial insemination by donor, through *in vitro* fertilization and by surrogate motherhood. There is very little research into the effects of these technologies on the family but several studies tackle the issue of secrecy. There is disagreement as to whether and how to share with the child the way in which he or she was conceived, which in part stems from the anonymity of the donor in AID and the inability therefore to give the child any useful information. There are obviously some differences with adoption here but also issues that are common, and with a greater degree of experience, more clarity will no doubt be forthcoming. Surrogacy is somewhat similar to adoption except that the surrogate mother makes the arrangements with the couple or individual mother who will receive the child, prior to conception rather than after the birth. The degree to which one expects there to be significant effects upon relationships between the couple and between the couple and the children born in these different ways is likely to depend in part on the myths surrounding biological parenthood. Where the blood tie and the concept of lineal descent is regarded as of overriding importance, all artificial methods of reproduction will be seen as 'second best'. When value is placed more on the relationships that are formed and where family relationships are seen as less differentially unique from other social relationships, then children born by these means need not feel in any significant sense different and in no sense whatever diminished. In fact it could be argued that the process by which family members join through adoption and technological means is a prefiguring of the 'new family' that transcends the tribal exclusiveness imposed by barriers of descent and blood.

Gay and lesbian relationships

The latter part of the twentieth century has seen the continuing effort to understand homosexuality within the spectrum of human sexuality. The increasing claim of many homosexuals to be treated as couples and to form family groups means that this debate must necessarily be part of any effort to wrestle with family life in the last decade of the twentieth century. With the highlighting of the debate, subtle changes occur in terms of the way homosexuality is perceived and these in turn may influence the degree to which people feel able to own or, on the contrary, feel compelled to disown a homosexual identity. It is hard therefore to be at all clear about the incidence of homosexuality within the population, which is variously calculated as 2%, 4%, 6% or 10%.

Definitions, aetiology and terminology are all hotly debated issues. The term homosexuality is regarded as in itself a derogatory and 'medicalized' term by many, which inevitably implies pathology. The term gay, largely adopted by homosexual men, has recently been challenged by the more politically assertive gay rights groups who argue instead for a return to the older and previously derogatory term 'queer'. Lesbians have progressively differentiated themselves from gay men, in terms of history, the social formation of their identity and their future needs and interests. For many feminist lesbians, their choice of a female partner is a political stand against the abuse of women by men and a demonstration that women can exist sexually and procreatively without them. Criss-crossing all the discussions are the sub-agendas of these two changing alliances – where sometimes the emphasis is on the similarity of homosexual issues and their difference from heterosexuals and sometimes the similarity of women's issues and their difference from those of men.

One aspect of the debate that has received much attention, particularly it seems amongst Christians, has been aetiology – the search for the roots or 'causes' of homosexuality. Like the search for causes in other walks of life it will certainly turn out to be the least important aspect of the whole discussion. The bishops in their report, *Issues in Human Sexuality* (1991), aptly refer to 'the mystery of its causation, a mystery, reflected in the diversity of theories on the subject' (p. 32). A major parameter of the debate has been the nature/nurture controversy. For example, Moberly (1983) arguing from a psychoanalytic perspective locates the origins of homosexuality in unresolved trauma in the individual's remote past. Specifically, she links the aetiology of homosexual orientation and preference to a disruption of attachment to the parent of the same sex. It is a scholarly and carefully argued thesis which views the choice of a partner of the same sex as a reparative choice leading to the restitution of the normal developmental process of identification with the same-sex parent. The difficulty about her analysis, from the gay or lesbian point of view, however, is that she clearly views homosexuality as 'deficient' in some developmental sense and that although the same-sex pairing is a proper attempt to meet essential unfulfilled needs, she views all such relationships as inherently self-limiting and merely a step on the road towards the full relational capacity of heterosexuality.

The opposite thesis, that of fundamental genetic difference, has been put forward most recently by researchers at the University of California Medical School at Los Angeles and at the Salk Institute, California. Simon LeVay suggests that there is some evidence to show that the interstitial nucleus of the anterior hypothalamus (involved in sexual arousal) is smaller in gay men than in heterosexuals. Likewise Laura Alan and Roger Gorski from UCLA found a size difference of 34% between the anterior commisure in the brains of gay men and heterosexuals. Whilst an argument based on genetic difference more definitively exonerates homosexuals from having to take responsibility for their choice of sexual preference, it could nevertheless open the way for a hunt for a 'cure' as surely as a psychogenic explanation.

An aspect of the discussion which relates to the debate about causes is the degree to which homosexuality is a ubiquitous human experience. Whatever their views on other related matters, most people would now agree that there is a continuum between the two polarities of sexual orientation with many people falling somewhere in the middle. This means that there is much greater diversity in people's sexual experience than used to be acknowledged and movement between different forms of family life – from same-sex pairing to marriage or cohabitation, or from a nuclear family experience to a homosexual relationship. There is a division in the gay and lesbian community between whether permanence, fidelity and exclusivity or impermanence and freedom of choice should be the essential ingredient of same-sex relationships. Plummer (1978) points out that the pervasiveness of the couple unit in our society as well as the continuing influence of traditional heterosexual marriage tend to exert pressure on homosexuals to form couple relationships. John (1993) argues persuasively for a permanent exclusive relationship comparable to marriage.

Demands by Christian homosexuals and others to have their relationships recognized as analogous to marriage and to receive social support in living a faithful, monogamous partnership, are challenged by the contrary demands of others to be allowed to form and re-form relationships in freedom, governed by different relational ethics. In practice homosexual couples show considerable diversity in the way in which they structure their relationships.

The change in patterns of expectation in traditional marriage undoubtedly affects the way in which other kinds of partnerships are lived so that we may expect both gay and lesbian people to have less role and task divisions in their relationships now than ten or twenty years ago. Lesbian relationships are also influenced by a history of hiddenness and accommodation within the dominant culture which has allowed women to form friendships and live together untroubled by intrusive questions about the nature of their relationship. They have therefore been less pressured by the persecution of homophobia though, by the same token, less challenged to claim their right to recognition. Lesbians are more likely to wish to become parents than gay couples, because of the social conditioning of women towards motherhood (and perhaps because of some innate differences between women and men in this regard). Parenthood may be achieved through bringing children into a relationship from a previous marriage, through adoption or through artificial insemination, and increasing numbers of lesbian partnerships and some gay partnerships are claiming their right to do so. The specific issues faced by homosexuals in their couples and family relationships will be discussed in chapters 8 and 9.

Communal living

There is a long history of interaction between the developing structure of the family and the desire to create a wider yet intimate relational system. The impetus for the development of communal living arrangements has been political, religious and ethnic as well as the influence of sexual politics. Some coexist or overlap with other forms of family forms in their own right. Christians have been well represented in this minority choice of family life-style and have created communal living arrangements of various different kinds. Some are collections of individuals, usually of the same sex, forming a traditional religious community. The individuals create a family identity and structure around the shared family history and family name (the Franciscan family etc.). They create peer relationships, designate one another as brothers and sisters and relate to a mother or father superior. They maintain their structure by vows, analogous to the vows of marriage. Other types of religious community are often collections of nuclear and lone-parent families and single people. They form a collective of sub-groups, where each sub-group becomes part of the wider community but individuals retain membership of another family form as well. The community live together but often in separate neighbouring houses forming a compound of related groups. Adult members of families usually take promises which bind them (but not permanently) to membership of the community family. Domestic chores and, less often, child-rearing tasks, are undertaken communally. Examples of this type are Little Gidding, Post Green, the Community of Celebration, Findhorn and the Israeli Kibbutz – whose motivation is often as much political as it is religious.

Similar distinctions occur between politically motivated communal groups. In these the desire to overcome the exclusive, possessive and inward preoccupations of the nuclear family are strong and groups of individuals or family collectives formed from nuclear and lone-parent families, cohabiting couples and singles create a common life based on varying degrees of shared income and goods. As in religious communities, those composed of individuals are more likely to be interdependent than those whose members retain membership of another sub-group within the community. Socially and politically motivated communes often extend their commitment to shared pos-sessions and to the sharing of sex. In some, every adult is free to have sexual relationships with everyone else; in others there is a convention of partner exchange within certain defined limits. The desire may be to diffuse the possessiveness of the monogamous union, to eradicate the deceptions that usually play a part in extra-marital affairs, and to promote greater equality between the sexes.

Ethnicity is also a factor in creating communal family life. Sometimes this relates more to the pressures of urbanization and housing problems than to the desire to live communally *per se*. Many Asian and Afro-Caribbean families in inner-city Britain, for example, live in old overcrowded multi-occupancy dwellings. This makes it possible for a large network of extended-family members to live together. This seems to be a matter of choice to some extent and has enabled the gradual reunification of families through successive immigration to be achieved with maximum degree of family support. It is often however a matter of necessity, arising out of limited resources and choice.

The travellers are an ethnic group where collective communal living has a very long history. It is for them a chosen and much prized form of family life. Close bonds are formed between the community group and families move together from one area to another by common agreement. Their demands on society are few other than the right to assemble and live together for periods of time between their periods of travel. Until 1992, every local authority had the duty to provide a suitable area for travelling people to congregate. At the time of writing, the government has announced the withdrawal of this obligation. It seems that travellers represent a form of communal family life which the dominant culture is finding it increasingly difficult to tolerate.

Definitions

These are some of the facts about family life as it is experienced in Britain today. We are now in a better position to examine some of the parameters that are often used for arriving at a definition of family. *Blood, law, habitation* and *bonding* can be used as categories of inclusion and exclusion from the definition of family, and we will look briefly at each. Within these categories we can then look at examples of a range of family types which bear some relationship to the real life experience of human beings as well as helping us move towards creating a theoretical framework from which to understand and then help families.

Blood-relatedness includes a variety of kinship groups and in theory this category is so inclusive as to be meaningless, as Goode (1982) notes: 'If we accept everyone as kin who is related by blood, through however distant a tie, clearly everyone in any society would be considered a relative of everyone else in the whole world' (p. 112).

For our purposes we must invoke the concept of awareness thus: given that I am related by blood to every other person in the world, of what blood–relationships am I aware? As in the case of each of these categories, other dimensions of inclusion have to be considered simultaneously with the concept of *blood-relatedness*. Thus we would be including as families, lone parents – mothers or fathers with dependent children – sibling groups, and adults with ageing relatives. Each of these three types may or may not live together and form a household, so that the category of *habitation* may be introduced alongside that of *blood-relatedness*; but habitation is not necessary for these groups to be included in the definition of family. In other words the two remain analytically distinct categories. Kin such as aunts, uncles, grandparents and cousins considered to be members of the *extended family* would also be included here. We would also need to include the *nuclear family* – families of *blood-relations* that form around marriage contracts between a pair of adults – so that again a second category, that of *law*, is being introduced alongside that of *blood-relatedness* while remaining independent of it. Thus within the general category of *blood-relatedness*, we would be including some families that are normally considered to be 'conventional' (parents and dependent children) and others which may not so easily fit our understanding of how a family should be defined (adult sibling groups and single-household groupings of parent and child/children). Although other categories may overlap, the salient characteristic of these groupings are their *blood-relatedness*.

Legal ties extend the definition of families to those created around a marriage contract between two adults and through the adoption of dependent children. If we extend the close definition of legal tie a little to include other forms of contractual arrangements, this will allow us to include as families groupings where adults foster children and where children are acquired through surrogacy and AID. A whole set of contractual relationships are initiated by a marriage contract and a great many people are bound into a legal relationship with one another after the marriage of a couple – a fact which we express by the terms 'in-law'. Thus mothers- and fathers-in-law, sisters- and brothers-in-law, become part of the family group when we use *law* as the defining category of family membership, as do step-children. *Law* as a category can and does exist simultaneously alongside *blood* and *habitation*, but it brings into family membership relationships not included by *blood* or *habitation* alone.

Habitation or household is part of our conception of what defines family life. Indeed, the Latin word 'familia' from which the word family comes, means household, and primitive cultures would have assumed that definition. We too assume that at least *some* of the people who are related by *blood* and/or by *law* will normally live together. However we do not necessarily expect *all* such persons to live together (i.e. all the aunts and cousins and all the in-laws) and we will need to *include* in our definition of family, parents and children who do *not* share a household. Young children for example may be away at boarding-school, students at college, relatives living abroad, as well as those who have left home permanently and formed their own households. On the other hand, the category of household allows for the inclusion of others in the family definition, not included by *blood* or *law.* Cohabiting couples often claim their relationship on the grounds that they 'live together'. The lifelong lodger or the elderly friend, the people that get described as being 'one of the family' and given the title of honorary aunt may also claim to be included through this category.

But few of us would be happy about confining the definition of a family to groups within the categories of *blood, law* and *habitation* alone. *Bonding* and emotional relatedness is a characteristic of family life that is considered to be important to a greater or lesser extent within all cultural definitions of the family. It is of course undoubtedly true that close emotional ties are emphasized more strongly in some cultures than others but in western culture the search for close, intimate relationships has increasingly become a primary driver in the motivation for belonging to any family group. Thus, in addition to one or more of the above categories, the desire for emotional *bonding* between people who are related by *blood* or *law* or who *live together,* is part of the definition of whether or not they can be defined as a family. However disagreeable the relationship between them may be, we define a group as a family in part because they share things in common (food, sex, chores, finances, time) and in so doing create an emotional relationship. We would not therefore include some people who live together (e.g. in lodgings or in an institution) as being a family, not simply because they are not related by *blood* or *law* but because they do not have an emotional relationship. On the other hand we would include people who live together 'in community', because they in some measure 'belong to each other'. The claim to be family is based upon claiming to share a degree of emotional relatedness which, though hard to quantify, is nevertheless experienced as real and important. Thus, we need to include here gay and lesbian couples, cohabiting unions, living-apart-together couples, long-standing friendships and any relationship that is subjectively experienced by the participants as involving affective *bonding* over time and where the behaviour of each person affects and is affected by each of the others. This defining category of emotional *bonding* is more untidy and perhaps more troubling than the others because it confronts us more sharply with having to make sense of the reported subjective experience of those who claim to be in families but whose life-style departs to a greater or lesser extent from some norm or ideal of what family life should be. Gay and lesbian couples for example claim to be families and to be allowed to adopt children on the basis of their emotional relationship.

In this category people claim that their family experience is represented by 'the relationships that matter most' to them. These relationships, of whatever outward form, are experienced by them as unique and irreplaceable. In Marris's (1974) phrase they 'seem to embody most crucially the meaning of our lives' (p. 185). Thus the extent to which a relationship is grieved for when lost and the extent to which it is experienced as irreplaceable provides us with a measure of its 'familiness'. This category, therefore, will include all the other types of families that are defined by *blood, law* and *habitation* and in addition, those that we can include in this subjective category of emotional *bonding*. For some people, the family pets would be included and greatly contribute to a person or couple's sense of 'familiness'.

The subjective experience of emotional *bonding* has come to be seen as of greater importance in all forms of family life during the twentieth century and the expectation that intimate relationships should fulfil this felt need is probably one of the factors that most clearly distinguishes our contemporary view of what a family is for from that of our predecessors. In other words we acknowledge that both subjective and objective criteria are necessary in developing a definition of family. We might thus summarize the foregoing and simply define a family as *an intimate domestic group, in which individuals are committed to one another by ties of blood, law, habitation or emotional bonds or a combination of all four.*

The picture that emerges for the future is that of increasing pluralism in family form. Yet as one talks and listens to people who are struggling, hurting, rejoicing, developing and 'becoming' in so many different kinds of structures, there is also a great *continuity* of needs and aspirations for the fulfilment of the fundamental hope for achieving loving, intimate and responsible relationships, which also allow freedom and growth to their members. The extremely rapid increase in cohabitation, both as a prelude to marriage and as a substitute for it, is likely to continue, so that the central relationship of many family groups is likely to be a cohabiting union. For those who do choose to marry, it may be increasingly important to augment further the particular character of marriage as an institution involving life vows and a permanent commitment to one other person. The preparation for and support of people making this choice must be more carefully considered. In particular, it must help couples to understand that the nature of lifelong commitment within marriage is not to a *status* but to a continuing momentum of *change* – both for the self and for the other. This crucial understanding is derived from our greater awareness of the meaning of the life cycle which involves passing through a series of discontinuous changes throughout our lives. It must be a preparation for the reality and not the fantasy of marriage.

But for many, marriage will not be the right choice for them. Some will want to choose singleness and some celibacy. Others will wish to form a variety of partnerships with differing levels of commitment. Some of these partnerships will want to take on the additional role of parenthood – some will not. Others again will choose the challenge of living in community.

'Thus the myth of the nuclear family in this country is not supported by either scripture, current statistics or sociological studies' (p. 15), comments Pothan (1992) succinctly and this requires us to consider how the Church might best enable this diversity of relationships to be supported and cared for. Marriage, with or without children, will continue to involve both the strain and the security of a commitment for life. Cohabiting unions will probably remain significantly less stable than marriages even though their increasing normalization will reduce some of the external stress with which they are currently associated. Periods of transition in and out of these unions will nevertheless cause considerable levels of emotional distress both to the partners themselves and to any children who are involved, and they will require a compassionate and skilful response. I would want to conclude that people are choosing to live in relationships other than marriage not lightly, wantonly or without serious thought, but because they believe that they often offer the best hope of enabling certain crucial and fundamental needs to be met, or some of the worst and most damaging effects of marriage and divorce to be avoided. By pressing people implicitly or explicitly to adopt models of family, which are not in keeping with their needs, we risk creating much of the misery and hardship which we say we want to help people avoid.

The decreasing rate of marriage, the increasing rate of divorce and the growth in cohabitation and 'living-apart-together' arrangements is likely to mean an increasing trend towards a matrilineal society. In some minority cultures in Britain, the mother–child relationship is already the central focus of many families but it seems likely that increasingly, lone parents, of which 90% are likely to be the mother, will be heading up households. Lone-parent families have been shown to be effective and resilient in meeting the needs of children, but they need to be embedded within a strong network of social and familial relationships, and they need the removal of the stigmatizing and stereotyping approaches of others, often betrayed in the language and imagery used to describe the so-called 'normal' family.

With more creative change in the relationships between women and men, more men may want to participate more fully in the care of their children. Again in our effort to increase the area of responsible relationship choice, we need to help fathers feel confident in the parenting of children, either alone or in role-reversed relationships with their female partners or in varying degrees of joint participation with them. Both demythologizing *and* valuing the differences between women and men will continue to lie at the heart of making new patterns of family life. Likewise, in our privileged multi-cultural society, both demythologizing *and* valuing the difference between people from every cultural and racial background will be essential tasks, so that inter-racial marriages and child-bearing will be seen as one uniquely valuable contribution towards creating unity, justice and freedom for all.

As we noted towards the end of chapter 2, people are deconstructing and reconstructing their models of marriage and the family. The transition period that results creates problems in defining the nature of 'family' in this final decade of the twentieth century. Elliot (1986) quotes Worsley (1977) as highlighting the fact that definitions vary over time, between cultures and within cultures and that we should be wary of 'giving the idea of "the" family some fixed "thing-like" quality, thereby perhaps smuggling in some notion of a universal or unchanging family' (Worsley (1977), pp. 169–70). Elliot continues:

> This approach to the problem of defining 'the family' is generally accepted and the old concept of 'the family' has given way to a new concept, that of families. Berger and Berger (1983, pp. 59–65) point out that this change in terminology recognises the empirical fact of diversity *and* reflects a shift in ideological position. It reflects, they say, the normative acceptance of diversity and a reluctance to accord any particular arrangement moral superiority as *the* family. (p. 6)

6

SYSTEMS

> Be silent and contemplate the dance. Just look: a star,
> a flower, a fading leaf, a bird, a stone . . . any fragment
> of the dance will do.
>
> ANTONY DE MELLO, *The Song of the Bird*

In chapter 2 we considered some approaches which have been used to understand the family and the way in which it relates to the social structures of society. The approach of psychoanalysis has been to its individual members; the approach of functionalism to its meaning and purpose for the social order; the approach of history to its development as an institution; the approach of radical politics to its power as an agent of change or of social control. But how does it actually *work?* What happens in a family when things 'go wrong'? What is happening when things 'go right'? How do we evaluate which is which? And how do we help families who are experiencing high levels of stress? These are the kinds of questions which we, as people concerned for the well-being of family life, are no doubt most interested in.

The difficulties involved in integrating a fully developed theory of how the family works are considerable. In fact we need to concede at this point that all such undertakings have so far fallen short of what is necessary. Vetere and Gale (1987) suggest that

> A workable theory must sort out the ways in which the family as a group differs from the family as a collection of individuals and must provide a specification for determining individual and family needs, the ways these are negotiated and the conditions under which they come into conflict and/or are changed. (p. 36)

However difficult this undertaking, it is nevertheless an essential task to discover at least a 'good enough' theory of family functioning because without one we will find it difficult to think about 'families' at all and instead, we will continually find ourselves discussing individual family members.

In the following chapters we will look at how to help families and couples, using ideas from an understanding of family groups as systems. These chapters are written for the non-specialist and assume very little knowledge of either the theory or technique of family therapy on which they are based. They do however assume that clergy and other licensed workers as well as others who are engaged in pastoral work are interested in acquiring more knowledge and skill as helpers and that this will include becoming more effective in responding to the many ways in which families, in their various different forms, may ask us for help.

The shift to perceiving behaviour and experience *systemically* is a huge leap in understanding and one which transforms one's approach thereafter to the way human beings 'tick'. But in a way there is nothing new about it at all. It represents the fundamental truth of life – that we are part of a vast, interconnected, interdependent universe, where all things have a dynamic relationship one with another and form a whole. It is a truth that has been articulated all down the ages by poets and mystics and theologians in every culture and every age. For John Donne, 'No man is an island entire of it self; every man is a piece of the continent, a part of the main.' For Paul, the whole universe struggles and travails together to come to fruition. Julian of Norwich sees the whole world held as it were in the palm of her hand, as though it was a hazelnut. Gibran's Prophet 'finds the roots of the good and the bad, the fruitful and the fruitless, all entwined together in the silent heart of the earth'. The Zen mystic proclaims that, 'Heaven and earth and I are of one root, the ten thousand things and I are of one substance.' For the ancient Chinese philosophers, reality, whose ultimate essence is Tao, is a movement of continual flow and change, with all phenomena caught up in this cosmic process.

And new ways of understanding both the physical and biological universe yield the same shift of emphasis from part to whole, from discrete entity to the interconnectedness of all things in one complex dynamic ecosystem. 'Most organisms are not only embedded in ecosystems but are complex ecosystems themselves, containing a host of smaller organisms that have considerable autonomy and yet integrate themselves harmoniously into the functioning of the whole' (Capra (1982), p. 297). And Capra quotes the American biologist Lewis Thomas to make the point further:

> There they are, moving about in my cytoplasm . . . They are much less closely related to me than to each other and to the free-living bacteria out under the hill. They feel like strangers, but the thought comes that the same creatures, precisely the same, are out there in the cells of seagulls, and whales, and dune grass, and seaweed and hermit crabs, and further inland in the leaves of the beech in my back yard and in the family of skunks beneath the back fence, and even in that fly on the window. Through them, I am connected: I have close relatives, once removed, all over the place. (Thomas (1975), p. 86)

All this stands in marked contrast to the individualistic way in which we usually construe our world. The systems approach by contrast challenges the view of the world which allows the individual to be 'diagnosed', 'treated', 'helped', or 'ministered to' as though he or she was a discrete entity. It challenges too the idea that individual family members can be set over and above 'the family' as distinct units of investigation, such as 'the child' and 'the family' or 'the family' and 'the parent', even though this isolated 'laboratory' approach to studying and treating children for example is still widely employed. It also challenges society's tendency (including the Church) to seek for linear causal connections in trying to determine 'who should be held responsible' for a particular event. Systemic thinking challenges the simplistic, unidirectional flow of much thinking about influence in the field of human relationships – for example, that parents are influential upon their children is a commonplace, even though it is difficult to specify exactly how this influence occurs.*
But that children are highly influential on their parents is less often acknowledged but is an obviously logical inference within the systemic paradigm. The behaviour of parents has indeed been shown to

* See for example Schaffer (1986).

be considerably modified by the characteristics and behaviour of their children and by the gender, health, personality, temperament and rate of development of each child. Children can therefore interact very negatively within the family system and create severe conflict between the parental and marital roles of the adults although that in itself is also an unsystemic description, required however in order to re-balance the unsystemic nature of the popular view. It is wise therefore to be cautious in subscribing to the myth often professed by Christians that children are beneficial to a marriage, or always 'a blessing from the Lord'.

Families are not systems. However, in several important respects they behave *as if* they were and, so long as one does not fall into the trap of confusing metaphor with reality, the exercise of applying systems theory to families is a very profitable one. Systems theory as a formal theory began to be widely discussed after the Second World War. Its origins and influences have been described at length in the literature of communication theory, family therapy, sociology and philosophy.* The practical application of these seminal ideas has provided fertile ground for theory building and for clinicians in their day to day practice, and their potential value is still being exploited in a whole range of methods of helping couples and families. For our present purposes, it is important to grasp the basic tenets of the theory and the way in which it can be made useful in our approach to families.

There are two kinds of metaphors that are frequently used by systems therapists. One set focuses on space; the other on time. Both yield some useful tools which we will explore further in chapters 9 and 10. In a recent article, Boscolo and Bertrando (1992) point out that in terms of the development of systemic thinking, the initial impulse was to throw out everything that suggested a continuing reliance upon the 'historical' methods of psychoanalysis. This meant that a time perspective was often lost, and spatial metaphors were favoured instead. It is now perhaps easier to be less trapped by these competing ideologies and in the next chapters we will examine systems ideas that derive from both the time and space perspectives.

* See for example, Emery (1969, 1981), Laszlo (1979), Wilden (1972), Bateson (1972, 1979), Watzlawick et al. (1968, 1974), Bradt and Moynihan (1971) and Hoff-man (1981).

If we consider a family as a system we are acknowledging that it, like other systems, is a complex arrangement of interacting elements together with the relationships between them. We can think of the family being made up of sub-systems (its individual members and the relationships between them) embedded in a wider social system (culture, neighbourhood, society) and relating continuously across both boundaries. In other words, individual family members are continuously influenced by their membership of the family system (and vice versa) and the family system is continuously influenced by its membership of the wider social system (and vice versa). We cannot separate out any of these complex interrelationships in reality although we often do (and must) for the purpose of description and analysis. However, such analysis is always an artificial and unreal activity (what Bateson (1979) calls 'chopping the ecology'), not least because it lends credence to the idea that the investigator (writer, observer, pastor, preacher) is able to take a position wholly outside the family that he is observing. He must indeed struggle to do so, but know always that he will fail.

Even family therapists who have adopted a systems model of the family in its broad sense, nevertheless can still get trapped into being 'unsystemic' in either their analysis of what is happening in a family or their efforts to try and help it with its difficulties. By being 'unsystemic', I mean being partial, limited and unable to see that the whole is always more than the sum of its parts and has an energy and purpose beyond that of its individual constituents. Although it is impossible to take a wholly meta-position to the family system which we are trying to observe or help, it is nevertheless important to try to do so in order not to operate from the partial and limited perspective of one or two of its individual members. Paradoxically, we are more likely to be able to retain this meta-position by being absolutely clear that we inhabit the same relational world as the family. Thus, when we sit down with a family to try and be of help, we become part of a new system made up of the family, the helper and the relationship between them. A therapeutic stance analogous to Carl Rogers' formulation of empathy is helpful, relevant and accurate. Paraphrased, this reads: 'We stand looking at the world through the eyes of the family, as if we were a part, without ever losing that essential "as if" perspective.'

The consequences of adopting a systemic perspective on a family are considerable. Most important of all, it allows us to consider the behaviour and experience of each family member as inextricably related to the experience of living in *this particular family* and in this *particular family's context*. This shift of perspective replaces a linear concept of how events are caused and how problems and difficulties arise, with one of curiosity about the relational pattern of interactions within the family and between the family and the outside world. A child's unsocial behaviour begins to 'make sense' as a function of a family secret that is shared between family members but not owned or discussed. A woman's compliant behaviour to a violent husband may become understandable in terms of the relationships in her family of origin.

A systemic view of causality shifts the 'blame game' into a new arena. It allows us to understand events in terms of a circular process that has become self-perpetuating and therefore without beginning and without end. This is in strong contrast to our ordinary 'common-sense' ideas of how relationships work and how someone must be responsible for beginning an argument, for example. A systemic, circular or recursive view of causality means that any behaviour can simultaneously be viewed as both cause and effect within the context in which the behaviour is occurring. The need to apportion blame is very strong in all of us and is usually located by family members in the 'other' or in the 'self' but seldom in the structure or processes of the relationships in which they are engaged. ('You' must be to blame or 'I' must be to blame, but seldom 'It must be something to do with the relationship between us'.)

But a systemic view of causality also affects the observer/helper – i.e. ourselves. It helps us to adopt the essentially objective, non-judgemental position without which it is not possible to engage in a therapeutic, health-giving, healing involvement with the family as a whole. If we are serious in our desire to offer help and constructive pastoral care to people who are experiencing difficulties in their personal relationships, we have to divest ourselves of our own preju-dices, hobby-horses and covert agendas and approach the family from the best possible vantage point in terms of their willingness and motivation to make use of us as an agent of change.

Systems theory emphasizes the ceaseless communication patterns which occur between family members. These are highly complex and involve the way in which sequences of behaviour are powerful on several levels in determining how family members relate to one another. It may take an outsider some considerable time before she can understand the shape and pattern of these sequences but because they are repetitive, circular and self-contained, they are also capable of interruption to the benefit of family members who have become caught into a self-perpetuating, destructive communicational sequence. Understanding a family systemically means beginning to understand the way in which it functions in its minute particulars and then introducing what Bateson (1972) called 'the difference that makes the difference'.

This emphasis on trying to understand and therapeutically interrupt 'the pattern that connects' means that there is a considerable emphasis on the 'here and now' in systems theory rather than on the 'there and then' emphasis of psychoanalysis. Wilden (1972) is correct in saying that

> The extreme difficulty of tracing back the evolution of an open system tends to turn the modern theorist or therapist away from any sort of archaeology of the subject (a past he believes he cannot change) and towards the future communication of the subject (which he believes he can modify more easily). (p. 97)

However, there is no inherent reason why this should be so because families can be as fruitfully understood systemically over their historical development as in their day to day interactions as a group. In fact it is often very important to try to understand the way in which past patterns of behaviour can be understood systemically in order to free family members in the present from perpetuating destructive patterns from the past. For example, the family may exhibit a pattern of behaviour over several generations which involves an adolescent becoming anorexic. The symptom may be expressed somewhat differently but an examination of family relationships over several generations may reveal for example an enmeshed, over-involved family system with relationships that are fused together across a generational boundary. This in turn gets handed on to the current family group so that they become 'stuck' in a pattern that was set up several generations earlier and which serves no constructive purpose for the family group now, even if it did then. The more important cutting edge of this analysis however is that because patterns get reworked in predictable ways over generations within family systems, a destructive sequence of behaviour can be interrupted in one time frame (i.e. in the present) with consequences for all the others, past and future. Thus, as Boscolo and Bertrando (1992) point out: 'Therapy if successful always changes the past, that is our memory of the past, and by helping the family with their problems in the present, they will also be more able to reconstruct the past in a more benign and constructive way' (p. 127).

The third major aspect of systems theory applicable to family life is the concept of equifinality. Because systems behave as wholes, change in any part of the system will cause the whole system to change. In other words, the behaviour of each family member is related to and affects every other member. This has direct and very clear consequences for our considerations of how best to be helpful to the family. If one member of the family makes a conscious decision to change his or her behaviour (cease drug-taking, stop truanting from school, leave home, change jobs or become a Christian) this changes everyone else's behaviour, perceptions and experience of that person and *therefore* changes the system as a whole, because everyone is now relating to everyone else's changed behaviour, perceptions and experience. This may or may not have a positive effect upon the family system as a whole or on the experience of all or some of its individual members, whether or not the changed experience/behaviour of the original family member is beneficial to him. This means that we need to adopt a cautious approach to helping introduce change into the lives of individual family members whose family system seems to be in difficulties, and even more where it does not. The changes of course, whether positive or negative for the other members of the system, are usually hidden, if the individual family member is being counselled on his own. To take a very simple but frequently encountered situation: changes for the family system contingent upon an individual becoming a Christian are considerable – their attitudes, beliefs, activities, friendship network, priorities and allegiances all undergo a profound change with related consequences for their family system and for everyone else's experience and behaviour. Such a dramatic and uncontrolled series of changes introduced unwittingly into the family system by perhaps a priest or pastor or other church member may be extremely beneficial or extremely destructive – but these effects will probably remain entirely unknown to the person who has given this family system such a powerfully change-producing input. By the same token, because of the principle of equifinality, engaging with one member of a family may be done in such a way that the whole system is propelled towards the changed patterns of behaviour that they have themselves deemed to be desirable. It is therefore perfectly possible (though quite difficult in practice) to help an individual family member from within a systemic framework so long as the system as a whole is being taken into account.

In a very economic way, the principle of equifinality properly understood can enable us to be highly effective in our efforts to help families. Because of the potentially unwelcome consequences which may arise from looking at the situation from the point of view of individual family members, those who adopt a systems perspective would normally much prefer to try to engage with the family system as a whole. It is usually much wiser and safer (if at first somewhat daunting) to move beyond the one person who seems to be in need of help to their wider family system. 'I think I could be more helpful to you by meeting with you and your husband together or you and your wife and the children' would be a typical way in which someone working from a systems perspective would try to move beyond the individual person who seems most in need of help.

If different initial conditions yield the same result, different results can also be produced by the same initial 'cause'. There is therefore a certain arbitrariness, from the systems point of view, in how a difficulty gets manifested or indeed dissolved. Families call attention to their difficulties in one of two ways: either through a symptom expressed by one family member or in a complaint about the nature of a relationship. The individual who experiences the symptom and its pain, does so on behalf of the family system as a whole. The distressed individual is therefore always a 'symptom' of the family group's difficulties and although an offer to help an individual member of that system will indeed produce change in the system as a whole, it is much wiser and more responsible to be able to facilitate these changes in such a way that everyone can be aware of and party to what is happening.

An important spatial metaphor from systems theory is that of boundary. Where does the family begin and end? Families do have boundaries, yet it is often difficult to work out where the boundary is. This is of course only a problem for the family if it is a problem for the family! In other words, thousands of perfectly happy, well-functioning families operate with very diffuse boundaries around their membership. Members come and go and the family system expands and contracts around them. In systems terms these families are relatively 'disengaged'. They may never be very clear about their boundaries until a life-cycle transition such as the wedding of a family member invites them to consider who should be included on the guest list. On the other hand some families are very clear about their membership and rather formal in their recognition of who belongs and who does not. These we can call relatively 'enmeshed' in the sense that they are involved with one another (and sometimes over-involved with one another) in a way that clearly differentiates them from 'those who do not belong'. From the standpoint of someone trying to help the family it is usually important to get some bearing on where the boundary is, because it will be important to involve everyone who is involved in the problems, in the efforts to sort them out.

Who is central to the cluster of concerns that the family needs to deal with *now*? This is the 'boundary' question that the pastor or counsellor needs to have in his mind. This may include a dead relative and it may include an elderly friend who lives five doors away, or a range of other likely and unlikely members of the system. This sense of having discovered the boundary which circumscribes the family's identity in time and space will be important in helping the counsellor to begin his work. For example, a couple lost one of their two young daughters in a motor accident. Two years later the family asked for help when they began to realize that they had 'got stuck' in the aftermath of that terrible event. After several tense and difficult family meetings, mother let drop that her widowed aunt had come to stay for a holiday. In enquiring further about the aunt and her relationship with the family, it emerged that she too had lost a daughter at the same age as the couple's. The aunt had kept her daughter's room intact, even though the death had occurred many years ago, and thereafter she had become a semi-recluse. It became clear that the mother in this family, out of loyalty to her bereaved aunt, to whom she was much attached, felt duty bound to re-enact her aunt's method of coping; the person trying to help them would therefore need to include the aunt within the boundary of the family if she was going to help it to move on. The advantage of course in this particular case was that it provided the opportunity to help the aunt too, although the invitation to the aunt was framed within a request to 'help me help the couple and their young daughter' with their bereavement.

We need now to consider the series of redefinitions that are made possible by a systems approach. In a sense as soon as a family asks for help, they have redefined the situation they are in. However difficult it is, they have implicitly agreed to engage in a new way of looking at things – an approach to their difficulties which involves looking at them, in part, from the point of view of another person (the helper or pastor or counsellor). That is why the very act of coming to a first family meeting with the outsider often releases immense energy for change. In fact some studies have shown that individuals and families who do not keep their first appointment and never go near the counsellor are nevertheless much helped by being given the appointment! A similar repeated finding occurs with people who are put on a waiting list.

But there are further extremely important aspects to this concept which it is useful for us to consider. One is the deliberate and 'gentle art' of reframing (Watzlawick et al., 1974). Reframing works on the principle of Korzybski's dictum that 'the map is not the territory'. There are, in other words, different levels of meaning in all behaviour and it may therefore be possible to 'reframe' a set of actions or behaviours that carry one set of meanings in such a way that they carry a completely different set, which then allows changes to occur in people's perceptions and actions in relation both to themselves and others. Watzlawick et al. (1974) have been particularly influential in revealing some of the possibilities of reframing. They define the idea as follows:

> To reframe then means to change the conceptual and/or

emotional setting or viewpoint in relation to which a situation is experienced and to place it in another frame which fits the 'facts' of the same concrete situation equally well or even better and thereby changes its entire meaning. (p. 95)

The fundamental premise is that uncomfortable and unhappy situations can often be changed by changing our perceptions of them, for, as Shakespeare notes: 'There is nothing either good or bad but thinking makes it so' (*Hamlet*, Act 2, Scene 2).

A special case of reframing is what is called the positive connotation. A central task for the person trying to help a family as a system is, as we have noted, to engage with the system *as a whole*. This is only possible if he studiously avoids taking sides and relates to every member of the system and to their behaviour in an equal and objective way. This means that even the most unappealing behaviour needs to be connoted in a positive way *in order to* interrupt the repetitive sequences in which the family has got stuck. The family is helped to perceive the interactive behaviour that is occurring between them differently by the special reframe of seeing the positive 'underside' of negative behaviour. Some of the problematic issues involved in adopting this position will be discussed at the end of this chapter, and are discussed more fully in Walrond-Skinner and Watson (1987). To take a positive view of the motivations and goals of everyone is saying no more than that the person trying to help an individual needs to adopt an empathic stance to that person, however destructive the behaviour which he is exhibiting. The *family* counsellor is faced with the more complex task of adopting an empathic position in relation to the system as a whole and he therefore requires some additional tools to help him do so. Suffice it to say at this point that reframing has a powerful impact on a family system that has become immobilized by its self-destructive behaviour and can often be the key to unlocking the rigid sequences within it.

Part of the theory on which redefinition is predicated is that words and labels hold predictive power. As Watzlawick et al. (1974) note, 'Some labels provoke difficulties, whilst others, achievable by redefinition, promote adjustment and harmony' (p. 156). Simple examples are the ways in which the determinative effect of labelling something by means of a noun is immediately changed if one converts the noun into its appropriate verb. Describing someone as a 'depressive' has quite a different feel about it to describing someone as 'depressed'. The effect of the description changes again if we add an adverb. There is all the difference in the world between calling Bill a 'depressive' and saying that 'Bill is *depressed about* his wife leaving home'. Nothing is changed in relation to Bill's subjective experience by this change, so long as it remains a change within the cognitive frame of the observer alone. However if the redefinition takes place within Bill's relationship with his daughter, his friend, his counsellor or, and especially, *his wife*, then the redefinition will inevitably and powerfully become 'a difference that makes the difference'.

People who are strongly committed to the Christian faith perspective on relationships may have particular difficulties with the systemic view of family functioning. They may be concerned that the individual gets depersonalized and lost within a framework that sounds mechanical in its talk of systems and structures of communication. They may be concerned about the dissolution of personal responsibility in the systemic view of circular or multi-faceted causality. And they may be concerned that to take equifinality seriously seems to involve an arbitrariness in what should be done and how, when trying to help a family and its members. None of these concerns are peculiar to the Christian's approach to using systems theory and they do beg real questions which, especially recently, family therapists have been trying to address.*

However, the power and effectiveness of the systems perspective does I believe outweigh its difficulties. It enables a family to be understood and helped in a way that does justice to the complexity of both its internal politics and to the impact on the family of its particular social, cultural and economic environment. It can be applied to a family group, whatever its outward structure or form. Systems theory is a macro-level theory capable of interpreting the way in which the individual's behaviour is affected by his membership of a family group and the way in which the family is impinged upon by its wider environment, limiting choice or providing opportunity.

It does of course need fleshing out to make it more accessible to the way we think about family life. Let us take one or two examples

---

* Trenchant criticisms of systems theory are summarized in Vetere and Gale (1987).

of the way in which some of these ideas from systems theory can be used in practice.

If we take the first idea – that the family is not just a collection of individuals but is a system of relationships, then we will want to call the family group together to work on its difficulties. Let us suppose that a middle-aged parent asks you for advice about her youngest child, a young woman in her early twenties. She is living at home, has dropped out of college, seldom goes out, has few friends and becomes easily upset by both her parents but particularly by her mother. Mother asks you if you would see her daughter to try and get to the bottom of what is wrong with her. Mother says she is at her wit's end. She feels a failure as a parent. There is a younger brother of sixteen who has just completed his GCSE exams with flying colours, but mother is only interested in talking to you about her daughter and getting you to help her. But instead of doing so, you invite the whole family to attend. The family is made up of father Dave, mother Ruth, daughter Carol aged twenty-two and son Colin aged sixteen. They meet with you at the prearranged time and you begin the meeting by conveying to them that you are here to listen to them, to help them to talk with each other about any difficulties they are having and to see if there are ways in which you can help them with these difficulties. At this point we need to pause and comment on the important and helpful messages you have already conveyed to the family.

1. You have suggested to them, by inviting all four of them to meet with you, that they are all involved in the difficulties that they are experiencing, rather than Carol being 'the problem'. You have thereby lightened the burden of labelling that fell on Carol and Ruth's perceived responsibility for her and, in exact proportion to the lightening of these burdens, you have engaged the more peripheral people, Colin and Dave.

2. You have constructed a framework for them to come apart from their normal environment (to meet with you, an outsider, in a strange place) yet remain within their normal environment (the family group, in which their difficulties reside). You have created a difference that makes a difference in their pattern of communi-

cation simply by yourself becoming part of the family but remaining always an outsider to it.

3. You have indicated that whilst you are happy to listen, to support, to help, it is they who have the knowledge and resources to engage constructively with their difficulties and to bring about change.

You might then, typically, go on to invite the family to discuss their difficulties. As they do so, you will watch and listen to the *process*, how the family communicates, who seems to adopt whose point of view, who talks most, who seems an outsider or the person/people being blamed for what is going on. As well as paying attention to the *content* (what is being said), you will begin to see how things go round in circles; you will begin to understand the steps that form part of this particular family's dance. You begin to become part of the dance yourself; yet you must remain a little outside, a little on the edge, so that you can continue to observe and understand the whole. In a sense, 'any fragment of the dance will do' for you to watch and try to understand. You may then ask them if they want to alter any of the steps in the dance or learn some new ones. This is presumably why they have come to you in the first place, yet it may be quite difficult at first to discern the direction in which the family is trying to move or to understand in what ways it perceives itself as stuck.

This is partly because there will be a number of different viewpoints to understand. Indeed, it may be precisely because of these many different viewpoints and conflicts between them that the family have come to you for help. You will want to help the family therefore to create some consensus about what it is they want to change and to take the first steps in moving toward their goal.

Working from within a systems framework creates a whole range of new possibilities. As we will examine in later chapters, the counsellor may still need to use ideas and theories derived from other approaches to pastoral care and counselling to assist her own mode of *being a helping person* and she may still need to use psychodynamic ideas to understand how the *shared unconscious* processes in the family group are expressed over time. But her basic framework for understanding the family is systemic because it is the family system as an interacting whole that she is trying to help. Before turning to the application of some of these ideas, we need briefly to recapitulate.

The family system is made up of *sub-systems* – that is, its individual family members and the relationships between them, and the family system itself is embedded in a *supra-system*, the environment – that is, an ethnic, cultural, socio-economic and historical context. The specific and particular characteristics of both family members and family context continually impinge on the way in which a family system functions. It is obviously not the case that a family system functions according to a set of 'rules' regardless of the temperaments, histories and individual characteristics of its members. Nor is it in any way true that we can disregard the family's context. On the contrary, the issues of poverty, wealth, homelessness, the pressure to succeed, anxiety stemming from the wider social and political context, issues of gender and race – all of these operate in different degrees and powerfully shape, influence and limit the family's and the helper's manoeuvrability. We need therefore to restate the point made in chapter 4 that in trying to understand and to help families, we have to examine a complex, multi-causal model which includes both individual (sub-system) and social (supra-system) factors and the transactional needs of the system itself in its recursive responsiveness to both.

Several questions are worth considering here. Does the systems perspective focus our concern on the family in isolation from its context? And does this lead us to 'iron out' the conflicts that exist in society which demand a political response? Is there a fundamental disjuncture of views between systems theory and the individual's idiosyncratic position within the family system? Does the individual get 'lost' in this preoccupation with 'systems'? And perhaps most crucial of all, does the power imbalance between victim and abuser get 'ironed out' in situations of violence perpetrated against women and children?

Both sets of issues have been raised and re-raised over the years. And both remain matters of crucial concern. In relation to family violence, Adams (1988) for example argues that

> Not only do interactive approaches blur the distinctions between
> violent and non-violent behaviour, they also give the tacit

115

> message that battering is an understandable, though unfortunate response to behaviour on the victim's part that the batterer deems as controlling or provocative. (p. 186)

I do not however believe that this is the case. The issue of family violence is exceptionally complex and our brief reflection on this central concern of family life in chapter 4 highlights its importance in helping families. I would want to argue however that systems theory does not in itself create the problem; it is a misuse and misunderstanding of the theory which makes it impossible to account both for individual responsibility and systemic meaning simultaneously. A man who abuses a child or a woman must be held accountable for his actions. Moreover if there is to be any possibility of his changing, the very first step in the process is that his actions must be fully owned. The man will not be helped to do this if a counsellor focuses exclusive attention upon the meaning of his behaviour within the context of his family relationships, so that his responsibility for his actions is diminished. Exactly the same problem has to be tackled by the Church and it is often the case that the same criticism can be levelled against the Church too. It happens sometimes that well-meaning premature intervention on the part of Christians can assure a man of God's forgiveness before he has fully owned what he has done. The Christian concept of foregiveness can, then, like the systemic hypothesis, be misused to dilute, confuse and exonerate the abuser from responsibility for his actions. Furthermore I believe that both frames of reference can be and *are* used in this way and nothing is gained by either systems therapists or Christians by denying it. (We need to note here that one of the inherent biases both amongst family therapists and the Church's ministry is its male bias, which is probably a very important variable to consider in what has been called 'the case of the disappearing victim'.)

The problem however lies not in the systemic understanding of these family patterns but in a disregard for their differential consequences. (Similarly the problem with some Christian approaches to forgiveness lies not in the theology of forgiveness but in a misunderstanding of its process.) The systems framework enables us to gain perspective, objectivity and purchase on the complex dynamics that continuously hold family members in relation to one another. It also

116

helps 'make sense' in relationship terms of even the most appalling behaviours. But to understand, to make sense of, does not mean to exonerate; nor does it involve a levelling down of the actual behaviours of family members to one common level of outcome. The *process* of battering a woman may be explicable in systems terms but the *consequences* of the process (battering) are of a different order than a whole number of other possible effects. The consequence then has to be evaluated in its own right, regardless of its systemic meaning or of the pattern that connects it to other behaviours and events within the system. As Meth (1992) points out: 'Understanding why the abuser is violent and knowing that this meets some of his needs for recognition and acceptance is relevant only after he has accepted responsibility for his behaviour without excuses' (p. 258).

This brief excursion into family violence has been made partly because it is such a vital matter in its own right and partly in order to restate a basic tenet of the systems perspective. It is essential that we reflect upon the dynamic relationship and interconnectedness of the family system, its individual members and its context. Without this multi-level perspective no approach to the family can be a truly systemic one.

7

CYCLES

> From what I have said it is abundantly clear that neither
> the future nor the past exists . . . it might be correct to
> say that there are three times: a present of past things,
> a present of present things and a present of future
> things.
>
> ST AUGUSTINE, *Confessions*, Book 13

A great deal of research suggests that families experience the greatest stress at points of major transition in their life cycle. It is at these points that families are most likely to seek help from friends, clergy or specialist professional workers and where we are most likely to be given the privilege of being able to respond. It is helpful therefore to consider the way in which a family system develops over time and focus some attention on the moments in its development when it is likely to be most vulnerable.

White (1991) has rightly pointed out that there has been a vacuum in theory building in this area and no rigorous theory of family development has as yet emerged. It is a very difficult task because although several groups of workers in the family field in America have adapted descriptions of the *individual's* progress through the life cycle and have identified the way in which the family group develops through its own life cycle stages in a reasonably predictable manner, it is nevertheless very difficult to keep one's eye on the dimensions of process in the minute by minute experience of the family simultaneously with the family's development over time, and thereby retain a systemic understanding of the ongoing life cycle of the family as a group.

Probably the most thoroughgoing description of the family life cycle has been undertaken by Carter and McGoldrick (1989) and their fellow authors and it is their work which provides the basis for this chapter. In the short time between the two editions of their book (nine years) they comment on the major changes that have occurred in professional reflections upon family life. There are three particularly important new considerations which they suggest must be taken into account: the increases in the incidence of divorce and remarriage, making these events a normal part of the family life cycle for almost half the population in the United States and at least a third of the population in Britain; changes in the self-awareness and aspirations of women with their effect on role relationships and the birth and deferment of children; and the awareness of different ethnic patterns of family life and a greater cultural variability. It is now much more overtly acknowledged amongst family theorists that gender and ethnicity interact with other experiences introducing greater complexity and difference into the life cycle of the family. Thus it becomes even more important to guard against introducing inappropriate assumptions about 'normality' which do not take account of cultural diversity and differences in gender. In addition, we have to be constantly aware of the effects of other influences in the environment on the family's life cycle, of poverty, homelessness, the pressure to succeed, individualism, consumerism, and the many anxieties that maintain their influence at a subliminal level. The environment impinges continuously on the family and vice versa and the interaction between the two needs to be uppermost in our minds when we are trying to look at ways of being of help.

The notion of a life cycle of a family system is essentially problematic. To begin with, the concept of life stages is a linear concept evoking the idea of movement from point A to point B to point Z. It also suggests the idea that, like the cycle of a washing-machine, satisfactory progress through the required stages will end in a state of completion, perhaps with an end product – a family group – fit for display on a television commercial – for washing powder! But the life cycle of a family system is much more to do with a dance to be experienced than a journey to be travelled, and so there is a continual tension between the ideas of circularity and pattern in the 'here and now' and development through time from the 'there and then'.

The interaction between the concept of the family as a system

119

which we considered in the last chapter and the life cycle of the family creates a very complex set of ideas. It means that we are trying to hold in our minds a vast network of relationships extending back into time and forward into the future, all having a dynamic inter-relationship one upon another in the present experience of the family. Carter and McGoldrick (1989) describe the practical effects of this complexity as follows:

> Three or four generations must accommodate to a life cycle transition simultaneously. While one generation is moving toward older age, the next is contending with the empty nest, the third with young adulthood, forming careers and intimate peer adult relationships and having children, and the fourth with being inducted into the system. Naturally there is an inter-mingling of the generations, and events at one level have a powerful effect on relationships at each other level. (p. 7)

Inevitably, there is always a dynamic interrelationship between the shared memory of what has gone on in the past and the current events of the family's experience. Often it is our own limited perspective which fails to engage both the vertical dimension of the family's experience over time and the horizontal axis of its systemic processes simultaneously.

Ceremonies, rituals and rites of passage

These periods of transition have sometimes been described as 'rites of passage'. Each involves a period of crisis, which is followed by a 'plateau' period during which the family accommodates to the changes that have taken place and, where necessary, undergoes a reorganization in its relationships and roles. The transition is usually marked by a variety of rituals and by one central ceremony – the ceremony being the point at which the Church or representatives of other faith communities become most obviously involved.

Friedman (1989), writing from the perspective of a rabbi as well as a family therapist, makes the excellent point, however, that the ceremony does not equate with the whole rite of passage – it is not all there is to it – and to reduce the whole of the event to, for example, the wedding ceremony is to miss out on most of its potential. This avoidance of the real significance of the event in the life cycle of two families, by reducing it to the ceremony only, is a very arid approach to pastoral work indeed and to argue that clergy and other Christian pastors 'have no time to do anything more' is to beg the question of priorities and choice. Although Carr (1985) is obviously right to insist on the unique aspects of the ceremony itself and the importance of the clergy person's role in it, there are also much greater possibilities for clergy here than the 'ceremony only' approach allows. Each transition through the life cycle needs its own rituals and ceremonies to mark and help master the event. Some of these are obviously available already as tools at the Church's disposal to help families. But we also need to be creative in our effort to think of new rituals as and when needed – for the formation of other kinds of partnership for example.

The rite of passage is made up of three distinct ingredients – process, ritual and ceremony. These are combined in varying proportions depending on the family's own culture and history – its unique 'ways of doing things', and also on the norms of the society to which the family belongs, and the nature of the life stage being negotiated. Each of these aspects interacts with the others so that, for example, a large and wealthy Mexican family faced with the death of one of its members will approach this rite of passage in a way that is determined by the unique configuration of family culture, social norms and life event. Such a death would be handled entirely differently by a white, 'chapel' working-class family in Wales and a black working-class family in Brixton and all of these would be different from a middle-class family in the rural south of England which had so contracted in size that it had now become focused around a few elderly members.

The process by which a family will negotiate a transition from one stage in its life cycle to the next will also be affected by its own internal culture and dynamics, by the interplay of several different life crises that may occur in close juxtaposition to one another, and by the way in which similar transitions have been handled in the past. One member of the family is selected as the focal point or central figure to represent the family transition, but as Friedman (1989) points out, 'So central is the role of family process in rites of passage that it is probably correct to say it is really the family that is making the transition to a new stage of life at such a time rather than any "identified member" focussed upon during the occasion' (p. 119). It is indeed the family, for as we noted in chapter 6, the theory of family systems advances the notion that change in one member of the system always involves changes in the system as a whole. This process of crisis, change and adaptation offers unique opportunities for clergy and others to facilitate the constructive development of the family and to help it move on to the next stage in the life cycle. Rituals and ceremonies enable families to manage change by allowing its more threatening aspects to get expressed symbolically. Imber-Black (1989) and others have pointed out that they can also help a family to manage the loss, contradiction and conflict that often surfaces during a life-cycle transition and they may be seen as 'the visible and condensed drama of the life cycle transition they mark' (p. 149).

Reflections from the past

The manner in which the family is able to negotiate a transition in its life cycle will also depend upon the degree to which other major transitions in its remote or immediate past become reactivated. Shared memories of other major family events or the way in which similar transitions were handled in a previous generation will affect the family's approach to the current transition. In the same way, anything that helps a family to manage a transition adaptively will contribute not only to its well-being in the present, but will also have a benign effect on future generations.

Sometimes a family will consciously create the therapeutic juxta-position of two major events in such a way that the family is helped to complete the process of transition. For example, Mary, the middle child of a family of three grown up children was tragically killed in a car accident. Her elder brother John had remained rather aloof from the family since the accident and had distanced himself from his parents. Mary had been particularly close to her younger brother Alan who still lived at home. On the first anniversary of the accident, the parents and Alan marked the event by going for a walk along the river which had been a favourite place of recreation for all five of them. To the parents' disappointment John had refused to come. Soon afterwards Alan got engaged to Wendy and the couple announced that they were to be married in a year's time on the exact date of Mary's accident. As the family continued in their efforts to come to terms with their tragedy, it became increasingly apparent that Alan and Wendy's decision, first experienced as an insult, could be the means by which the family could begin to move on. The wedding, two years after Mary's death, became a ritual ending for the mourning period at which many of the same family members and friends who had come to Mary's funeral could gather once more – to remember, to grieve and to rejoice. Alan's own special closeness to Mary made him the appropriate, perhaps the only possible, means by which the family could allow themselves to let go. Because of the nature of the event, wholly different yet intensely reflective of the past, John was able to participate with his wife and children and rejoin his parents and brother.

Moving on

One of the most significant transitions in the family life cycle is the movement of the young adult out of his family of origin into a phase of independent life. As with every family transition, the family member who undertakes this movement first usually has the hardest time of it, and the family as a whole 'shudders' with the greatest shock waves. Parents and young adults have to renegotiate their roles to allow them to relate now to one another as adults. The parents may need to deny the meaning of their child's new found adulthood because of the way it reflects their own progressive ageing. This will often make it hard for them to let go. Likewise, if the young adult fears the challenges of adult life he will cling to a dependent relationship with his parents.

A major trap at this stage is the precipitate entry into a close substitute relationship which offers the hope of a buffer between the dependence of childhood and the independence of adult life. But the young adult needs to differentiate himself successfully from his family of origin – he needs to become his own person – before moving into his family of procreation. Young adults who cut themselves off emotionally or geographically are just as unable to separate as those who cannot leave home or those who move prematurely into a substitute relationship. The task of the family counsellor in this situation may be to 'coach' the young person in finding ways of relating to his parents that do justice to his adult status. It may involve meeting separately with the parents to help them accomplish the symmetrical task of relating appropriately to the young person.

Children who run away from home are often caught into a relationship with their parents that has got 'stuck' in a dependent mode that more appropriately relates to the time when they were young. Younger children sometimes anticipate their movement away from the parental home because they experience strong contradictory feelings about growing up both within themselves and in their parents' attitude. This shared interlocking ambivalence can often be helped by some family meetings with a counsellor, to support and 'steady' the family system as it moves through the anticipated transition. For example, a couple asked for help because their fifteen-year-old son had run away. Whilst the parents were very frightened and upset, it turned out that they had in fact demanded that he leave, because he would not agree to comply with the 'family rules'. On further probing, the counsellor discovered that the rules the parents were trying vainly to impose related much more appropriately to a ten-year-old boy than to a fifteen-year-old. Moreover, the older brother (a rather shy dependent boy who seldom went out and had no friends) had been recruited by the parents to act as both 'spy' and go-between, informing the parents about his brother's behaviour and carrying messages back and forth after he left. After meeting once or twice with the parents to build up some trust with them, the counsellor arranged several family meetings during which she encouraged the parents and the boys to negotiate about the rules that were needed for all four of them to live together satisfactorily until it became an appropriate time for the boys to leave home. These included things that the parents did which the children did not like, such as father smoking in the shared living-room and mother insisting on preparing food which nobody liked, as well as the boys' behaviour disliked by the parents. Alongside these family meetings, the counsellor also met with the boys separately to coach them in relating to their parents less reactively and to develop a stronger alliance between them. She also met several times with the parents to help them to become used to focusing on their marriage and thus to prepare them for the time the boys would leave home.

Becoming a couple

The transition from being a single adult to forming a couple is a major transition for the whole family system, not just for the couple involved. It may be completed in three different ways: through marriage, through gay or lesbian coupling or through heterosexual cohabitation. The transition may occur at different points in the family's life cycle and may be repeated by the individual several times during his or her lifetime.

There are some common features in each of these three forms of coupling but there are also some distinctions. In each case there is always a 'leaving behind' in order to make a new 'cleaving' possible. What is left behind may be the individual's family of origin, or a previous couple relationship or the independence of being single, or a combination of all of these. There are, too, always adaptations to be made to the new and unfamiliar world of partnership with this particular person. For one or both partners, a change of domicile will have to be made, and one or both partners will have to leave the known and familiar material world of place and location and all that is emotionally connected with that, and move into strange and unfamiliar territory. Particular issues have to be faced where one partner is moving into the home of the other. There may be many reminders of a previous couple relationship, but even if there has been no obvious previous incumbent of the role which the new person now fills, there may be a sense of diffidence at making changes in what has been someone else's home.

There are obvious differences too between the experiences of different types of couple. The transition to marriage is marked by a variety of rituals and a public ceremony. But it is not necessarily true that the entry into a cohabiting relationship or a gay relationship is unmarked by any ritual or ceremony. Pratt's (1992) and Jenkins' (1992) ideas that people casually fall into a cohabiting relationship without a second thought are not borne out by my own experience of talking with such couples. Like marriage, cohabitation occurs as a response to other events that are happening within the wider family system and the decision to cohabit makes a major change in the couple's relationship and often too in the relationship between the friends and families of both partners. It is often ritually marked in some way by the couple, through a party with friends in the new home, through a holiday just before 'entering in' to the new home together afterwards or through the purchase of some shared treasure.

Gay couples too usually want to mark ritually the beginning of their new relationship. Some gay couples view their relationship as precisely analogous to marriage and, for them, there is a desire for a ceremony, along with other rituals to mark this rite of passage from singleness to full committed partnership. (Stuart (1992) provides a useful collection of possible ceremonies.) One of the differences may be however that marriage provides a more open, public opportunity for rituals and ceremonies to be celebrated and for the whole extended network of family and friends to participate (or not!).

In its preoccupation with marriage as the only form which coupling should take, the Church has got itself into a curious position. It prevents some couples (gay and lesbian) who feel ready to make a publicly recognized formal commitment from doing so, whilst hastening others (cohabitees) who do not wish to do so into a commitment that they are not ready to make. As we noted at the end of chapter 2, the need for both freedom and commitment, for individual self-differentiation and for intimacy in a bonded relationship are continuing human needs, but they are needs that oscillate in the way that they are experienced, depending upon the inner experience and emotional development of the individual, the external circumstances that impinge upon her experience and the needs and constraints of the family system. The task of clergy, counsellors and others who may be involved is to help couples achieve the best accommodation they can between freedom and commitment, differentiation and intimacy, within the form and pattern of partnership that they have chosen to live.

In many cultures, the choice of a partner for marriage is arranged by the two families involved and in multi-cultural Britain some individuals will experience this process. Its advantage is that it is more likely to ensure some measure of compatibility on the part of the two families and the commitment of both families to help and support the couple's relationship.

Most couples make their own choice of partner although this choice is limited by the circumstances of a person's life, which limits the number and kind of potential partners that are available. People often meet their partners in the work place, so that for those who are unemployed there is a further limitation on the pool of potentially available partners. People who are physically or mentally disabled may be limited in their ability to go out to meet people and their needs in this area are often completely overlooked. People who are only children have less opportunity of gaining relational experience with their peers at a young age and may, as a result, be more diffident in making relationships in adult life. Family custom and tradition will impose other limitations too such as class, race, age and educational background and although it is possible to move beyond these limitations, most people in practice do not do so. The helper's task is not to interfere with the choice that the individual has made – of partner or structure or both – but to enable the couple to overcome the challenges of this transitional experience in such a way that they and the wider family system of each of them, joined together through their relationship, can move on to the next phase in their development.

Because of the greater variety of family patterns now being chosen, marriage does not hold the same position as a status passage-marker as it did, in the process of achieving maturity. Nevertheless, because of its legal and culturally defined position the transition to marriage as distinct from other kinds of coupling has particular components for the experience of the family system. For one thing, it bestows new roles upon everyone and new relationships between them. It also reawakens shared memories of similar experiences throughout the family system, rumblings and reverberations of happy and fearful times. Because of the threatening implications of discontinuous change, families often fall back on the comfort of folk wisdom at these times. Old folklore like 'not losing a son but gaining a daughter-in-law' defends family members from the threat of loss. The marriage itself may be an unconscious defence against loss in another part of the system and the timing of a marriage is often influenced by such events and is an unconscious compensation for them. It is always interesting during marriage preparation to reflect with a couple on who has died or left the family in other ways and when these losses occurred. Marriages and pregnancies often occur when the family system is looking to replace some crucial losses in its fabric of relationships.

The experience of marriage for the man and the woman will be markedly different. Bernard (1972) pointed out over twenty years ago that this difference is so great that it would be more appropriate to talk about two marriages that exist in every marriage – his and hers. Men thrive on marriage, whereas in almost every respect married women are less healthy, psychologically, emotionally and physically, than their single counterparts. Moreover, men and women have different expectations of marriage. Thornes and Collard (1979) found that women's expectation was primarily for intimacy and men's for sexual fulfilment. They also found that women make considerably greater adjustments to marriage than do men, and, not surprisingly, express a greater level of dissatisfaction with their marriages. It is probably one of the major challenges of the decade to work out ways in which the healthy adult selves of both men and women can be united in marriage in such a way that the woman as well as the man can continue to grow and develop. In chapter 8 we will explore some of the predictors of poor marital adjustment and the way in which the pastor or counsellor can be helpful to couples in difficulties.

Parenthood

The timing of the movement towards a parental phase of family life is now much more flexible. Couples of all three types, married, homosexual and cohabiting feel much freer both to have and to defer having children. Many single people also choose to have children. For them the passage through the life cycle of forming a couple may never occur at all or it may occur after they have moved into the parental phase. These choices are obviously greatly influenced by the tremendous advances in reproductive technology which allows children to be planned and, if desired, prevented altogether. More couples of all kinds are choosing to have their children at a later stage and advances in medicine and surgery are allowing post-menopausal women in their fifties and sixties to conceive for the first time.

The advent of a child in a couple's relationship dramatically alters that relationship in ways which can barely be foreseen. The two-person system becomes a triangle with all the new relational possibilities that that affords. In fact the family system's progress through its life cycle is most obviously marked by what can broadly be called its crises of accession (the joining of new members) and its crises of dismemberment (when members leave by growing up, separating, divorcing or dying). The arrival of each child means that each person's role in the family and each person's repertoire of prospective relationships is extended or changed. The first child to arrive has the greatest impact. It changes the relationship between the couple in terms of their roles (from couple to parents), in terms of their expectations of one another and in terms of the tasks to be accomplished. Each subsequent child changes the relationships of the parents with each other child and amongst each of the other children.

The birth of children roots a couple in the cycle of the family's relationship with its past and in a whole new future stretching out in terms of new generations to come. The couple's own hopes and aspirations for the future, perhaps barely articulated until now, become focused in the tiny new person. How she or he will respond to these expectations, hopes and dreams will determine in part some of the joys and the difficulties which must be mediated through the relational pattern that develops between parents and child. If the parents need the child to live out too many of their own unfulfilled hopes, the child may be unable to discover her own unique identity. Sometimes the child is burdened instead by unresolved conflicts and events in the family's past. The sins of the fathers can indeed be visited upon the children in such a way that a past family member's role and its conflicts is 'offered' to the new member, to act out and resolve.

Some of the difficulties that have to be faced during this stage include: how to juggle the occupation of a marital and parental role simultaneously without either of them becoming overshadowed by the other; how to give proper attention to the need for one or both parents to invest energy in a job and simultaneously manage the home and the child care; how, in a two-parent family, the parents can work together as a team in their management of the children and, in a one-parent family, how the single parent can manage all the tasks of care and control that are demanded, as well as providing for the family's economic support; how to provide for the needs of children when neither parent is in a waged occupation and how to manage on state benefits; how to manage the conflicts and tensions without acting them out in violence towards the children; how parents and children can renegotiate the relationship as the children grow older so that they can begin to move towards adult relationships between them; how to avoid recruiting one or more of the children into conflicts that belong to the marital pair or to the relationships of one of the parents with his or her family of origin; how children can survive the physical, emotional and psychological dangers of early childhood sufficiently to grow up secure in their own identity and able to form healthy relationships with others; how to maintain appropriate boundaries *between* generations in terms of sexuality and intimacy; how to create the possibility for enriching relationships to develop *across* the generational divide, including relationships between children and grandparents.

Given this complex array of physiological and emotional tasks, it is indeed a considerable cause for wonder that so many families manage these stages of family life so successfully. There are always several crises to negotiate. The birth of each child requires everyone to shift around and 'make space' for the newcomer. Frequently the child who had previously occupied the position of the youngest finds the task of 'making space' quite stressful and the jealousy experienced by this child or sometimes by other children in the family greatly increases the stress experienced by parents. The job of 'making space' is one which is maybe hard for parents too, already hard pressed by the demands of other children, jobs, or the strain of poverty and unemployment.

However, the presence of young children in the family allows parents to rediscover the child in themselves. Children teach parents how to play and be playful and in the process the parents may be able to repair the privations or deprivations experienced in their own childhood. As well as being stressful, children can in a very real way be healing and reparative for parents, periodically enabling them to regress and work through earlier developmental stages of their own lives. But young children can, by the same token, create envy in parents for whom childhood was painfully violent or abusive. They may feel competitive with their children in terms of what they themselves were unable to have. One or other parent may also feel excluded because of the close bond that is formed between the child and their partner. The excluded partner is usually the father when the child is very young, but powerfully excluding pairing relationships can be set up later on between fathers and their adolescent daughters with consequent rivalry between mother and daughter. Sometimes these relationships will become overtly incestuous.

The child's gender may have important symbolic meaning for one or other parent. A woman has often been socialized to experience a deep sense of inadequacy if she cannot produce a male child. This may militate against her ability to make a satisfactory relationship with her daughters. The difficulties which women experience in relation both to their own mothers and to their daughters appear to be qualitatively different from those experienced by boys because it is more difficult for the little girl to separate out from her first close relationship when that person is 'like' rather than 'unlike' herself (Chodorow, 1978). All of these aspects of the early child–parent relationship may contribute to the conflict which erupts between parents and their young child, leading in some cases to physical violence or sexual abuse.

The complex dynamics which surround the issue of physical and sexual abuse have been studied by psychologists, family therapists and feminist writers. Fathers, mothers and children all have a part to play in the scenario which gets acted out through physical violence, and incestuous or abusive intergenerational sexual contact. Child sexual abuse has recently attracted a considerable amount of professional attention and concern. A full discussion of the issues involved is obviously outside the scope of this book. A brief comment only can be offered at this point, namely that intergenerational sexual activity must be regarded as a divergence from the normal processes of family development and always as a serious interruption in that development with destructive consequences for everyone involved and especially for the child. It is a set of activities which need considerable understanding and help and a positive programme of prevention. In chapter 4 we looked briefly at the intra-and extra-familial factors which contribute to the sexual abuse of children. At this point we need to add to the picture the contribution made by the child.

The difficulty in exploring the part played by a child in its own abuse is extremely complicated. On the one hand, the arrival of children in the family has a multiplicity of consequences for all other relationships within the family, particularly for the relationship between the couple. These may include serious *negative* consequences which in turn may interact with residual needs in one of the parents (usually the father) for sexual contact with the child. On the other hand, such contacts are often rationalized to the point of denial or 'normalization' or they are excused by an argument which evokes the image of the child as 'seductress'. The child is both exploited and then blamed for the need to exploit her. Children do of course require from adults close, warm and intimate physical contact as part of an optimal environment for encouraging their psycho-sexual maturation. Children who are deprived of this may learn inappropriate 'seductive' ways of expressing their need and trying to get their needs met by adults. They cannot however be deemed to be 'responsible' in any moral sense for their own abuse or in any sense be regarded as the causative agent in the appallingly high incidence of abuse that we are witnessing today. Glaser and Frosh (1988) make the point sharply:

> Over and over again it has to be restated that child sexual abuse is a common phenomenon *in reality*, that the victims of child sexual abuse are *victims*, that children do not have the power to seduce grown men against their will, that children who are looking for affection are desiring precisely that, and are not 'in fact' asking for sex. (p. 35)

Alongside this absolute fact however, we have to retain a concept of family relationships that are both truly systemic *and* wholly cognizant of the power inbalances of gender and age that exist within the family group. And therein lies both the difficulty and the challenge. To claim, rightly, that the child's needs are paramount, must not become an excuse for reverting to simplistic linear thinking or adopting a punitive approach to the perpetrator of the abuse. A systemic understanding must be retained alongside the need to protect and rescue the child and to punish those guilty of a criminal offence. Relating the events that have occurred to the systemic processes of the family group and identifying the relationship of these to the family's wider social and cultural context will be the only way in which the complexity of the child abuse can be properly addressed.

The passage through this period of the life cycle ends with a major transition whereby young children move through adolescence to adulthood. It is often one of the most unstable periods in the family's life cycle for several reasons: children move unpredictably back and forth between being children and becoming adults, making it difficult for parents to know how to respond; parents may take time to master the necessary shift from being parents of young children to being parents of near-adult children; there is often a painful juxtaposition of experiences between the children's growing sexual and creative potential and the waning of reproductive and working capacities in the parents; the family itself is at an adolescent stage in its formation when parents as well as children feel compelled to act out unmanageable areas of their unmet needs. Each parent may need to begin a new sexual relationship with a younger person as a way of feeling assured of their own continuing attractiveness. A woman may demand a great deal more space for herself and the development of her own identity as a person, not simply as someone else's daughter, mother or wife. Out of this period of instability and change, the family moves through the transition to a new phase where children leave home and parents become once more identified primarily as a couple, or a single parent moves to being on his or her own once again.

After children leave home

The transition from becoming parents or a parent of young children to letting them go as adults creates new challenges and demands which might be summarized as follows: how to readapt to being a couple (or single person) without the day to day care of children; how to develop new adult-to-adult relationships between parents and children; how to develop a pattern of relatedness that can be sustained over the geographical distance that probably now separates the families; how to allow new members to join – the children's partners and the grandchildren; how to manage the increasing dependency of the other generation.

Because of the increased longevity of both women and men, this period of life now often lasts as long as the child-rearing period. It can helpfully be divided into two: the period between when the last child leaves home until the parents become more dependent and the final period of extreme old age and death. In the first part of this period the family may experience a time of consolidation: re-investment in the marital relationship; a freedom to experience a good sexual relationship without fear of conception; the development of enriching relationships across four generations; the opportunity for developing talents and interests that have hitherto been insufficiently exploited. It can, on the other hand, be a period of stress, conflict and disintegration. Couples who have invested too heavily in their parenting relationships to the detriment of their relationship with their partner may find that the loss of the children reveals a barren and unsatisfactory partnership which has lost the 'glue' that the children have provided for it. This 'empty nest' experience creates an overwhelming sense of loss and makes other compensating factors hard to find. Second only to the very early period of the marriage or other form of partnership, there is a high incidence of divorce during this period after the children leave. In fact these disruptions may pave the way for new and satisfying relationships to be formed in later life, many of which take the form of cohabitations and living-apart-together arrangements rather than remarriages, providing each partner with the opportunity to develop towards the maturity of old age as individuals and within new relationships.

The experiences of women and men, different from and similar to each other at every stage of the life cycle, may involve different challenges in this later stage. Whilst for some women the loss of the direct parenting function is overwhelming and no other purpose in life can be envisaged, for others there is a tremendous release of energy, interest and creativity and the desire and the opportunity to 'catch up' on the years when the needs of the self were subordinated to these tasks. For a man, premature redundancy or the realization that the peak of his occupation and promotional prospects has been reached may bring depression. Or it may provide the opportunity for early retirement which, as for women, may release him from a lifetime of a monotonous and duty bound wage-earning role.

If the threat of these changes and challenges cannot be absorbed, either partner may develop physical symptoms or resort to alcohol or become anxious or depressed. If a long-standing marriage breaks down during this phase, men respond much more adversely than women and cope much less well with the return to single status. In terms of his continuing physical, psychological and mental health, a man's capacity to remain in a good marriage or other partnership is perhaps the most important single variable. Part of the task of this phase is to develop a new way of relating to adult children and to their children and to the older generation. The complexities of this four-generational system will be further taxed or enriched, depending on how it is handled, if one or both members of the couple separate and form new partnerships and begin new families. The number and complexity of the potential relationships that then occur will take some while to get used to!

Old age

The final phase of the family's life cycle is not of course final at all. Yet it represents a way of expressing the fact that the original couple, who have become parents and grandparents, are now themselves approaching their own old age. They will have to cope with the death of their own parents which today often occurs when the couple are themselves in their sixties or seventies. Where conflict with this older generation has not been resolved, the couple can be left with severe and debilitating guilt which may be quite unrelated to the actual relationships that existed in the past.

Older family members may benefit considerably from wise counselling at the point of their bereavement from someone appropriately aware of the psychological mechanisms involved in 'letting go'.

When the family is unable to deal with losses in the grandparental generation, the unresolved conflict may erupt in other ways. Bowen (1978) has drawn attention to the chain reaction that can get set up in families after the death of a pivotal member of the older generation and the extremely destabilizing effect that such a death can produce. The entry of the original couple into their final phase of life in this world will usually involve the chronic illness or loss of one or other partner. Women are four times more likely to lose their partner than men and this loss will be experienced more harshly if the woman's emotional, relational or financial world is also very depleted. In another case, a realignment in relationships may draw her closer to children and grandchildren and provide her with a new and satisfying role in the family.

For both parties the fact of grandparenthood creates an extraordinary change for everyone in the family, especially of course for grandparents themselves who have this role 'thrust upon them' sometimes quite unwillingly. Becoming a grandparent and a great-grandparent is another marker in the long road towards old age and may be resented as such. For many however it offers a whole new variety of possibilities. Mead (1972) comments in relation to her own experience of the role: 'In the presence of grandparent and grand-child, past and future merge in the present' (p. 311). The arrival of grandchildren and great-grandchildren provide evidence of con-tinuity, stability and purpose in the continuing life of the family system stretching into the future.

The death of elderly family members who have become the grand-parental generation signals a ripple (or convulsion) for the whole family system, whereby roles and seniority are reallocated. The death of the last member of the older generation is a particular milestone. The involvement by the whole family in the experience of death will enable its meaning to be better assimilated and for the different bereavement needs of family members to be expressed and worked through. Although the processes of bereavement are now much better understood, families may still sometimes want to shield young children from a family death. It cannot be emphasized too strongly that children can be helped to cope with the trauma of death if adults around them are honest, open and able to allow the child to approach the experience at his own pace, and if they offer him explanations appropriate to his level of understanding.

> What happens when I die?
> Is there an after life?
> And what is it like?
> These are the Great Spiritual Questions.
> No one escapes them.
> There are no exceptions.

Jonathan Andrew (1992) in speaking from his experience as some-one with AIDS, points out the difficulty for the Church in meeting these universally engaging questions. Yet the Church should have more to give the family at this point of death than at any other moment in its life cycle. The opportunities offered by the funeral ministry are rich with potential. The rituals associated with this rite of passage are powerful in helping the family manage this event. Involving many of the family in planning and carrying out the ritual, according to the customs of the religious and ethnic grouping to which the family belongs, will greatly help the family system. Many Afro-Caribbean families will want an open coffin, an opportunity for respect to be paid to the deceased and special rituals at the grave-side, including the filling of the grave by family members and the singing of spirituals. Asian families may need a prolonged (by western standards) and expressive period of mourning. However as Friedman (1989) comments, the 'celebration' (or in this case the funeral service) is not the whole event. The family can be greatly helped at this moment of emotional reorganization if someone can help it to work through the meaning of the change and to reconnect with its history and its future. Reminiscing and recalling the family's sense of its own history is something which helps reorientate it in time and space. In addition, however dimly perceived, most people have some sense of the continuity of life beyond death. Since this concept is so central to our Christian faith, death ought to be a moment when we can help family members create metaphors and imagery that will encapsulate the meaning of this continuity for them. Some of these metaphors will be to hand in the Bible; others can be sought from poetry. Still others will already reside deeply within the family's shared consciousness from the past and only require the prompting of an outsider or the provision of some framework for them to become usable.

Families who cannot handle the death of their members may become stuck. This may express itself in the symptomatic behaviour of one member of a family – often someone who has had a particular relationship with the deceased, either positive or negative. Or the family may displace its difficulties onto others outside its own membership. The family may for example want to recruit members of the congregation into a continuing observance of the family member's death, especially if the deceased has also played an important role within the congregation. Or there may be a need to 'fix' the memory of the deceased by gifts of ornaments or other artefacts to the church. There may be a difficult balance to be kept for the clergy involved, in encouraging the healthy use of such 'remembering' without allowing it to become fixated and fossilized for the whole community.

Until recently, there has been a severe depletion, in many of the

Protestant Churches, in their repertoire of rituals for those who mourn, because of the reduction – almost to nothing in some cases – in the liturgies for the dead. In Britain, Roman Catholic and some Anglican Christians have maintained the practice of offering a Requiem Mass for the departed as well as the corporate observance of All Souls' Day. Catholic countries in Europe retain further practices as well as customs which involve the visiting of graves on All Souls' Day and the exchange of flowers within families. The extensive participation in the annual act of rememberance for the dead which characterizes Mexican society with its special days for remembering children, adults, those who have died violently etc., is enacted each year in 'The Days of the Dead'. Whole families and whole communities share in this communal remembering, which involves a mixture of religious and secular rituals including the preparation and enjoyment of special food shared at the end of the prescribed period.

Recent liturgical reform within the Anglican Church has encouraged much more frequent use of memorial services, for individual families and for groups of the bereaved at intervals during the year. In addition the new services suggested for All Souls' tide encourages churches to recognize the community's need to come together to share their family experiences of death on an annual basis within the containing framework of a liturgical event. The many painful individual experiences of death and bereavement within separate families can be greatly assisted by such corporate communal acts. The lack of such opportunities has over the last half century been displaced onto the outwardly similar but symbolically extremely different event of Remembrance Sunday. Restricted to the remembrance of those who died in battle, these services do nothing to heal the unremembered hurts of most of the population who yearn to make sense of their loss, their own continuing life and the possibility of a life to come. Instead, they side-step people's deep attachment needs, displacing them on to symbols of national life, and in so doing provide a pseudotherapeutic route to attaining healing and comfort.

Green (1987) points out the many opportunities which are afforded by liturgical acts to enable people to understand and manage the significance of crucial life experiences. He discusses the power of the Church's liturgical acts, both to reveal and to conceal meaning, and in helping people to handle the ambiguous nature of much human experience – especially the final one of death. The affirmation of a family's continuity beyond death as well as its continuity within an earthly life cycle is one of the Church's major contributions to the healing and strengthening of the family system's experience.

Several other transitional experiences affect a minority of families and have considerable significance for their passage through the family life cycle. We will look briefly at three.

Migration

Migration is an experience that repeatedly influences the life cycle of many families within ethnic minority groups as well as some families amongst the ethnic majority. McGoldrick (1989) comments: 'Migration is so disruptive in itself that we could say that it adds an entire extra stage to the life cycle for those families who must negotiate it' (p. 83). In Britain, many Afro-Caribbean families experienced a major transition in their family life cycle with the arrival of the first members in this country in the 1950s. Those who are now in their mid-life, with adult children of their own, will easily recall the month, the year and the boat which brought them here as children. Their experience since then has often been of a family in motion, with members moving back and forth between the island which remains 'home' in some real and relational sense.

Those who migrate have to negotiate two sets of cultural norms, often two different languages, two different histories and often two sets of loyalties. They have to try to hold two ways of understanding the world in some sort of balance. Families whose members migrate may respond by identifying fully with one culture to the detriment of the other. Families whose language and religion separate them more sharply from their new neighbours are more likely to remain identified with their original culture. Others may cut off from their country of origin so that children have less chance of remaining in contact through visits or a period of schooling, during which they can live with their grandparents, cousins and other extended family members.

For families who migrate as young adults with young children, there is, as McGoldrick points out, a likelihood that the parents will acculturate more slowly than their children, creating a problematic reversal of influence and authority within the family. This may be more accentuated if the children are adolescents when the family arrives, learning English quickly and becoming the parents' interpreters.

A major issue for all families separated from the older generation is how to provide them with care and support at a distance. In addition to the usual life-cycle issues that have to be faced, the family may have to cope with its guilt and anxiety over the older generation alongside its problems of adjustment to a new culture. In addition, they are deprived of the ongoing support and contact which grand-parents could provide. Families who have been forced rather than chosen to leave their country of origin, such as the Vietnamese 'boat' families or, more recently, families fleeing the old Republic of Yugoslavia, will have had no time to assimilate the shock of the move or to cope with their bereavement. The loss of country may be combined with multiple losses of relatives, friends and other loved ones.

Families who have migrated two or three generations ago may make it easier for children to reclaim their cultural inheritance from the country that their grandparents left. Adolescents may identify strongly with the 'old' culture as a way of differentiating themselves from their parents' assimilation to the new. Inter-generational conflicts may get worked out through this division of cultural loyalties, with younger members adopting the music, dress and customs that make them simulatenously the same and different from their family.

Divorce

As we noted in chapter 5, separation and divorce are now so prevalent that they have become part of the experience of family life for over a third of all families in Britain. They need therefore to be considered in terms of the family life cycle. To consider divorce as a transition within the family life cycle more easily helps those who must endure the process to cope with it constructively.

The degree and the manner to which the family system as a whole is affected by divorce depends on what stage in the family life cycle the divorce occurs. Peck and Manocherian (1989) comment: 'The disruption [of divorce] is associated with shifts and changes in membership and boundaries, requiring a major reorganization of the family system' (p. 346).

Divorce is least disruptive for couples who divorce soon after marriage when they are still young and have no children. They have fewer roles and relationships, and less shared history to disentangle and the absence of children means that the complex tasks of continuing parenting do not have to be negotiated. Families with young children are both most divorce-prone and also most adversely affected by it. Wallerstein and Kelly's (1980) study showed that pre-school children (other than young babies) are most severely affected by the confusion and emotional insecurity of the divorce crisis. The non-custodial parent may grieve for his lack of day to day contact with the children and the custodial parent may find the adjustment to a lone-parent family hard to make. The essential tasks are the separation of the marital and parental roles and the provision of as much stability and continuity as possible in relationships with grandparents, other relatives and friends.

When children are adolescent, they may more easily get caught into loyalty conflicts. They may have to cope with the confusion of seeing a parent begin a new relationship when they themselves are experimenting with their own newly developing sexuality. They may be recruited into a co-parenting role, or a role of confidante by the custodial parent, which hinders the pursuance of their normal developmental tasks. When children leave home, the couple experience the stage in their marriage which is next most divorce-prone. The major change that occurs when children leave, after a prolonged period of parenting, creates the need for major readjustment which not all couples are able to make. Divorce at this stage may be a little easier for children to tolerate but it is often much more difficult for the couple and the wider family system because of their prolonged shared history. If one or other parent is unable to make a new start, the young adult children may find it difficult to continue tackling their own movement into new relationships and jobs. The important task at this stage is to ensure that both parents establish their own separate good relationship with children, cutting off from as few members of the family and friendship network as possible, whilst moving forward to make new friends and develop new work and social opportunities for themselves.

The whole family that became one system through the couple's marriage is now affected by the breakup of their relationship. Not only grandparents, parents, siblings and the couple's own children, but also the friendship network that has been developed around them all get caught up in the crisis.

Ahrons (1980) views divorce as a transitional, time-limited crisis, which interrupts the developmental tasks that are occurring at a particular stage of the life cycle. Like all transitional crises, everyone involved undergoes a period of disequilibrium and rapid change. He proposes a five-stage model for understanding the process of divorce. Stages 1 and 2 occur before separation and mark the point when first one spouse (stage 1) and then both (stage 2) begin to face up to the idea of divorce and make the decision. The majority of divorces are non-mutual, with one person wanting the divorce more than the other. The extent to which the decision is taken suddenly by one partner, will increase the stress experienced by the other and make the process of separation even more traumatic. At stage 3, the divorce takes place with a range of accompanying feelings which almost always include ambivalence on the part of *both* partners. The more that the partners disagree about the wisdom of the decision to divorce, the more traumatic and difficult the process is likely to be. In general women are more expressive of their pain during the immediate separation period and then recover more quickly from the crisis than men. Stage 4 is the period when the whole family system has to face the reorganization of roles and boundaries that results from the divorce. If the couple have children, they have to work out how to sever their marital roles whilst continuing and supporting each other's parental roles. New norms have to be established around contact and relationships with grandparents, relatives and friends of the ex-spouse's side of the family. Stage 5 begins when the family has successfully negotiated most of the tasks involved in the previous stages and has achieved a new equilibrium. The whole process may typically take two to three years but in fact often takes longer.

The end product of divorce in terms of family structure may be one of three possibilities: a lone parent household, a single person, or a remarried family. Many people who begin the post-divorce process as a single person or in a lone-parent household move to become a remarried family (either as a remarried couple or a family with children or other dependants). It is however important to under-line that for some, the experience of becoming single and alone again or of remaining as a lone-parent family will be their permanent situation, either through choice or necessity. The goal of divorce is not remarriage and the automatic link between the two will be more effectively severed if the status and normality of being single or a lone parent can be more securely established, allowing remarriage to be an open and less compulsive choice.

Brown (1989) suggests that there are three distinct phases in becom-ing a lone-parent household after divorce: the aftermath, the realign-ment and the stabilization. Each phase has its own distinct characteristics. She concludes that 'It is a process that, when success-fully complete, results in a family that can function well whether the mother decides to remarry or not' (p. 373). It is in fact very important to affirm the lone-parent family as complete and viable in its own right, rather than on its way to becoming something else. The same kinds of adjustments and needs are often contingent upon widowhood.

Some single women who become lone parents may do so out of choice and thus be better prepared to cope with what is involved. Many find creative solutions to providing male role models and relationships for their children and view this potential difficulty as an opportunity to be selective and diverse. Many young single mothers have good support from their parents and extended families which gives opportunities for mother to have contact with other adults, and for her child (children) to relate to other children in the family. Many also have good support from their partners even though they are not living together (Phoenix, 1991). However, as Ferri (1976) has pointed out, the main difficulty for lone-parent households is often coping with the attitudes of others:

> Far from being conducive to the re-integration of one parent families into the social fabric, the ambivalent and often negative attitudes which society adopts towards such families seems only to isolate them and add to the multiple difficulties they face. (p. 149)

Remarriage

However, the majority of people move into remarriage and have to tackle a range of complex tasks, again dependent upon where they are in the life cycle when remarriage occurs. McGoldrick and Carter comment:

> So complex is the process whereby the remarried family system stabilizes and regains its forward developmental thrust that we have come to think of this process as adding another whole phase to the family life cycle for those involved. (p. 399)

People marrying for the second time may come from very different life-cycle stages. In general, the wider the discrepancy between the two experiences, the greater the difficulty in negotiating the transition. Moreover, a remarried family may have to deal with several life-cycle stages simultaneously. For example, a young wife may be step-parenting her husband's teenage children before becoming a mother herself. The couple may be experiencing nappies and sleepless nights in relation to their own new-born, whilst at the same time becoming grandparents. On the other hand, couples with no previous children still have to deal with the integration into the wider network of each other's family and friends as well as continuing the process of disengagement from their previous marriages and relationships.

The most complex situations are those when both new partners bring children to the marriage from previous marriages and where these children are at the stage of being either young or adolescent. Each child has to cope with new relationships with the step-parent and their family and friends *and* the loss of their own parent as a full-time parent. At the same time they must learn how to forge a continuing but new-style relationship with their non-custodial parent and, in parallel fashion, form new relationships with step-siblings, step-grandparents etc. Some researchers suggest that young children have most difficulty in dealing with divided loyalties. Wallerstein and Kelly (1980) and others show that step families with teenagers experience most difficulties.* Where remarriage happens in later life, grown-up children may resent the disturbance to their childhood memories caused by the intrusion of their parent's new

---

* Visher and Visher (1979).

spouse. If the new partner has not been married before there may be a clash of expectations. The new spouse may hope to be parent/grandparent by proxy to the partner's children whilst the adult children may refuse to accord the newcomer any status or title other than 'my father's new wife'. Serious conflict may arise over the drawing up of the couple's wills and there may be a profound sense of betrayal experienced by grown-up children at seeing their emotional and financial inheritance redirected.

In chapter 8 we will consider the early phase in the family life cycle in a bit more detail – that of choosing a partner.

8

CHOICES

'And the two will become one.'

Matthew 19: 5

One Flesh Separate Persons was the title given to the English version of an early and influential text in the field of family therapy.* It describes the challenge and the struggle of all couple relationships as well as the hope to which almost every human being on some level aspires. Becoming one with another person is the awesome, ecstatic possibility which is contingent upon our separateness. It holds out the greatest hope of fulfilment and the deepest threat of failure. It is the riskiest of enterprises because in daring to become one, we necessarily expose the most vulnerable and tender aspects of ourselves to another.

We offer ourselves for the healing of acceptance but risk the untold damage of wholesale rejection. Because the difficulties of this undertaking can be severe, they are often denied and hidden away under a froth of romanticism, especially in the case of traditional, heterosexual marriage. The Church colludes in this evasion. It wrings its hands at the muddle and pain but it also denies the value of other kinds of couple relationships as well as avoiding the hard work that is necessary to help people find the fulfilment for which they yearn.

In this chapter we will look at the process involved in choosing a partner, at some predictors of difficulty in different kinds of partnership and at some ways of helping those couples who choose to marry prepare for their marriage.

* A. C. R. Skynner, *One Flesh Separate Persons* (London, Constable, 1976)

Choice of partner

Choosing and being chosen are concepts that are at the heart of our Christian faith. We believe that every human being has 'been chosen' by God for the privilege of life and that all human beings are presented with opportunities for choosing between life and death throughout their lives. To be *chosen*, and to be free to *choose* are also aspects of human experience that are highly determinative of the individual's self-esteem and fundamental experience of self-worth. *Not* to be chosen by one's fellow human beings (even within the confines of a training exercise, or a game or social event) can evoke a painful loss of self-worth and an acute experience of rejection. Likewise to have all freedom to choose removed and be compelled to interact with people whom one has not chosen can be a suffocating, frustrating and debilitating experience. The act of choosing and being chosen by a partner may evoke the ambiguity and pain of half conscious memories from the past, of other moments of choosing and being chosen or being cast aside. The desire to choose and the fear of not being chosen can therefore abruptly precipitate couples into a relationship which is based more on their fear of being alone than their desire to be together. Paradoxically, the compulsion to choose and to avoid not being chosen may play a major part in limiting the freedom of each partner to direct the process consciously.

These fears and desires partly arise from the innate human need to form an attachment bond with another person which replicates the primary bonding of early childhood.* They arise partly from the social pressure to become a couple that exists within our culture. The two are obviously interrelated and the second is a social externaliz-ation of the first. Thus the ability to make a free choice of partner is limited first by these general social and psychological pressures to choose lest one is ultimately not chosen. However there are several other ways in which our choice of partner is limited beyond the practical ones of availability noted in chapter 6.

A considerable number of studies have confirmed the fact that partners are attracted to one another on the basis of *assortative mating* – that is, in terms of similarities in personality, attitudes, beliefs, education, socio-economic class and a whole range of other variables

* Bowlby (1969, 1973, 1980)

(Tyler, 1988). The opposite hypothesis, that couples are also attracted on the basis of dissimilarity, of *complementary mating*, also seems to be true but within a different set of variables, a major example being the gender variable, since most couples make their choice of partner from among those of a different gender. Moreover, research conducted over many years at the Tavistock Institute of Marital Studies suggests that people choose their partner in relation to a variety of unconscious needs which include the need to reunite themselves with 'lost' repressed parts of their own personalities, both parts that have been idealized and are split off and parts that have been disowned (Dicks (1967), Pincus (1971), Clulow (1985)).

The projection onto the partner of aspects of the self which have been disowned and the subsequent attraction to the partner's 'difference' suggests that on an unconscious level at least, the pull of opposites is also an ingredient in the process of choosing a partner. For example, a shy and socially incompetent man may be attracted to a vivacious outgoing partner, not only because she represents some promise of a socially enriched existence but also because she can 'hold' for him, through his projection, latent aggressive aspects of his own personality which he both fears and needs if he is to function more fully and ably in his social environment. The therapeutic task here would be to help him to regain for himself the part that he has disowned and projected onto her, so that he can become a more whole person himself, rather than relying on 'his other half' to make him complete. However the former may well be a route to the latter and part of the promise of partnership is that it holds out for all of us the possibility of what Dominian (1991b) summarizes as 'sustaining, healing and growth'.

The influence on the choice of partner of previous relationships is also very strong, again operating mainly on an unconscious level. Pincus (1971) points out that

> Although there is often a wish to start afresh . . . and to escape the frustrations and disappointments of unsatisfactory early relationships, a strong unconscious tie to the first love-objects may help to determine the choice of a partner with whom the earlier situation can be compulsively re-enacted. (p. 14)

The influence of our relationship with our parents and of our image of each parent plays an important part in our choice of partner. Various interpretations have been made of the influence of the parental relationship. In general however, it seems that a person is likely to choose a partner who resembles, in terms of personality, the parent with whom he or she was most closely bonded as a child. By the same token, people will tend to avoid partnering with someone who resembles the parent with whom they had a more distant or hostile relationship. In a controversial study, Moberly (1983) has suggested that gay and lesbian partnerships are influenced by the need to reverse the process of disidentification with the parent of the same sex. She hypothesizes that the normal process of early identification with the same-sex parent was interrupted in early childhood by the parent's absence or emotional unavailability, and the choice of a same-sex partner is therefore a restorative choice aimed at healing the trauma caused by an earlier deficiency. The problem about Moberly's analysis is that it 'implies an environmental rather than a biological etiology for the conditions of homosexuality' (p. 65), which in view of the increasingly suggestive evidence to the contrary, is difficult to sustain. However, in so far as *all* our partnership choices are likely to be governed in some measure by the unconscious drive towards healing the past, there may well be environmental factors that coalesce around early relationships with the same-sex parent, which are influential upon the choice of same-sex partnering.

Predictors of difficulty

There are a variety of circumstances that act predictively upon the likelihood of a couple experiencing difficulties in the future. Some of these predictors apply to a specific type of partnership but most apply to all types and militate against the successful adjustment of the pair. As we noted in chapter 7, losses through death or divorce occurring in the wider family systems of both or either partner can influence the system to increase its membership. However, the close juxtaposition of such an event usually has a negative influence on the ability of a new couple to create a satisfactory lasting relationship. Sometimes, even with a considerable amount of premarital counselling, the disruptive effects of recent unresolved losses are impossible to counter.

For example, a young couple in their mid-twenties came for preparation sessions prior to what was to be a second marriage for him and a first for her. His first marriage had broken up a few months after it had been contracted and he had returned home to live with his parents. It came to light during the preparation sessions that he had gone through with this marriage in a highly traumatized state because his sister had been killed two days before the wedding was due to take place. The family had decided that the wedding should go ahead, but neither he nor his parents nor siblings could do more than go through the motions. The honeymoon was not surprisingly a disaster and a few months later the marriage had come to an end. During the marriage preparation, considerable attention was paid to these events alongside the parallel consideration of the experience of failure and guilt at the breakdown of the first marriage. Meetings were held with his parents and a ritual was carefully constructed to assist the process of arrested mourning which continued to affect the young man. At the same time, equal attention was paid to the young woman's traumatic separation from her family of origin at the age of four and her yearning to repair the relationship that she had lost with her mother. Nevertheless this second marriage also broke up, leaving the young man back in his parents' home and the young woman again alone. The strength of the counterveiling factors preventing this couple from successfully forming a relationship involved the deep ambivalence towards the marriage on the part of both the couple and their families of origin. Whilst urging their daughter and son to introduce replacement members into the family, each family feared the threat of new loss and change which would have been an inevitable consequence of the new marriage.

A high level of unresolved conflict in one or other of the partner's families is also predictive of difficulties. This is partly because the desire to escape from the conflict may be the primary driver in forming the new relationship. It also provides poor role models for handling conflict in the new relationship. Chronic destructive conflict within the parents' marriage or within the sibling group or between the older generation makes it difficult for the new couple to know from experience that the conflicts that inevitably occur in all close relationships can be handled, worked through and used as an opportunity for growth. Kobrin and Waite (1984) have shown that there will be an increased risk of marital instability if marital patterns in either of the extended families are predominantly unstable. Again, although the facts of the legacy of the past cannot be altered, the new couple's awareness of their possible effect can be awakened and some of their perceptions about these difficulties can be changed. However, divorce does tend to run in families. In addition to the reasons already noted, Hart (1976) suggests that the experience of having divorced parents may reduce the individual's aversion to divorce. She suggests too that parents who have themselves been divorced may be less active in discouraging their children from undergoing a similar experience.

Important early work by Toman (1969) showed that the partners' position in their family constellations – their sibling position – would affect their ability to adjust to each other in a partnership. For example, an only child who marries or who forms a partnership with someone from a large family, clearly brings a very different experience of family to this new relationship from that of his partner. He will have had very limited experience of relating to his peers or handling the wide range of interpersonal dynamics that occur within peer relationships in families. On the whole, people who have extremely dissimilar experiences in their families of origin are more likely to have difficulties with the new partnership, compared with those who have similar or complementary experiences. For example, a man who is the eldest of several brothers and a woman who is the eldest of several sisters are likely to have difficulties forming a partnership because both will be accustomed to being 'leaders' and neither will have experience of a peer relationship with the other sex.

The degree to which prospective partners have been able to separate from their family of origin and to resolve the conflicts inherent in their childhood dependency will have an important bearing on the success of the new partnership. An inability to separate emotionally may be indicated by a need to stay close geographically to one or other of the parental homes, but the need to cut off and live on the other side of the world is also often an indicator of unresolved emotional closeness. The task of the new couple is to become intimate with one another without being fused so that each person can also remain differentiated without becoming isolated. Intimacy and differentiation – one flesh but separate persons – is the overall emotional task to be achieved. This is made very difficult indeed if one or other partner has been unable to achieve closeness without fusion with his original family.

Sometimes the problem is expressed by one or both of the partners going back each day to their original home. This may not show up as a difficulty at first (and indeed it may not be one). However, problems arise when either partner believes that they must choose between making an emotional investment in the new relationship or being disloyal to their parents. This may become evident in conflict experienced by the clash between the way his or her family 'did things' and the way the partner's family seems now to 'do things differently'. Negotiating the different cultures of the two families of origin and creating something that is new and different without denying the influence of either family is a formidable goal for the new couple to achieve. It may be an insuperable one if the chief loyalty of either partner remains with his primary relationships of the past. If a high level of conflict is activated in the family system by the impending marriage and remains unresolved, the residue of this conflict will continue to reverberate around the system with highly destructive consequences for the stability of the new marriage. If the bride's mother finds her daughter's choice of husband impossible to accept, because of the resonance this has for the way her own marriage disappointed *her mother*, the new bride will have continually to renegotiate this conflict or else cut off her relationship with her mother, with all the negative consequences that will be involved.

Couples who marry very young have repeatedly been shown to have a high risk of marital disruption. However, as we noted in chapter 5, the average age of marriage is increasing, thus reducing the influence of this particular factor. Couples who conceive a child very early on in their relationship are also at greater risk. Contrary to the received wisdom in some Christian circles, children nearly always have a deleterious effect upon a marital or other partnership. This means that it is important that the relationship has had a reasonable amount of time to settle down before the more complex relationships with children have to be negotiated.

Particular problems are likely to arise in most heterosexual partnerships, both marital and cohabitational, around the way in which gender roles are perceived and exercised. Again there will be greater problems in adjustment when the partners have experienced very different role models in their families of origin. The continuously developing self-definition of women requires a continuous response from their male partners, and women who continue to work outside the home after forming a partnership are likely to be unwilling to undertake major responsibility for domestic duties as well. All the research shows that they do, however, continue to do so and that this contradiction between the expectations on the wife as both housekeeper, child-minder *and* wage earner is a major source of marital conflict. Other factors are probably also related to the way in which gender roles are perceived. Cherlin (1979) showed that, in the United States, the greater the wife's income in relation to her husband's, the greater the risk of divorce. Likewise, the risk is greater when better educated women are married to less well educated men.

Finally, the greater the degree of difference that exists between partners, the greater degree of difficulty in negotiating the relationship and the greater the risk of breakdown. This is a general factor that seems to hold good across practically every variable – education, social class, age, religion, race, nationality, occupation and recreational interests. Goode (1971) suggests that those who are alike in many respects will share a similar and approving circle of friends and acquaintances which will support and foster their relationship. Those who do not share sufficient similarities may not so easily get this support. In view of the great cultural diversity, mobility and variety that are likely to be permanent features of our contemporary social experience, we need to pay considerable attention to difference as a variable associated with marital breakdown and to consider ways in which difference can be evaluated as an increasingly positive and enriching aspect of our social and relational lives. In particular situations, such as inter-racial marriage, the important point to make is that the person helping the couple prepare for their relationship considers with them the ways in which their differences may create stress and the ways in which conversely they can be used creatively. According to a survey in 1981 (the most recent figures available) about 1% of marriages were between partners of different ethnic groups (Coleman, 1985). In terms of both the preparation and counselling of interracial marriages, McGoldrick (1989) makes the point that the counsellor's role will be that of 'culture broker, helping family members to recognise their own ethnic values and to resolve the conflicts that evolve out of different perceptions and experiences' (p. 86).

Couples who cohabit rather than marry tend to be more unstable. They therefore require more help but probably receive a lot less. This is partly due to the ambiguous nature of the partnership even today when many more couples cohabit as an alternative to marriage. One of the reasons why cohabiting relationships are less stable is because of the lack of recognition and support given to them in the community. Often people begin cohabiting without revealing the new or changed nature of the relationship to anybody but a small number of close friends. The ceremonies and rituals for beginning or continuing a cohabiting relationship have to be created from scratch or borrowed and may be inadequate to express the full significance of the relationship.

The reasons why the couple have chosen to cohabit instead of marry may be well thought out and represent an ideological stance against the perceived restrictive institution of marriage – especially as experienced by women. Or, the couple may believe that cohabitation is a life-style that is appropriate to their circumstances (e.g. they are students or at a point in their careers where they are unwilling to make a long-term commitment). For them cohabitation may be a responsible choice. On the other hand, the reasons may be muddled and confused and hold within them the seeds of the relationship's destruction. For example, one or other partner may find the prospect of any kind of commitment to another fraught with difficulty because of his or her unsatisfactory early experiences of intimacy. In addition, sources of conflict are likely to include the specific reason why many couples choose cohabitation rather than marriage – the freedom and lack of permanence that the relationship both offers and requires. Skolnick (1978) for example suggests that 'if boredom and the feeling of compulsion are the occupational hazards of marriage, insecurity and jealousy are the corresponding hazards of the free couple' (p. 224).

Macklin (1983) suggests that a further problem is that the sexual stereotyping often considered by women to be inherent in marriage, is also hard to avoid in cohabiting relationships. The couple may therefore have to contend both with the problems of gender inequality *and* the disappointment that this problem still exists. It obviously takes more than merely altering the *form* of the relationship to overcome this fundamental relational difficulty between women and men. A further difficulty, peculiar to both heterosexual cohabitation and to same-sex pairs, is the lack of ritual and other means of ending the relationship. This may encourage the couple simply to drift apart and create another relationship on the rebound from the last or form a new relationship in which they are destined to repeat the same unresolved problems. This should alert clergy, when preparing couples for marriage, that it is as important to help the couple work through the residual grief and guilt from a previous cohabitation or gay relationship as it is to help couples disengage from a previous marriage. In this respect, the dynamics are the same.

The relationships of gay and lesbian couples are predicated on gender symmetry. An inherent difficulty is therefore likely to be the way in which the partners create difference and organize their role relationship. Freed from sexual stereotyping, they nevertheless have to create a workable model for managing the roles and tasks of the relationship. Predictors of difficulty are therefore an unresolved competitiveness in relation to work, domestic chores and sex. Like cohabiting partnerships, there are no prescribed rituals to support the relationship nor to mark the transitions within it, and no structure for bringing it to an end. Tensions between the couple and their families of origin because of opposition to the relationship may reduce the amount of social support available to them. As with married couples, such hostility is a poor predictor for the relationship's success. If the couple cut off completely from one or other of the families and if the friendship network is small, the relationship will be forced to supply most of the emotional and social needs of each partner which may become too great a burden for the relationship to bear. The management of the stigma still associated with homosexuality and the homophobia within society may create added stress and the way in which this is managed will be highly influential in predicting the success of the relationship. If one partner wants to 'come out' whilst the other does not, such a deeply divisive issue may be hard to resolve. Likewise, for lesbian couples in particular, the question of whether or not to have children requires the same kind of negotiation as it does for heterosexual couples. However, the couple will know that they will be bringing up children in an unusual social situation and will need to address in advance the possible difficulties associated with doing so. A major area of potential conflict between gay couples in particular may be the relative priority placed by each partner on the sexual and the emotional sides of the relationship. Again, the continuing inability to resolve the relative importance of both aspects may create chronic conflict between them.

Preparing for partnerships

It may seem odd to end this chapter with a section on how to help couples prepare for their partnership. However, I believe that a prior consideration of the many difficulties that couples encounter may act as a spur to undertaking more thorough preparation with a couple to help them embark on a new relationship. I believe that fewer opportunities would be wasted if the would-be counsellor gave more consideration to what actually makes relationships work and what creates obstacles, rather than what the counsellor thinks may be the obstacles!

People form partnerships in order to defend themselves against the deep seated fear of living alone in the world. They also find partners in order to complete what they sense is incomplete in themselves. In the early part of this chapter we considered some of the unconscious determinants of partnership choice in more detail. These choices are strongly determined by unconscious needs, by social norms and by family expectations. But this does not mean that couples cannot be helped to reflect upon their choice, to consider the potential of their partnership and to anticipate and prepare to meet the possible difficulties that they may encounter.

Various writers have made the point that, desirable as it might be to engage in premarital counselling, few couples are likely to present themselves for help before they actually experience difficulties. The big exception to this otherwise correct observation is the still con- siderable number of couples who approach clergy with the request that they be married in church, thus opening out the opportunity to prepare the couple for their marriage. Very few couples indeed refuse the opportunity to engage in marriage preparation. The problem often lies in the diffidence, embarrassment and downright resistance that many clergy demonstrate towards engaging in this task. Even when it is considered to be part of the clergy person's role (or the role of those to whom it is delegated in the parish) it often founders for the following reasons:

1. Too much time and emphasis is given to preparing for the wedding rather than the marriage. 'Wedding preparation' is a strategy of avoidance on the part of the clergy person and merely colludes with the couple's own fantasy that marriages are all about weddings.

2. A didactic approach is taken: a series of mini-lectures and discussions are arranged, using outside experts such as the bank manager, the doctor, a legal adviser etc. This approach simply serves to infantilize the couple and is a strategy on the part of the clergy person for avoiding the real issues in marriage preparation.

3. The wider systems perspective on the family and significant events that have occurred in the past are avoided.

4. Opportunities for actively helping the couple to resolve difficulties and conflicts that are currently occurring within or between the families are ignored.

5. The use of rituals and sacraments for healing the unresolved hurts of the past, including the guilt engendered by the breakdown of previous significant relationships are largely under-used.

Whilst the wedding ceremony itself undoubtedly holds enormous symbolic importance and, if well prepared for and conducted, will remain a powerful referent for the marriage, its full potential can only be harvested, as we noted in chapter 7, if it is seen in the context of the family system as a whole. Friedman (1989) puts the point like this:

> Ceremonies celebrate. From an emotional systems point of view, they are not in themselves efficacious. Rather, their effect is determined by what has already been developing within the emotional system of the family. Ceremonies do focus the events, however, in that they bring family members into conscious

contact with one another and in that they bring processes to a head. (p. 124)

They perform this function whether the clergy person is aware of this fact or not. However, if he or she *can* be more aware of it, and of its potential, it will then be possible to use the marriage preparation for helping the couple and the family as a whole, in negotiating this transition in their life cycle. As Friedman (1985) again comments:

A wedding is like an iceberg: only one eighth of the moving mass will be visible, but the process and decision usually have the impetus and momentum of generations of build up. (p. 179)

Marriage preparation should therefore help the couple to understand and engage with current areas of conflict and help them understand and work through unresolved conflicts from the past. Obviously, if the couple are preparing for a new marriage after divorce, or after another previous significant relationship, the issues that were salient in disrupting that relationship need to be understood as fully as possible.* The clergy person needs to hold, at the forefront of his or her mind, the need that we all have to repeat compulsively the old patterns from the past in all our new relationships. Good marriage preparation provides perhaps the only opportunity for a couple to receive competent help which may interrupt their need to do so. Couples may often need some help in resolving the guilt or loss they still experience which, for Christians, may helpfully include the use of the sacrament of reconciliation and/or a ritual for dissolving and forgiving vows or promises made to a former partner.

* See Walrond-Skinner, *Family Matters* (1988) for a fuller discussion of this process.

9

❦

STORIES

There were always those amongst us who had just returned from the world of the Living. They had returned inconsolable for all the love they had left behind, all the suffering they hadn't redeemed, all that they hadn't understood, and for all that they had barely begun to learn before they were drawn back to the land of origins.

BEN OKRI, *The Famished Road*

In chapters 6 and 7 we examined two ways of looking at families in terms of their behaviour in the present (systems) and their inheritance from the past (cycles). Between them they provide us with a model for accessing the interior life of the family group. It is a two-dimensional model, relevant to all families – to our *own* families and to *all* families, whatever their outward pattern and form. It is therefore a model which helps us to see that there is a continuum of experience between families who seem to be coping and those who, at any particular moment, seem to be coping less well. In this chapter, we will examine some of the ways in which the family as a group can be helped, and look at some examples. We will look at the way in which change occurs in families and ways in which an outside helper, pastor or counsellor can participate with the family in helping positive change to take place.

Change

In all living systems change occurs through sudden leaps whereby the system moves to a new level of integration which then becomes irreversible. The normal passage through the family life cycle and the unexpected crises that impinge from the outside world both create pressure for change. If change occurs in either the family's external environment or within its membership the family system itself will *necessarily* change. This change will occur through a sudden discontinuity, in response to mounting pressures from within or without. This pressure will create one of two possibilities. Optimally it will result in a new transformation – the sudden appearance of a whole array of new patterns that did not exist before. Hoffman (1989) cites as an example the kaleidoscope which keeps the same pattern until, as the tube turns, a small particle suddenly shifts and the whole pattern changes to form an entirely new one. 'The most interesting feature of a kaleidoscope,' adds Hoffman, 'is that one can never go back!' (p. 93). Or, the system will break down or 'resist' change, by diverting or absorbing the pressure to change. An example is the electrical system of a house which when overloaded or when short-circuited will trip.

Similarly, the transformations that occur in families in response to change may appear and in fact often are quite smooth and trouble-free. But if the number of changes, or the intensity or pace of change is too great, the family system like an electrical system will short-circuit or experience overload and an interruption or block occurs in the family's adaptive mechanisms which would normally move the system on towards a new transformation.

In an electrical system a circuit-breaker comes into operation to prevent the whole system from breaking down. The circuit-breaker will be triggered when the system short-circuits or when it experiences overload and, in modern house wiring systems, the very slightest overload will usually trigger this mechanism. Thus the safety of the system (and the inhabitants!) is protected to a very high degree. Put another way, the sensitivity of the system is so finely tuned that its defensive strategies come into play to protect it from harm at very low levels of overload.

Unlike the relatively simple example of an electrical system however, a family system will normally undergo a period of disequilibrium, confusion and stress, during which it invokes its own 'circuit-breakers' or defensive manoeuvres. These are in themselves experiments in an effort to bring about adaptation in response to the pressure for change. The family routinely makes use of several mechanisms during this period. They all have *the dual effect* of signalling the family's acknowledgement of its need to change and, *simultaneously*, its fear and resistance to doing so. In the stories which follow, several of these mechanisms will be illustrated and in each situation the task is to help the family regain its own natural momentum towards achieving a new transformation. The task is to help family cease diverting its energy into these compromise 'solutions' and make the leap instead to a new systems reorganization. The pastor or counsellor will try to do this by the minimal amount of intervention on her part needed to release the family's own momentum for change. At the end of the chapter we will review a hierarchy of levels of involvement in which the counsellor might engage.

We will focus now on three defensive strategies which families often use when confronted with the pressure to change: the choice of one family member to be 'the problem person' or symptom bearer; the blurring or dissolution of the family system's boundaries and the use of family myths. These are different defensive manoeuvres but like the examples of overload and short-circuiting in an electrical system, they produce the same result – an inability to make the leap to a new level of functional organization.

Often all three of them combine to hold the family in a state of immobility during this time of crisis before a new step forward can be taken. The counsellor will want to consider the different ways in which she may be able to offer help. This will often involve getting the family to sit down and discuss its difficulties together and its various patterns of relating and then helping them to create small differences, by trying out something new which will begin to interrupt old patterns of behaviour and foster new ones. Sometimes it will involve helping the family to understand the meaning of its past, so that it can be free to relate differently in the present.

The Jones family

It is frequently the case that when a family gets stuck, it 'produces' a symptom within one of its members. One person in the family who is predisposed to carry this role becomes the symptom-bearer for the whole family. The symptom itself and the symptom-bearer both serve a dual function for the family system: they signal the fact that the family is trying to negotiate a change in the way it functions *and* they prevent the threatened change from taking place. Sometimes a family has to make use of a series of different symptoms and symptom-bearers before it can move on to its new level of transformation. For example, a couple, Ted and Janet, came for help because of their concern for their eleven-year-old boy John. He was an extremely anxious child, refusing to go anywhere unless one of his parents accompanied him. He was seriously overweight and ate continually but only within a very narrow range of foods. He slept in his mother's bed whilst Ted slept in the spare room. John's symptoms and difficulties reflected those of his mother. She was grossly overweight and seldom emerged from the house both because of her difficulty in walking and because the children on the estate made fun of her. John would usually go to school because his father (who worked evenings only in a café) spent some time in the school each day as a volunteer helper and could therefore provide him with the necessary support. During the course of the year John had, however, started to refuse school as well and despite a great deal of effort and a series of elaborate bribes, his parents had been unsuccessful in getting him to return.

John was the youngest of six and the other five children had all left home some while ago. John had therefore been brought up effectively as an only child. During the earlier phase of this family's life cycle, two of the children had been taken into care (although it was never made clear exactly why) and Janet's pervasive fear was that John 'would be taken away' from her as well. It became clearer during the counselling sessions that Janet was much less insistent on John going to school than Ted and that John was in fact urged to go to school by his father but encouraged to stay at home by his mother. The symptom, like all symptoms, was in fact precisely chosen to hold the family system poised between the possibility of change and the prevention of it. By staying at home, sleeping with mother and refusing to grow up, John was allaying his mother's fear of losing her youngest child and his father's symmetrical fear of having to become a husband again. Yet by adopting a symptom (school phobia) that was very likely to result in his removal from home, he was creating a situation whereby the system might be forced to move on to its new transformation – the couple letting go of their children and the children moving on to fulfil their own age-appropriate needs.

The symptom had a great deal of subtlety about it because it also served to distance the parents and their approach to the problem which in turn maintained their shared defensive need to avoid change. For if John went to school he was staying with his father, and if he failed to go to school he was staying with his mother. Either way one of the parents was able to retain a close relationship with John which allowed them to avoid dealing with the difficulties that existed in their marriage.

The parish priest and another member of the ministerial team worked together to help this family. Their first effort was directed at helping John and his parents avoid the 'catastrophe' of him being taken into care. They helped the parents to work out some agreed rules whereby they would work together to get him to go to school on certain days (when there were congenial lessons and activities) but not on those days which caused John particular anxiety and stress. The intention was to engage the parents in a different kind of experiment with change from the one they were trying at the moment, but one that was sufficiently limited and unstressful as to be likely to succeed. By getting the parents first to agree between themselves and then to negotiate an agreed plan with John, it was possible to help them experience some success in their efforts to get John to go to school and to begin to feel a bit more potent both in relation to John and in the face of the threat from the outside 'authorities'. On the other hand, the agreed plan only involved John in having to go to school *some* of the time and not so much as to disrupt the system's defensive pattern. It continued to allow John to remain at home with Janet *some* of the time and to go to school with Ted *some* of the time. It encouraged John to move a *bit* faster towards more age-appropriate behaviour but it did not challenge him to move faster than he was able and thus risk him adopting an even more regressive pattern of childish behaviour. Moreover, it enabled the Education Department to see that some 'improvement' had occurred, and thus prevented them from challenging the family to adopt the total change it had previously required, which they were unable to manage.

On the surface level, this simple strategy proved remarkably successful. It created a difference that made a difference within the system's current capacity for change. John began to go to school two or three days a week and became 'suddenly' interested in swimming. This in turn was partly as a result of him 'suddenly' beginning to lose weight and therefore feeling less conspicuous in his bathing costume. All this meant that he was quite keen to go to school some of the time and his parents' pride in his (and their) achievement lessened Janet's resistance to letting him go. At about the same time (or simultaneously!) Janet decided to have some driving lessons, passed her test first time and was suddenly liberated from the confines of the house but within the protective care of a car. At the same time, John decided to sleep in his own room and Ted returned to the marital bed.

The next few months thus saw a great flurry of activity. The family pronounced that everything was 'much better' and felt that there was no need for further meetings with the ministry team. The system had reorganized itself on a slightly new level and seemed able to function again without experiencing undue pressure to change either from its own members or from the outside authorities. Part of the success of this set of changes was due to a small amount of outside help, which included supporting the parents' effort to exercise their parental role more successfully and building their self-esteem. The ministers were able to role-model a relationship of co-operation, mutual care and trust and an explorative approach to family difficulties. Their relationship to this rather small and isolated family unit probably also had the effect of supporting and containing them sufficiently for a variety of spontaneously occurring new opportunities to be taken up by the family.

About two years later, however, Janet phoned the priest (who had now left the area) in great distress. Ted had been arrested for fondling one of his young nephews and had been removed from the house pending his trial. Ted had lost his job, John had returned to his mother's bed and was again refusing to go to school. In system terms, the family had, it seemed, produced a new and more complicated symptom and a new symptom-bearer – again perfectly expressive of the family's need to move towards a new stage in its life cycle and its inability to do so, with children leaving home, the couple functioning more fully as a marital pair and less as a parental pair and with their sexual relationship reinstated. Its effort to move forward was simultaneously altered, a fact expressed by Ted engaging sexually across the generational boundaries, having lost even more of his sense of identity and self-esteem through his unemployment, and his 'failure' to parent John or to be accepted as a husband by Janet. No further help could be offered by the minister because of the distance involved but one would hypothesize that the next piece of work needed to help this family take a new step forward would have required a different focus. It might have involved working on the blurred generational boundaries, evidenced by John's relationship with Janet as well as by Ted's abuse of his nephew; and some direct work on the marital relationship, alongside the recognition of Ted's behaviour as culpable and damaging to the nephew involved. It would also have required some work with the extended family to help understand what had happened, repair relationships and work towards prevention and growth.

Intergenerational sexual abuse is a particularly powerful example of the blurring of family boundaries. Often the pastor or counsellor is able to repair and strengthen these boundaries by the way she organizes the counselling sessions. She may divide them up between the different sub-systems in the family, modelling some of the changes that need to occur in a safe but symbolic way. For counselling families systemically does not entail seeing all the people involved all of the time. As we will see in the following stories the counsellor saw a variety of different groupings while working with each of the families – sometimes a couple, sometimes an individual, but always from within a systemic perspective.

Vital family members are often unavailable in the literal sense (because they are dead or abroad, etc.) but, as in the case of the Thomas family (described below) it is often necessary to include their memory and to 'recall' them back into the family symbolically, because they hold the key to the family's current difficulties. Thus, we need to discern the boundary of the family system with some care and make sure we are including everyone who is involved in the current difficulties.

We also need to discern the different sub-systems in the family correctly – the couple, the sub-groupings amongst children and/or the older generation and others. We need to work out with the family (as in the case of the Jones family) the ways in which the family's environment is playing a part in its difficulties. Is there a fight going on between the parents and the school about a child's behaviour, non-attendance, poor performance etc.? Is the family on income support and needing help with negotiating a loan or grant? Is the family preoccupied by the racism of its neighbours? Is the family trying to juggle the relentless demands of employers on husband and wife which leave them no energy or time for either their marriage or their parenting roles?

Boundaries between the different sub-groupings in the family need to provide a predictable framework to allow children, parents, grand-parents and others to function within their different sub-groupings. But they also need flexible exchange of roles where necessary. Children need to be able to parent their parents sometimes, for example; grandparents and others need to form close relationships with parents and children. There must therefore be enough structure to make it possible for adults and children, older family members and more distant relatives to fit into a reasonably predictable pattern, but also to allow flexibility so that new and unexpected circumstances, such as illness, can be handled by different family members occupying different roles.

Families also construct and cling to myths and stories from the past to help them both avoid and manage change. Byng-Hall (1979) defines family myths as 'all those shared family images and stories which help give the family its continuing identity' (p. 103). Like symptoms, triangling and boundary problems, family myths serve both to reveal the need for change and also to prevent it from happening. Thus the purpose of the family myth is both to conceal and reveal important but anxiety-provoking truths about the family's past and present. Sometimes the myth will relate to the family's present functioning. 'We never have arguments or anything like that in *our* family' may conceal the hidden violence in one or more family members or hide from present family members a violent and destructive drama in the family's history. Myths about what it means to be masculine or feminine can be particularly powerful and create considerable stress for family members encountering a clash between the expectation of their family's transmitted history and their current need to engage in appropriate egalitarian gender relationships. Part of the function of a family myth may be to guard a family secret, protecting family members from the full force of its power but enabling them not to lose touch with it entirely.

Family myths can usefully be explored by using a genogram – a kind of family tree which maps three or four generations of the family system and its progress through the life cycle. It is a very useful way of helping couples who come for marriage preparation. A genogram provides a picture of the family's structure as well as a way of mapping its recurring patterns in the form of family constellations (the number, position and gender of children); alliances (who is close, distant, estranged or in conflict with whom in each generation); the roles people carry (sometimes, for example, there is a clear expectation handed down through generations as to how mothers should behave or eldest children or youngest, etc.). It is often possible to see at a glance 'the pattern that connects' the current family with the family's history over several generations. This exercise in mapping the family's past has several effects. It may root the family more securely in its own history which can give security, especially to small and fragile units who are unclear about who exactly they are or what they represent. The act of 'telling their story' to an attentive, curious and compassionate outsider enables them to hear it again 'as though for the first time' and gain confidence in its meaning as their own unique *formative* story which has helped to create them now in the pattern of family that they have become. It can provide an 'explanation' to the family as to why things are how they are which may help them to feel less guilty, threatened or immobilized by their current situation. In this way it can become a means of giving them the confidence to move on instead of allowing the past to determine and hold the family stuck in its present dysfunctional pattern.

The Smith family

The Smith family came for help with their family problems on the advice of a professional colleague of Mary the wife. Mary had recently returned to work after the birth of their fourth child. The couple were in their early forties. They had married very young and neither had separated very fully or well from their families of origin. They were experiencing increasing tension and violence in the relationship, which had come to a head when John had started a homosexual affair and given in his notice to his employer. The eldest child, James, eleven years old, was refusing to attend school and spent his time mainly with his widowed, maternal grandmother from whom his mother was estranged. Sessions commenced with the whole family, in which the two youngest children (aged three and one) played happily with toys and paints, and the two older ones (aged ten and eleven) sat looking anxious and unhappy whilst Mary and John engaged in ever more violent rows. In between the verbal violence that took place during the family meetings, the couple would describe their frequent times of rapturous love-making, holidays and deeply loving sharing times together when they would read, write poetry and make music. The two groups of children seemed to portray the two opposite experiences of their parents' marriage.

The crisis in the family was about John and Mary's need to develop aspects of themselves over and above the need to nurture the children, or to be young and passionate lovers. But the children's need to experience their parents' love and responsibility for them was a continuing need and both needs must find some means of being accommodated. After several family meetings, James, while continuing to spend most of his time with his grandmother, sheltering from the emotional storms at home, resumed his schooling and began to attend regularly. His original symptom had done its work in calling attention to the family's difficulties and was therefore no longer needed.

The counsellor then began to meet with John and Mary on their own and explore the two contrary needs that existed in the marriage. On the one hand, their symmetrical need to *leave* the relationship, in order to express newly discovered parts of themselves which they could not express inside the relationship, and on the other, their need to *preserve* their relationship, albeit in a new form. They both imaged their nearly twenty-year marriage as a kind of beautiful fairy tale, played out between children, which could no longer be believed. Now they had reached their forties, it seemed time 'to grow up'. For Mary, this meant discovering herself as a woman, returning to work and beginning to publish her poetry and novels. For John, it meant stepping off the bread-winning treadmill, and expressing the part of himself which had never been allowed to surface, his homosexuality.

The marital sessions focused partly on the relationships with their families of origin (especially on Mary's unsatisfactory and empty relationship with her mother) and partly on negotiating a new marital relationship between their two adult selves. For Mary, this included daring to stop clutching and clinging to John (her mother and lover combined) and daring to let him go. For John, this meant daring to leave his 'mother' (Mary), leave home and venture out into a new relationship. This breaking apart of the marriage in order to regress into a needed earlier developmental stage was essential if each were to become their own person and come to this or other relationships as mature adults. But it was terrifying in its implications of loss and abandonment. For each of them it involved the provisional step of drawing in a third party – a lover for John, a new search for creative expression for Mary, as a means of enabling them to separate.

But for this couple, their symmetrical need to stay in relationship with one another as well as to separate, was also developed through their emerging relationship with God. Neither Mary nor John professed any orthodox religious belief nor came from families that did, but gradually both John and Mary began to express their different spiritual needs as these began to emerge out of the chaos and the pain. John took himself off to a large and traditional cathedral, where he could sit anonymously at the back and let the music and words wash over him. Mary began writing intense, angry and erotic letters which she would first read to John and then post to the counsellor. The substance of these was a reaching out for God who could then be abused, blamed, clung to, adored, bathed in and let go, but who could also be returned to, to 'show' him her next faltering step forward in her growing experience of confidence and self-worth. As she wrestled with coming to terms with the realities of her inadequate experience of being mothered she wrote:

> I am beginning to feel I can mother myself. If I have God with me I don't need a mother. It is a good feeling (merging into my right side for some reason – a Centre, but still off-centre). I don't have God in me yet – but I know the worst can happen and I will survive.

This was of course braver talk than she could sustain in action. Before Mary could hold on to the experience of feeling 'better inside'

169

and be able to mother herself, she experienced much despair. As the inevitability of the marriage breakup came nearer, Mary's God became larger and her experience of him more intense, and she filled several pages a week with an account of her relationship with him.

> I am rooted in this mess – crucified. I will have to stay here, nailed like Christ to the cross. S'okay. I'll make it. I do just about resurrect each time. *But just tell me the fucking arms of God are there.* I've nearly lost it all . . .

For Mary, Christ was a remote, persecuting figure, a man who called people on and out of relationships into the pain of loss and sacrifice. He was a man, like her husband who had promised love but had now withdrawn it to follow some higher, purer ideal (ascetic for Christ, homosexual for John). Christ pointed to crucifixion and renunciation. God the Father on the other hand offered her the mothering that she had lacked and the sustaining compassion she required to enfold her through the loss of John.

For John, the attraction was to the young manhood of Christ and more generally to a place of aesthetic beauty, the cathedral where he could take his lover and where, anonymously, they (John, Christ and the lover) could unite in a mutual acceptance which was denied them in the outside world. His place of work, his wife and his friends all criticized him for abandoning Mary and the children but in the healing triangle created with God he could find a way forward, a means of passing from his childlike relationship with his wife to an immature but potentially more adult relationship with his lover. Both his relationship with God and with his lover were provisional, but were nevertheless movements forward in this development to full personhood.

As John and Mary progressively separated, their link became their newly but independently discovered relationship with God. Different and wholly unorthodox in its expression, their relationship with God became the container for their newly developing relationship with each other. They were able to talk through the pain of the changes between them and the way in which God – important to each of them in a mysterious way – held them in a connecting and unbreakable tie. Mary was able to express 'how good life can be without John' but also the sadness. 'It's an out-of-the-Garden sort of good. Post-innocent so very sad really . . . Paradise lost is so difficult.'

Their increasing separation was modelled and 'practised' in the shape of the counselling process, with separate meetings between the counsellor and each of the couple as well as joint meetings and occasional meetings with the whole family so that the parents could reassure the children of their love and continuing joint concern. As they began to feel more certain of their new, separate identities they became increasingly committed to investing effort and emotion into retaining and supporting each other in their parenting roles. As the separation became clarified and experienced as bearable and workable, the children became more able to function in age-appropriate ways. As Mary began to forgive her mother and relate more easily with her, James could stop trying to hold mother and daughter together and spend more time with his friends and hobbies instead.

At the end of two years, counselling came to an end. John had settled into a permanent living relationship with Colin, alongside regular loving contact with Mary and the children. So far as I could tell, he ceased to have any further need of an overt relationship with God and felt able to accept himself as well as take responsibility for his family in a different, but nevertheless productive way. Mary had enrolled for a higher degree and had developed a realistic faith in God which contrasted with her use of him mainly as a means of holding her through the painful transition in her relationship with John. The development of her faith both enabled and mirrored the enormous strides she was able to make in mature self-acceptance, identity formation and a progressively more adult relationship with John, the children, her mother and the outside world.

The Thomas family

The Thomas family were referred by a member of the congregation where the family regularly worshipped because of their concern about Jane's inability to sit through to the end of a church service. During the Eucharist in particular, Jane would suddenly get up and leave the church in obvious distress, saying to anyone who might be near that she was too guilty to remain in the presence of God. Peter and the children would follow her home after the service but the matter was never discussed between them. As the counselling sessions got underway it emerged that this family was expressing its anxiety at reaching the point in its life cycle when the young children were needing more independence through starting school and moving into the outside world. The family felt unable to cope with this new challenge and expressed its anxiety through a dramatic cluster of symptoms which focused in the mother Jane.

Jane had experienced two periods of hospitalization for post-puerperal depression after the births of the two children. On the first occasion she had been admitted as an involuntary patient with a severe psychosis. On each occasion she had experienced terrifying fantasies of being found wanting and judged by a vengeful God. Sometimes, her own father and God had seemed to become one and the same, with God the Father and the father both threatening her with unspecified but appalling punishment for her unspecified but appalling failings. By contrast, she sometimes experienced herself as being 'God's Chosen One, sent to deliver the world from its sin', except that she was unable to do so because she was a girl. At other times, she believed herself to be the Virgin Mary and the child she had borne was Jesus, except that it could not have been because both her children were daughters. Whichever route the fantasy took, she was found wanting, unable to fulfil God's purposes for her and trapped in a terrifying and dangerous world through which God would wreck his vengeance on her.

During the course of the next three months, family sessions were held with the four members of the current family, together with a series of marital sessions with Peter and Jane on their own. It became clear that Jane's fantasies had an immobilizing effect on the whole family. The children were not allowed to go anywhere unless they were with one or other of their parents, in case their destruction was to be God's chosen means of revenge. Whenever possible Jane kept them home from school and she refused to allow them to go swimming with the school, in case they caught a virus, or to play with their friends at weekends in case they hurt themselves, or do anything much other than stay at home and watch television. Fearful herself of the outside world, Jane became a powerful figure within the home. She exercised strong control over her husband's efforts to discipline the children, criticizing him if he so much as raised his voice or corrected their table manners.

The family sessions were devoted to looking at Jane and Peter's genograms. Peter came from a large family and was the youngest, the only boy after four sisters. Both his parents were now dead and he had little contact with his sisters. His father had been an invalid for much of Peter's childhood, while his capable and necessarily dominant mother had run the household and gone out to work as a secretary. His experiences of his family of origin predisposed him to be compliant with the role required of him by Jane's own disturbed early experiences. But his compliance did nothing to help to change the 'stuck' situation of the current system, nor did it enable either the children or the adults to move into more age-appropriate behaviour.

In examining Jane's genogram, it became clear that her father had been a remote and rather frightening figure. Her mother, with whom she had been very close, was effectively 'removed' from her when she was three because of the birth of twin sisters, of whom she had remained, until the present time, extremely jealous. Her father had been distant and demanding, her mother helpless and compliant. As a child Jane had felt excluded, lonely and frightened. When she was eighteen one of the twins had experienced a severe psychotic breakdown, for which she had, unaccountably, been blamed. She felt herself to be the failure of the family, disappointing her father's academic hopes of her and flouting the religious practice of her parents by leaving home at eighteen to live with her future husband. For Jane, fathers were remote and potentially vengeful people, whilst mothers were unreliable, impotent and withholding. Younger siblings were competitive and hostile, yet she was still held responsible for their well-being and care. Being female was unacceptable and appeared to 'cause' disappointment, disruption and breakdown.

Over the weeks, Jane was slowly able to relate her psychotic fantasies of a destructive God, whom she could never please yet who held her responsible for the misfortunes of others, to her unhappy experiences with her parents and twin sisters. Peter and the children began to see how Jane's frightening behaviour was understandable, framed in this context, and began to feel freer of Jane's over-protectiveness and fears. Peter began to take on a more assertive role in relation to both Jane and the children, and as Jane began to understand the needs of her own father better, she was able to allow Peter to become different. She began to see that men could be assertive and authoritative and express their own personhood without being the violent destructive people she experienced in her father.

The family myth revealed through the genogram centred on the notion of maleness being both normative and strong but also omnipotent, destructive and greatly to be feared. The content of the myth had at its heart a contradiction – the idea that children must (but are unable) to make things safe and OK out there for parents. Because only males had any power, this necessarily meant male children. There was therefore a need to find someone else to make the world feel a safer place – the contradiction being that this 'someone' ended up being an even less potent instrument of succour and strength, doomed to be a disappointment, doomed to be punished for their inevitable impotence.

The family began to understand the way in which Jane's father had himself inherited a pattern of scapegoating in his original family and had brought to his own family the need to have successful, potent sons through which he could 'change the world'. It turned out that father had been a 'replacement' child born some years after the death, in infancy, of his brother, whom his parents had idealized; they had projected onto him enormous unrealistic expectations which Jane's father was now expected to fulfil. His own scientific career had been mediocre, yet he clung to extravagant visions of how the world could be changed for the better through scientific discovery. As Jane, with Peter's help, began to identify with her father's disappointments and sadnesses and the burden he had had to carry in relation to his own parents, he began to seem to her more human-sized, less Godlike, more available and loving and less remote, demanding and vengeful. It was clear that she had begun to see these possibilities shortly before he died and had just begun to hope for a new relationship with him when the 'punishment' of his death had interrupted this process and possibility. It was at this point that family counselling had begun.

Part of the work involved loosening Jane's projections onto God, simultaneously with her beginning to realize that her human father was indeed human in his weakness and pain. The circular interaction between her perceptions of God and her father was gradually disentangled and, as Peter grew in confidence, he was more able to introduce the softer image of a Father-God which he had absorbed from *his* parents and to enact a strong and sensitive version of masculinity within his marriage. His ability to be himself was further activated by feeling less immobilized by Jane's conflicting demands of him for protection and impotence simultaneously. And as she became able to relate to Peter as a real human being and Peter able to respond, their sexual relationship resumed. It symbolized an expression of relatedness between human bodies in the real world rather than the need to relate at a distance only in terms of their projections from the past.

As she experienced God as less of an angry tyrant and more of a loving being, Jane experienced her father as less demanding and critical and as more of a loving parent who had wanted the best for her. She now became freer to grieve for a real person and at the same time to begin to discover that the reality of God was different from that of her own vengeful projections. Jane had begun to realize that her growing confidence in a loving God enabled her to believe that he held her father in his safe keeping as well as Peter, herself and the children. She could therefore still tell her father all the loving things she would have liked to tell him before he died. I suggested that she write down in the form of a letter what she would like to have said to her father, and later that she write her father's reply. Both letters revealed her forgiveness and acceptance of what she had experienced, as well as the knowledge that she was herself forgiven and accepted. She had grown in autonomy and in acceptance of her own feminine personhood and she could now experience her father (and her Father) as wanting for her her own unique fulfilment and happiness. Now that God was no longer a vengeful tyrant she found she could entrust her children to the life of the world around them as well as accepting her husband's greater assertiveness and autonomy.

During the later sessions the family reflected on its experience of belonging to a wider family and, in the final session, they brought this new sense of connectedness into clearer focus by offering prayers for each member of the family, for those who had died, for those with whom they had been out of touch and for each other.

It is difficult to avoid suggesting that families have to struggle, like an autumn salmon, to leap the waterfall of change. Families like other systems do not have to 'try to achieve' new levels of transformation; these will occur when the family lets go of the provisional solutions that stand in the way of change occurring naturally. Like trying to empty one's mind in meditation, like trying to find inspiration for a work of art, like trying to find the right word for a sentence, the new condition will suddenly occur. This will often become possible through a variety of odd, unconnected and serendipitous events which will create new information and possibilities for the system, and make a new 'rearrangement' possible. Somewhere out of nowhere and usually quite inexplicably, the family will become 'recalibrated' and it will begin a new phase of continuous movement and change within the temporary permanency of its new condition. The pastor or counsellor is always more of a midwife to change than a primary agent of it. It is therefore a very good plan to be parsimonious in one's approach to a family and to undertake the minimum amount of intervention compatible with helping it to take one step forward towards its new integration.

In the following pages I have set out a 'ladder' of approaches whereby the would-be helper can begin by considering the simplest level (the first) and work up as and when needed in helping the family with the difficulties it is presenting.

1. Some families simply lack confidence in their own ability to organize their lives and want the counsellor to lend them a little *strength, support* and *affirmation* for who they are and what they are trying to do. For example, a lone parent and her child may benefit from meeting with an interested outsider to talk about themselves. He or she becomes part of this small and fragile system as a friendly temporary member (preferably *not* as a substitute parent) to confirm by his interested presence the family's value and 'right to be', to listen to its concerns and to encourage it along its passage through whichever life-cycle stage it has reached. By the very process of sitting down and 'playing' with mother and child, the outside helper provides recognition of this relationship as a viable family unit and by her attitude of curiosity and interest she affirms its identity and value. This task of recog-

nizing and valuing will form a major part of any pastor's work with a family unit that is trying to manage a socially discreditable identity. Gay and lesbian couples for example will particularly benefit from and probably chiefly need from the helping person an unwavering commitment to the value and importance of the relationship between them. This will often be the sufficient therapeutic ingredient which helps them on their way.

2. Some families may be uncertain about the ways in which they are handling a situation – regarding parenting, gender roles or sex. They may lack information or be unable to decide between the different merits of some course of action – how to handle some conflict in the extended family or how to weigh up the conflicting demands of one's elderly parents in Nigeria compared with the needs of the young children here. The family needs time and space to *explore in a cognitive way* the relative merits of different possible plans and perhaps to review the process by which they will ultimately make a decision.

3. Some families will be experiencing a considerable amount of conflict and family members will be needing to work out different ways of relating to one another. As we have noted, conflict chiefly occurs at certain predictable times during the family's passage through the life cycle and will often be particularly high when the system is adapting to crises of accession or dismemberment. An outside helper's task may be to enable the family to *re-structure its relationships* around the new membership or new circumstances that it is having to face. Step-families can often be greatly helped by some meetings with a family counsellor to work out their many new family roles *vis-à-vis* one another and in relation to the outside world.

4. Some families will have become chronically stuck in an intergenerational pattern of defensive relationships, whereby quite severe symptoms are being expressed by one or more family members and severe conflict between them. Often one or more members have received help individually from a counsellor or therapist and whilst symptoms may abate for a while, they seem to recur or erupt in another member. An outside helper may need to meet with the family over quite a prolonged period and work with them on these cross-generational patterns *enabling*

177

them to gain understanding and insight into what they mean. This may of course mean helping the family to receive more intensive help from another person or agency.

5.   Some families will be chronically stuck and have already tried to use outside help from a family counsellor and often a whole army of other helpers too! These families may have developed a finely tuned aversive reaction to any outside helper and whilst on one level they convey a desire to change, on another they are skilled and practised in disqualifying any attempt to make change possible. Within a parish context, different members of the family may approach different members of the ministerial team or one family member will seem to have an insatiable need for different pieces of advice, none of which he acts upon! An outside helper may be able to help these families by a *variety of 'uncommonsense' strategic approaches* by which the family system is helped to change by the family counsellor taking a position that appears to be on the side of 'no change'. With these families it may be particularly important (as it is in all situations) to resist the compelling urge to 'do something to help them at all costs', rescue one or other family member, find a 'solution' to the problems, or make things better – all of which would risk the outside helper, like all the other helpers that have gone before him, being used by the family to 'prove' that change is impossible, and thus to prevent it from happening. By resisting the system's efforts in this way one may well be helping them effectively to change.*

* For further discussion of this approach see Weeks (1984).

10

GROWTH POINTS

> 'With your body and your speaking
> you have spoken for everything,
> robbed me of my strangerhood,
> made me one.'
>
> LEONARD COHEN 'Owning Everything'

The life of a couple's relationship is always influenced by the wider system of relationships that exists in the rest of the family. However, there are also specific issues that concern the couple as a sub-system and these will now be considered. Much of what is said in this section also applies to cohabiting and homosexual couples but the latter also have special needs which will be considered separately.

Marital counselling

Helping marriages and couples who are cohabiting that are in trouble requires some knowledge and skill. More important still however, it requires a willingness to become involved with them in a dispassionate and non-judgemental manner. If the would-be counsellor has a desire to help and an unjudging eye, then she will be able to acquire the knowledge and skill that is necessary. If she has not, then no amount of knowledge and skill will enable her to be helpful.

There are three ways of structuring the counselling process:

1. Working with one of the partners alone.
2. Working with each of the partners separately with either the same or separate counsellors.

3. Working with the couple together, with one counsellor or with two counsellors together.

Counselling one of the partners without involving the other is a viable possibility so long as it is undertaken within an overall systemic framework. In other words, the counsellor must continually bear in mind the fact that he is intervening in one part only of the threesome which is made up of the husband, the wife and the relationship between them (A + B = 3).

As we noted in chapter 6, to create change in any one part of the system changes the system as a whole. Thus it may well be possible to discuss with the husband how he might be able to modify his own behaviour in his relationship with his wife. Or it may be possible to coach a wife in working on the conflictual relationship with her mother which is skewing her relationship with her husband.

An effective example of this method of work is described by Bennun (1991). In situations of domestic violence, individual meetings with the abused partner will almost always be required although it will be important to keep in one's own mind at every point the fact of the individual's situation. The counsellor's first duty is to ensure the safety of the physically abused adult – normally the woman – and she needs to do whatever is necessary to help her find a place of safety, support her through the trauma of leaving her home or help her set in motion whatever is required to protect her in remaining at home. Feminists have rightly criticized the apparent neutrality of the position taken, in theory at least, by systemic workers. To disregard the power imbalances that exist in families between parents and children and between women and men is to disregard a fundamental reality of wrestling with family life. In these situations it is usually necessary to see the wife on her own with a view to moving hopefully to seeing both members of the couple first separately and then together. In situations of severe physical abuse, this may, however, be an impossible goal to achieve.

In other situations, I would want to counsel caution against trying to help one of the partners alone. This is partly because to see one member of the pair separately appears to be such an obvious solution to the problem when the other partner will not come to see an outside helper. And it is also such an inviting approach for clergy to adopt, who routinely become involved with a distressed member of a partnership (usually the woman) whose husband does not in any case come to church. Thus, the clergy person has a much easier and more obvious route into the relationship with the wife, whom he already knows, compared with the husband, whom he does not.

The pitfalls are, however, many and it is more likely that one is going either to be quite ineffective or be actually harmful to the relationship by seeing one member of a partnership alone. By being ineffective one is getting in the way of the couple receiving the help they need. But the major risk in this way of working is that one will get drawn into taking sides with the person one is seeing against the other partner and thus be actually harmful to the relationship itself. The more involved one becomes with one side of the story, the more difficult it is to think and act systemically, that is, with an awareness of the effects of one's intervention into the partnership as a whole, and the more likely will be the disruptive effect on the relationship between husband and wife. Whichever member of the partnership is not being seen by the counsellor is likely to become progressively more distressed. He or she may begin to resent the attention the other is receiving and also fear that the counsellor is getting a very negative picture of the part he or she is playing in the relationship. He or she may be jealous of what on some level is perceived as their partner's 'affair' with a third party. Thus the counselling may replicate the actual problems that are being experienced in the marriage. Gurman and Kniskern (1986) provide highly suggestive conclusions to this effect.

The second possibility is to see both partners separately. This gives each partner the opportunity to share some things with the outside helper that they might find hard to say in front of their partner. It also allows the helper to work on issues at some depth which he feels belong more to the psycho-dynamic make-up of the individual than they do to the relationship system. Obvious areas of work here might include the residual difficulties that one or other continues to experience in relation to their childhood or young adulthood before they met their partner. This kind of work may be done by a single counsellor working concurrently but separately with the partners or it may be done collaboratively, one counsellor working with the wife, one with the husband, with the possibility of foursome meetings at intervals.*

The third possibility is to see the couple together. This is my own preference and my own routine approach when a couple asks for help. This enables the counsellor to engage not only with each of the partners, but also with the relationship between them as it gets expressed and as it unfolds in the 'here and now' of the counselling session. Different approaches to working with couples together are helpfully reviewed by Paolino and McGrady (1978).†

To work on the relationship of the couple as they interact together in the session by no means precludes helping them to look at their relationships with their families of origin. On the contrary, for all the reasons outlined earlier, it is often, in fact usually essential to help the couple reflect upon issues that remain unworked through in the individual's earlier relationships. However, it makes all the difference in the world to do this work in front of the *partner*. The couple can then be helped to understand links between events that have gone on in the past and the current difficulties that they are experiencing. Husband and wife can often work co-operatively in trying to understand issues that have been difficult in the families of origin of each, even though these very same difficulties pull them apart within their own marriage.

For example, a couple was experiencing great difficulty in handling the triangular relationship formed between husband, wife and their grown up son. The husband felt an outsider to the relationship between his wife and son, who shared many interests together. The couple were helped by spending time looking at a similar relationship triangle in the wife's family of origin. When she was a teenager, she and her father formed a close, companionable relationship that excluded her mother and provoked considerable hostility between mother and daughter and husband and wife. Looking back, she felt that she had lost out by having this close relationship with her father at the expense of her mother as it had prevented her from, as she saw it, developing a relationship with her mother at all. The husband

---

* The model and practice of this kind of collaborative work was developed by the Tavistock Institute of Marital Studies.
† The specific help which can be offered to couples with sexual problems is outside the scope of this book but is well reviewed by Guirguis (1991).

was, however, able to see that she had in fact benefited from the strong relationship formed with her father as well as losing out, so that in terms of their current relationship difficulty, both husband and wife were able to move a little nearer to each other's positions and stand a little more inside the other person's shoes, by reflecting on a mirror image from the past.

In conjoint marital work, the pastor or counsellor is always in the position of himself forming a triangular relationship with the couple. The advantages of this triangular situation need to be exploited and the disadvantages reduced.*

An obvious difficulty for the counsellor is how to avoid becoming 'piggy in the middle'. Each member of a couple in conflict will work hard to draw in an outside helper onto his or her side in order to help defeat the partner. Alternatively, both partners may turn on the outsider and make her the scapegoat instead. Every move she makes to help them may be disqualified and the harder she works the further removed she feels herself to be from the issues that are important to the couple. However, if the helper is able both to *experience* these forces and also *resist* them she may be able to use the process to explore with the couple the moments when they are feeling anxious enough to defend themselves in this way. This may then make it possible to explore the underlying anxiety in their relationship. Alternatively, without any exploration at all, the couple may simply be strengthened in their relationship by their experience of uniting together against the counsellor! The value of such a process should not be discounted. Again, the counsellor may find herself being called upon to play a particular role – a nurturing, unchallenging mother for example, or a destructive one. Clues to the way couples perceive one another and the relationship of these perceptions to their experiences in their past may be discovered through the way they relate to the counsellor.

Triangulation is an important means of handling conflict between couples. Because of its ubiquitous nature it will be used here to explore the kind of conjoint marital counselling to which I want to draw attention. Triangling is a process whereby a third party is drawn into a twosome either temporarily (e.g. in the form of conver-

* Broderick (1983)

sation about someone or something else) or for a more prolonged period (e.g. an extra-marital affair). It is a defensive reaction of all twosomes faced with external or internal threats to the relationship. Triangulation serves the dual purpose of stabilizing the twosome and expressing the problems that the relationship is experiencing. For example, in the simple everyday experience of inviting some new acquaintances for a meal, the host couple and the visitors will look for some topics of conversation that will 'hold' their relationship together. Sometimes one can look back on such an evening and be aware that the two groups created such an engaging 'third party' that the distance between them remained as great at the end of the evening as at the beginning. The focus on the topic held them together and apart. In fact, third parties act as emotional distance regulators, helping the couple to deal with their ambivalence about intimacy and differentiation (cf. Byng-Hall, 1980). They stand between the couple as both barrier and link.

The triangling dynamic often involves mother or father putting their parenting roles first and their marital roles a far second in their order of priorities, and the children are then used to prevent closeness from developing but at the same time are needed to sustain the other partner's involvement in the relationship. Children may evoke envy, jealousy and competition between husbands and wives. For example, a middle child who had been severely asthmatic from early childhood had evoked a strongly protective response from his mother which lasted up until he became adult. The husband felt progressively excluded from an intimate relationship with his wife and the situation echoed his experience in his original family when he felt himself not to be his mother's favourite child. The couple came for help long after the children had all left home, because of the husband's depression.

Husband and wife may both feel envious of their own young children in terms of the attention and love they receive from their partner. Each may then vie for attention by becoming 'one of the children', a situation which gets reinforced by the partner's negative attention to this 'extra' child. The couple is then reduced to fighting both with the children and with each other. An outside helper may need to spend a lot of time creating a warm, containing environment and forming a nurturing parental relationship with both partners.

Her own work in providing space for their relationship away from the children and in valuing and affirming each member of the couple may be the major axes of the therapeutic work. By providing emotional food for the child within them both, she may be able to help the adult spouse and parent to function, freed from the burden of their unmet needs.

Quite often a couple tries to deal with its conflicts through an extra-marital affair. One partner has the affair but it is the needs of the *relationship* that are being expressed and which the affair is organized to meet. Surprisingly little work has been done on examining the psychological ingredients of extra-marital relations. An affair clearly represents a search for something that is missing in the relationship, which one partner believes can be found more easily elsewhere than through searching for it in the marriage. However, as Vaughan (1989) points out, it also has a societal component. The ambivalent social attitudes that prevail in society both encourage affairs to happen and make them more difficult to come to terms with when they do.

Kell (1992) suggests that an affair is an attempt on the part of one of the partners to create more honesty and immediacy in the marriage. If the partner can create an oasis of honesty *somewhere* he may perhaps be able to free that part of himself that has been trapped and cut off in the marriage. It may also provide an opportunity to offer love within a relationship that has clear limits, thus avoiding the anxiety aroused by the limitless commitment and expectations of the marriage. However, as Kell points out, the partner 'is faced from the outset of an affair with his yearning for wholeness and his escape into splitting' (p. 164).

Just as the events that occur between parents and children or spouses and in-laws require systemic explanations and solutions, so do the dynamics involved in an extra-marital affair. The helper's concern must be finely tuned to the realities of the three people involved. Moreover, whilst it may be appealing to become sympathetic to the rage and despair of the 'wronged' spouse, such a move is neither systemic, ethical or therapeutically fruitful. *Both* partners have contributed to the need to triangle in a third party and both partners need to own their responsibility for this development, value the opportunity it affords and work towards a systemic solution that attends to the needs of everyone. This does not of course mean that such a painful dilemma can be resolved so that 'everyone can win and all can have prizes'. My experience of counselling couples in this predicament is that the work is painful and often quite pro-longed and involves the continuous reworking of areas of conflict, projection, forgiveness and blame.

The problem may be presented to the counsellor in one of two ways – either openly, with both partners fully aware of the facts or covertly by the partner involved with the third party, without the knowledge of the spouse. In this latter situation, the person having the affair is often asking the counsellor to help him or her dispose of one or other of his partners. If this is the case, the counsellor may need to work separately with the partner having the affair until he or she can be brought to the point of deciding to make a break and then to begin the work needed on the marriage, moving to conjoint work (i.e. with the couple together) as soon as possible. Very often however, the married couple come for help at the point when the affair has become known to the other partner. Conjoint work can then begin straight away. Good questions for the counsellor to have in mind are: Why did the affair start when it did? Why has the couple come for help now? What function does the affair serve within their relationship and within the relationships of the wider family system?

If at all possible, the counsellor should see the third party, if only to clarify that he or she understands that the couple have come to the counsellor for help which may well have consequences for the partner's relationship with them. The counsellor may need to encourage the third party to get some counselling help and support for themselves and, if they are also married, for their marriage. Sometimes it may be possible to have parallel conjoint meetings with the extra-marital couple alongside the meetings with the married pair and, occasionally, it may seem desirable and possible for all three people or the two couples involved to meet together with the counsellor. Perhaps more than in any other situation, the counsellor needs to provide a strong container for the expression of everyone's fears of disintegration and abandonment. If the experience has enabled the couple to face up and work on some of the latent conflicts in their marriage for the first time it may be possible for the affair to be reconstructed as an opportunity for growth rather than as the epitome of failure.

But the same must hold for the third party too. If that person is single, the relationship may have been their one precious opportunity for a costly commitment of faithfulness and love. My experience of counselling people who have been involved as third parties in the marriages of others has filled me with respect for their sensitivity and grace. The necessarily non-possessive position that a third party has to adopt if the affair is to continue at all, may provide some useful input into a marriage where the non-aligned partner has over-whelmed the other with unmanageable emotional demands. As a result, the system as a whole may be able to develop a greater ability to create intimacy without either fusion or flight. The emotional tasks of learning to respect boundaries, learning to share and to respect another's needs are essential ingredients within all relationships and may become usable via this relationship within the marriage.

A couple may also use a job or other outside interest to form a triangle within their relationship. Again husband and wife are both drawn together and pushed apart by the third party of the triangle. For Christians, such a third point may often be the faith of one of the partners, or in the case of a clergy marriage the clergy partner's ministry. Both can be highly threatening and extremely destructive to a marriage. The non-Christian partner or the clergy spouse may feel highly competitive with his or her partner's ministry or faith. Compared with the degree of threat posed by an extra-marital affair, God is usually experienced as a much more powerful opponent!

Whybrew (1984) provides a very clear theoretical framework for understanding the particularly potent triangles that can develop between the clergyman, the wife and the congregation. (These dynamics do I believe relate considerably more sharply to *wives* of clergy men than to *husbands* of clergy women for a variety of reasons at present – but this may change when more women become clergy.) Any of the three participants can experience themselves at different times as the third point in the triangle serving a function for the relationship between the other two. For example, the wife can be used as a distance regulator in the relationship between her husband and the congregation. A very frequent example is the wife's experi-ence of being cast in the role of mediator between two warring factions. She is used by the congregation as a messenger girl to convey wishes and needs to her husband – their priest; and she is used by her husband to gain support and help in dealing with a congregation by which he feels progressively more isolated and attacked. The counsellor needs to 'coach' the husband to deal straight with the congregation and help the wife to resist the seduction and ambiguous power derived from her 'go-between' role.

Alternatively, the congregation may play a major part in stabilizing a dysfunctional clergy marriage. The husband spends every hour of the day and night engaged in an 'affair' with the Church, whilst his wife feels progressively more isolated and alone. The story of the clergy wife who rang the vicarage door bell to seek an appointment with the vicar has more than a grain of truth in it. Married clergy who say that they cannot take regular time off each day, a day off each week or their holidays, are simply describing, in code, an unhappy marriage which they do not know how to change.

The third kind of triangle is the triangle that revolves around the wife and the congregation. The wife feels required to live out the hopes and expectations of others. These expectations may circumscribe her behaviour in various subtle ways – by constraining her to attend church, take part in certain activities or to refrain from activities as in Joanna Trollope's *The Rector's Wife*, such as filling the supermarket shelves for a living! Whilst fewer wives of clergy experience the grosser forms of these projections now, the wives of couples who come for help with their marriage are often still caught into the uncomfortable position of being 'a clergy wife' and therefore somehow 'not me'. There is sometimes a complex relationship between the covert need of the husband to dominate and control his wife which creates in him an unconscious collusion with the projections from his congregation. In each case, counselling needs to focus on helping the couple to free each partner, by increasing their individual self-definition as well as increasing the quality and intensity of direct communication between them within the relationship. Helping the couple to identify the ways in which each can be sucked into forming triangular relationships with the Church, and helping them to understand the reasons for this process that lie within their relationship, will free them to re-invest in their marriage to the benefit of everyone.

Divorce counselling

It is a matter of some delicacy for the counsellor to determine with a couple when and how they might be best helped by working towards the ending of their marriage. All of us who are committed to the belief that marriage is a relationship entered into 'for better, for worse, for richer, for poorer, in sickness and in health, until death do us part' will find areas of resistance to be negotiated within ourselves that must continually be acknowledged and reviewed. I have come to believe, in my quite prolonged experience of being alongside couples whose marriages are coming to an end, that there is a sense in which divorce is always a turning back, a sense in which it is always experienced on some level as a life-threatening abandonment for both partners and a sense in which it is always an interruption in the pursuit of kingdom values. It always represents a loss with the concomitant grief and guilt of that loss which is some-times experienced almost entirely by one of the partners but more usually shared at some level by both. That does not at all mean that I believe divorce to be unique in this regard, nor that it cannot be and often is a turning point for the individuals involved, or even 'a kind of inspiration and source of wisdom to others – clean amputations of rotting relationships that are splendidly on the side of life' (Furlong (1981), p. 26). Divorce may simply be the most colossal liberation, a heart-felt relief and a blessed escape from a violent and destructive marriage. Given appropriate support, it will often become the gateway to new growth which would have been impossible without this parting and this pain.

The Church can play an important part in helping people through this life transition, enabling the family system as a whole to manage this crisis of dismemberment in as functional and growth-promoting a way as possible. Moreover, the Church has some unique expertise to offer in helping couples to make use of rituals to mark the end of a particular kind of relationship and the movement on into another. Clergy and others need to consider how they can help individuals and couples through the sacrament of reconciliation to gain relief from their guilt, mark the dissolution of vows, and remember what now lies in the past with thanksgiving as well as with sorrow.*

* See for example Grainger (1987).

Sometimes couples who come for help saying they 'have come to the end of the road' may, with appropriate help, be able to work through their difficulties even when they are quite severe. Other couples discover, through the process of counselling, that their marriage has already ended. The counsellor needs to offer a flexible response, unhampered by fixed positions which derive from her own emotional needs. The prospect of engaging with a divorcing couple may be highly evocative of the counsellor's own countertransference (her feelings derived from her own family experiences of abandonment and loss and/or her emotional reaction to the people she is trying to help). Often this involves her own emotional need to hold together a relationship that is breaking apart because it evokes in her fears of actual or threatened disruptions in her own relationship in the present or past.

The couple too will usually be highly ambivalent about separating. Sometimes one partner will express most or all of the need to opt out, sometimes it will oscillate between them. Sometimes one partner will cling to the smallest ray of hope that the relationship still has a future, and the difficult task of the counsellor is to help him or her to face up to what is actually happening. Facing up to and making a decision to separate may be the goal to which the work needs to be directed and it is important to be clear about this for two reasons. First, it prevents the counsellor experiencing an overwhelming and inappropriate sense of failure for not succeeding in reconciling the couple. Second, and more importantly, it enables couples, who find making the decision to separate impossibly painful, either to implement or to carry through, to move beyond the endless debilitating vacillation of neither leaving nor fully re-joining the relationship. Individuals will react differently to the crisis of divorce, depending upon their age, gender, psychological make-up, previous experiences of separation and degree of support available.

As with marriage, the whole family that has become one system through their marriage is affected by their breakup and needs to be borne in mind. Not only grandparents, parents, siblings and the couple's own children, but also the friendship network that has been developed around them are all caught up in the crisis. This was brought home to me recently, when attending a wedding reception along with four hundred other guests for a couple from Sierra Leone.

In one of the speeches, the couple were told that if they should ever consider divorcing, they could only do so if they reconvened the whole four hundred of us together to witness the separating of what we had witnessed being joined together today! Oddie (1990) comments:

> In a volatile separation period, extremes of emotion contribute to job-losses, accidents, overdosing, homelessness and violence, symptomatic of what may be perceived as a hostile world. The divorce counsellor's role, though by no means restricted to the emotional dimension may at first be to contain fluctuations in feeling over the crisis. (p. 69)

An important component of the work will include helping the couple cope with the multiple bereavements that have to be experienced, and their need to express guilt, anger, confusion and the pain of loss; the need to retrieve from the past the positives that have been jointly created and held; the need to consider how on-going links can be maintained with significant others in the family system and the need to minimize the trauma for any children that may be involved. Wallerstein and Kelly's (1980) vitally important study leaves no doubt that for children, especially for younger children, the divorce of their parents is extremely traumatic.

It may help the couple to focus on the way in which others in their wider families have managed this transition and survived. Making these connections may also reduce the sense of guilt and isolation that is often experienced. Other family members and friends have trodden this road before and it can help the couple to be reminded of this. Structuring the sessions to include other family members, particularly the couple's children, may also be helpful. It will also be important to incorporate more frequent individual meetings with the husband and wife separately. The structure of the counselling will thus provide a model for the couple's own separation and their need to learn to function again as separate individuals.

The overall aim of divorce counselling is to help everyone move through the transition to the position of becoming a post-divorced family. Brown (1989) suggests that

> whether the custodial parent marries or not . . . the family will

191

> benefit from a view that defines its members not as a family 'in
> transition' to another two-parent nuclear household, but as a
> family 'in transition' to a different structure of organisation,
> a bona fide family form. (p. 371)

This is an extremely important point, as the tendency in our society,
as we noted in chapter 5, is still to see lone-parent households and
single people as incomplete and in transition between two nuclear
family formations. This view may encourage divorced couples to
move prematurely into new marriages or new cohabiting unions with
the likelihood of them having to endure yet another traumatic
breakup. It is extremely important therefore that the ending of the
couple's marriage is handled as effectively as possible. The likelihood
of this occurring can be greatly enhanced by the couple being referred
at an appropriate point for conciliation or comprehensive
mediation.

Conciliation services and comprehensive mediation

In 1974 the Finer Report drew attention to the fragmented and
costly adversarial methods of bringing marriages to a legal end,
and proposed instead that a new process involving negotiation and
conciliation be adopted. As a result, groups of workers from counselling, social work and the law began to develop the procedures of
conciliation and mediation, whereby the legal and emotional aspects
of the divorce process could be handled in tandem. The first conciliation service was established in Bristol in 1979, and the considerable
development of conciliation and mediation practice since then has
provided important new methods of helping couples manage the
divorce process more co-operatively.

Conciliators and mediators are specially trained and operate within
a carefully limited framework. They offer an alternative to the legal
process and an opportunity for parents to resolve their disputes, in
particular over the care and custody of the children. Comprehensive
mediation (Parkinson 1990, 1991) is, as its name suggests, a more
inclusive process, covering not only issues surrounding the future care
of children, but also matters to do with finance, property and the
division of assets. As Parkinson points out, these issues tend to be

closely linked, both in practical and emotional terms. For our present purposes, it is important to note that conciliation and comprehensive mediation, both major developments in services for families during the last twelve years (Parkinson 1986, 1987), are both specialist services with which all who are concerned with helping couples should be acquainted, so that they can encourage them to make use of these services when appropriate.

Marital/divorce counselling is a related but separate activity which should lead, wherever possible, to a referral for conciliation. Part of the helper's skill is in referring people appropriately for the kind of integrated emotional/legal approach which conciliation and comprehensive mediation provides. Because these services are not yet universally available, part of the Church's responsibility does also, I suggest, involve campaigning for their wider provision and more secure public resourcing.

Gay and lesbian couples

Gay and lesbian couples may face particular problems in getting help when their relationship encounters difficulties for several reasons. The prevalence of homophobia in our society and within the Church may make it difficult for their needs to be perceived or responded to. Second, the skills required both to work with couples *and* to help gay or lesbian people may be split between agencies specializing in one or the other. The same issues which reduce the amount of available help operate within the culture to put extra pressures on gay and lesbian relationships. Gay and lesbian people who are open about their relationship may experience overt prejudice, harassment and discrimination, for jobs and housing, which naturally puts added pressure on the internal dynamics of the relationship. Gay and lesbian people who do not 'come out' are forced to live continuously a kind of double life. They cannot acknowledge to others the central relationship in their lives and therefore cannot involve other people in supporting them or rejoicing with them.

The relationship is disqualified in a variety of subtle ways. The couple may never be invited out together as a pair nor be expected to turn up together at the functions or ceremonies at the work place of either. Each is pushed into pretending that they are single with neither the freedom of singleness nor the structure of coupledom. In addition, a new factor for gay couples arising out of the AIDS crisis has been how to respond to an epidemic which has initially attacked gay men in large numbers. Many gay couples have to face the appalling experience of knowing that their partner will die but also knowing that they themselves are HIV positive. The emotional complexity of this situation may be met by a variety of responses, ranging from despair and suicide to denial or to a desire to abandon the partnership. An outside helper will need considerable resources of knowledge, skill and compassion if he is to provide an adequate containing environment.

A second major problem may arise from a married person's discovery of his or her homosexuality and consequent desire to leave the marriage and form a gay partnership. In chapter 9 the Smith family provided an example of this situation. The counsellor may be presented either with the new gay partnership or the shattered marital relationship or both. The counsellor will need to review, with the couple, the variety of triangular relationships involved and the needs and resources within each of them which will help them to make decisions and follow them through. The tendency for each member of the triangle to split off parts of themselves in order to defend themselves from the anxiety engendered by this complex situation, is high. The counsellor may need to work in parallel with the marriage and with the newly formed gay partnership and subsequently, if the marriage breaks up, with the ex-wife/husband and/or with their children. The children will also need help in understanding and working with this new situation and the counsellor may also need to offer some family sessions.

Lesbian couples share some of the difficulties encountered by gay couples but also encounter issues that are specific to women's particular psycho-social conditioning and development. Common difficulties shared with gay couples are how to deal with homophobia in the community generally and how to gain acceptance for the partnership within the two family systems of each partner, sufficient to retain enough emotional connection with them, or at least to minimize their hostility and rejection. Another important therapeutic issue involves the symmetrical nature of the relationship. Although gender roles are largely socially determined, their absence in a gay or lesbian partnership can be problematic. The partnership may have to work out how to distribute roles and tasks co-operatively and avoid the competitive, runaway conflicts that often arise between couples who share many similarities. Hite (1988) found that lesbian relationships offer a high level of satisfaction. They often arise out of ordinary friendships and continue as enduring, committed relationships long after sexual activity between the couple has ceased. Because of the lack of validation for the relationship in the outside world, an important aspect of the counsellor's role will be the recognition and affirmation of the relationship itself with the consequent strength and support that this can lend. Simons (1991) comments:

> The work in the counselling sessions consisted initially of my playing the role of 'witness' for a relationship which was very close, caring and intimate but which was 'not meant to exist' . . . central to successful work with this couple was the provision of a mirror for their relationship, validating the joys of connection, the fear of loss and the sadness of change in the face of invisibility. (p. 212)

In other words, a major task of the counselling is the safe 'holding' of the precious but invisible reality of the relationship, a witnessing to the fact that the couple are indeed one and that this is indeed good.

At no time is this more important than when one of the couple is coping with the loss of the other, through death or separation. None of the mechanisms of social support that are available to a bereaved widow, mother or son operate for a gay or lesbian person and grief must often be suppressed because the relationship that is mourned was always invisible. It may only be the counsellor who is available for the bereaved person to share the depths of their grief at the loss of their partner and nowhere else perhaps will they receive the reassurance that the relationship did indeed exist and had great value. It is important for outside helpers to avoid denying the value and importance of such a relationship when one or other person moves into a new heterosexual partnership. The guilt and sadness resulting from the breakup of a homosexual relationship is not different in degree from any other kind of separation. Anyone who has entered into a relationship with another where the self has been offered and has now been withdrawn will experience a painful range of feelings associated with the guilt of that withdrawal. A counsellor who denies the individual's grief and guilt when they are moving into a heterosexual relationship, merely betrays his own homophobia.

Prevention and cure

> We could reasonably expect to find specialist parts of the established health and welfare professions acting as agencies engaged in couple therapy. Because couples' problems are so widespread and so damaging, we could expect to find these specialised services very widely available. In fact we find no such thing. (Barkla, 1991)

Barkla's point is reinforced by Dominian et al. (1991a) in their carefully argued research pointing to the now very well documented links between marital disruption and physical and psychological illness. However, the fact of the matter is that there is a great paucity of direct services on offer both to help couples who are already experiencing difficulty and to support and educate those before difficulties occur.

In the 1990s climate of under-resourced public services, it is quite unrealistic to expect Social Services Departments, the Probation Service, or GPs to offer very much, although all of these do have some involvement in helping couples in crisis. Likewise some large teaching hospitals have specialist departments offering help with marital and sexual difficulties. Two small specialist units offer a high quality service and also undertake influential research, namely the Tavistock Institute of Marital Studies and Jack Dominian's Unit, One-Plus-One. But by far the greatest number of couples are seen for counselling by Relate and the smaller organizations, catering for the special needs of Roman Catholics, and for Jews and for some other ethnic minority groups. The change of name of two of these agencies to Relate and to One-Plus-One, indicates an acceptance that couples in difficulties no longer form a homogeneous group and that they may be married, cohabiting or homosexual.

In addition to the agencies, a growing number of individual practitioners are training in marital work and the counselling of sexual dysfunction, and take fee-paying clients. However, since a low income is one of the factors that is inversely related to a healthy partnership, fee-paying services are not likely to do more than scratch the surface of the deep well of personal pain and unhappiness that relationship difficulties represent.

There exists I believe an enormous vacuum that needs filling. People prepared to acquire the necessary training to undertake both preventative and therapeutic work with couples are needed to fill it. Many more people are needed and those 'many' could appropriately include many more clergy and lay Christians. I am not suggesting that clergy abandon their role as clergy in order to become counsellors, but simply that they become more effective in the pastoral ministry that is theirs already.

Moreover, there are many ways in which agencies and individuals including the Church can promote educational as well as therapeutic approaches to helping couples. These are preventative approaches aimed at supporting couples in their relationships and extending their repertoire of coping skills so that they can better withstand stress. The emphasis in these approaches is on growth and development, often using a self-help approach to sharing knowledge and skill.

Marriage enrichment is one of the best known, allowing couples to

> take an honest look at their present situation. In recognising and valuing the strength that they each bring to the marriage they come to accept and trust one another more deeply and begin to see how further growth is possible. (Association for Marriage Enrichment, 1983)

Marriage enrichment courses are also run by Relate. The model adopted is normally a weekend away with a group of couples and a pair of co-leaders. Some organizations offer a support group with regular meetings for couples who face a particular issue such as a mixed marriage between a Roman Catholic and a non-Catholic partner.

The Anglican Family Life and Marriage Education organization, which emerged from the House of Bishops' Marriage Advisory Panel, has developed quite vigorously in most dioceses. Each diocese emphasizes different approaches and focuses on different aspects of family life. There is no one common emphasis other than providing educational opportunities for couples and families. Some areas run courses for couples or encourage couples in parishes to meet together regularly and to form groups on the basis of being at a similar stage in the life cycle (for example couples with young children, couples with teenagers etc.). Others run parenting courses, bereavement courses and courses in debt counselling to help couples in financial difficulties. Relate offers courses in divorce experience, helping people to learn from the breakdown of their marriage in order to try to avoid entering into a further unsuccessful marriage. The Jewish Marriage Council offers some courses and discussion groups on personal relationships both for young people, for engaged couples and for newly married couples, as does the Catholic Marriage Advisory Council. The Lesbian and Gay Christian Movement offers some opportunities for gay and lesbian couples to gain support for their relationships.

It is a curious fact however that efforts to *prevent* distress in relationships have an even lower profile than efforts to help relationships that are already experiencing problems. It may be much easier to define the issues and the focus for counselling couples in distress compared with the uncertainty of how to intervene preventatively in an effective way. Should the approach be to help children in school learn what goes into creating healthy fulfilling relationships? Should this be done at college level? Should it target those who have formed stable partnerships already? Should it involve ongoing programmes or limited self-help opportunities? Questions of funding, confidence and credibility loom large and there seems to be a general lack of focus in the preventative field. There are exceptions. In the effort to prevent the spread of AIDS, for example, a considerable amount of time and energy has been expended. But it seems difficult to raise the same commitment to undertaking preventative work with marriages and other committed relationships. As Dominian (1991a) comments: 'Counselling cannot form an effective part of a preventative strategy if it is regarded as a last resort before divorce. Sadly, this has been the case. Other preventative approaches need to be examined and employed' (p. 30).

11

§

STRUGGLES

Be patient toward all that is unsolved in your heart.

RAINER MARIA RILKE

The miracle of new life that emerges out of chaos and pain can best be understood, not from the point of view of the helper, but from those who have undergone the deepest of struggles. The helper and the struggler may, of course, and usually do participate equally in the difficulties of living in and out of relationships, but in this chapter the focus is the viewpoint of the person who at this moment is in the eye of the storm.

Three stories, two of them written in the first person, bring us back and 'earth' us again in the painful realities of the experience of how life is. First a brief picture of Olivia.

Olivia

Olivia comes from Ghana. She has lived in this country for eleven years. She is bringing up her three children alone – three boys aged eleven, six and two – all flourishing attractive children, high-spirited, full of fun – all a credit to her.

But she struggles to cope against several competing pressures. Her tiny council flat consists of two bedrooms – one measuring seven foot by six foot, a living room, tiny kitchen, bathroom and loo. It is part of a concrete complex built in the late sixties, joined together by galleries and long dark corridors. Olivia's flat is at the end of a row and overlooks the one-way traffic system where the traffic joins one of the main roads into Brixton. The flat is regularly infested by cockroaches and although the council does its best, the infestation is never completely eradicated. Olivia copes so well that she is the one person that everyone else depends upon. She has become the unofficial baby-minder for friends and neighbours, allowing them to shop or work for a few hours. But her mother needs her too. She has just returned from Ghana bringing with her Olivia's younger brother. He has learning difficulties. Olivia's mother cannot cope any more. She herself feels isolated and alone here, speaking little English and here only in order to do the best for her youngest son. She asks Olivia to provide him with the care be needs. And so he comes to live in the tiny overcrowded flat too.

And then the harassment begins. There is no particular reason for it. The children cause no trouble. The community in the flats is racially well integrated. But it is the last straw for Olivia. Bottles of milk and pots of yoghurt smashed against the front door. And finally an egg. To anyone else an egg might well have been taken in their stride along with all the rest. But probably unbeknown to the person responsible, a broken egg to Olivia, coming as she does from Ghana, means quite simply that a curse has been put upon her. She tries to laugh it off – but her spirit has become fearful.

One day a woman called and announced that she was Olivia's partner's wife. The woman lived a few doors away and had just discovered Olivia's existence. She was calm and cold and controlled. She said that Olivia should leave at once. The shock for Olivia was intense. Her partner of six years standing – the father of two of her children – her loved, dependable mainstay in life, had left – but leaving behind him the betrayal and duplicity of his hidden, proximal marriage. . . . She thinks about the broken egg, she feels its menace and she longs to leave her cramped and derelict flat, now bereft of its meaning for her as a secure retreat from a hostile outside world.

For Olivia, her therapist, her church, her faith in a God who stays close to her within the betrayal, is what has left her still human, surviving, coping with humour and grace, amidst her day to day uncertainties. The struggle continues – the resurrection is found – but only within the Cross.

Jonathan

Jonathan lives alone but is part of a large extended household of friends, which are this family. The following is part of Jonathan's story – extracts from a talk given to the Southwark Diocesan Synod, 7 March 1992, and a sermon preached on Passion Sunday at All Saints' Battersea 1992.

My name is Jonathan Andrew I am a gay man.
I have been living with HIV the best part of ten years.
I now have ARC and virtually no immune system.

My T cell count had dropped to 160
I was in deep trouble and I knew it
So I decided to fly out to New Zealand
and tell my father
I decided to come clean
I went and told the truth . . . and
the Truth began to set me free.

Within three weeks I was in the AIDS ward of Wellington
    Hospital
Admitted with bacterial pneumonia. I was in a lot of pain
I couldn't sleep and the drugs didn't seem to work
. . . and then I had another of those damn visions.

This time, in the early hours of the morning
A lady . . . with the most incredible smile
Towards a deeply beloved but none-the-less wayward son
Beloved . . . and this is important . . .
for his very waywardness
A smile which seemed to say:
'. . . and what sort of mess are we in this time?'
The pain left and I fell into a deep sleep
The next morning I woke up certain
that this . . . this AIDS ward
was the only place in the world
I was meant to be.

My father walked in and sat down
He looked at me slightly strangely and said
'You're supposed to be here aren't you?'
'Yes. Yes, I am.'

My diagnosis has utterly transformed my relationship with
    God
No longer a stranger
He has become my friend
He is also the very source of my being
He has transformed
my relationships
with my brothers and sisters
and with myself.

. . . and what I want from the church
is for it to walk with me on The Way
As I go through the process.

Soon after I was diagnosed
I noticed that there seemed to be
two separate debates taking place
In the Church:
The Sexual Debate
            – Should Women be priested?
            – Why is God 'Our Father'?
            – What about 'pulpit poofs'
            – (as the *Daily Mail* so delicately put it)
And in the Gay Bars
Some extraordinary conversations
were beginning to take place
The like of which I had never heard in the GBs before
            – why is this happening?
            – why are my friends dying?
            – why am I dying?
            – am I being punished?
            – what happens when I die?
            – is there an after life?
            – and, what is it like?

202

These are the Great Spiritual Questions
No one escapes them
There are no exceptions.
Everyone here has to ask those questions
and until they have
and begun groping for an answer
they are not going to be much use
You can't give away that which you do not have.

It seemed to me then
and it still does
that AIDS connected these two debates
about the mysteries of Sex & Death
Perhaps just perhaps
God's hand was in the middle of it
working his mysterious ways.
Mysterious it might be
but that is no excuse for its brutality
but then again getting nailed to the cross
isn't exactly pretty either.
This Xian faith business is not for the squeamish.

At the beginning of this health crisis
The Churches,
placing aside their doubts about sexuality
asked, quite rightly,
'What can we do?'
and back from many came the emphatic reply
'You can Sod Off.
You have caused quite enough damage to our people already'

But that didn't work . . .
because God had other things in mind
and the young men kept on asking
those damn awkward questions
they were not going to be cut off by
minor considerations, like:
Sex in church, or
God in Bars.

A priest in his Xmas Sermon two years ago
said of the boys in London Lighthouse
shaking his head in disbelief
'They keep on wanting to talk about Jesus'
Of course they do
It's called soul sickness
It's a hunger for God.
You can see it in the eyes of The People.

The call to God
is a call to prayer
I don't know about anyone else, but
my transformation came
when I stopped talking *about* God . . . and
instead
started talking *to* him.
I abandoned the God of the church
and went it alone.

Well . . . not entirely alone
three Women, dear friends, watched
as I put myself through the process.
They had enough faith
to trust God.
one of them simply said
'Before you read the mail
say your prayers'
Seek ye First the Kingdom of God.
. . . And what I want from the church
is men and women of great holiness
who can reach back
and guide a fellow pilgrim through
So . . . Every morning
I went out into the Park to pray
just chats with My Mate
There was no where else to go
. . . and the more I prayed the more I wanted to pray
and the miracles began to happen.

It was to him in those chats
that, eventually, I took the Great Questions.
You see . . .   the bars don't have the
                answers
                nor does the church
                in a sense there are no
                answers
                here is only
                a relationship.

I used to get very angry with the church
I still do sometimes
but I get most angry with people
who provide glib religious answers
to questions they haven't even asked
Abandoning the Parable of the two men
who went up into the temple to pray they
confuse humility with humiliation
and the damage caused by their spiritual arrogance
is . . . well . . . eternal.

I now know that I make my own pilgrimage,
and I am utterly convinced that the way through
is a direct, personal & deep
relationship with my Creator.

And my friend?
Well . . . I walked into a church one day
and discovered that you had been talking
about him all along.

I know that he will be with me
holding my hand when I am in London Lighthouse
and that when it is over
he will carry me through the gate.

. . . and, part of me, longs for that day
longs to go home

and do you know . . . I'm not scared any more
None of this means that I will be excused
my Gethsemane
Nor my Calvary
But death has for me, quite literally,
lost its sting.

No longer do I live in fear
I live
I live
in immense hope
. . . and that is good news
In fact I believe that it is
The Good News.

Now what I would like most of all is for
you to:
Go Tell My People . . .

Just tell them
Emmanuel.

Rachel – early morning reflections

And the perspective of somebody who has been a clergy wife and
has survived – is surviving – the breakup of that relationship:

It is about survival to start with. We live in a vicarage. We have
no money. I have no job except as a freelance journalist which
has brought in money for holidays and extras. I've been a vicar's
wife. The 'Church' was good and gave me six months to move
out. They would help to find me somewhere to live. The
congregation were loving and supportive and I cried my way
through the service most Sundays and they understood. I took
in lodgers. I found a very demanding two day a week social
work job. Then followed three months of paralysis about looking
for somewhere to live. Perhaps it took that long to sink in that
he wouldn't be coming back. Should I go to the other end of

the country – right away from it all; away from him? Make a new start?

But where? I don't belong anywhere. The longest we ever spent in a vicarage was five years. So nowhere obvious to go. Nowhere with roots that I could call home. Two of the children had just started new schools – that must be the reason to stay, the anchor. And so that they could see their father, who now lived a few miles away.

Decisions. I've never been good at decisions. I phoned agents to send the particulars. Large brown envelopes lay unopened on my desk. Eventually I went and looked at some houses and flats. One would do. The process of buying and moving took three months. We moved out the week before the next vicar moved in.

And so I survived the first six months because there was so much practical stuff to do. Rather as you survive the first few weeks after a death. Like when my brother had died two years before. There was so much that *had* to be done, the funeral *had* to be arranged, his things sorted out, the house sold. (How I missed him now.)

Then comes the vacuum. The emptiness, the purposelessness, the loneliness and Why? The thinking over and over. How could he have given up all that we had? How could he have abandoned the children? How could he be missing all the day to day growing up and joys and upsets? How could he give up all that job satisfaction? That loving and supporting congregation who needed him? And me? Has he really found what he was looking for?

God, Why? What has been the meaning of all these years together? Years of faith and Christian ministry. Years of work and sacrifice and relative poverty. What now? What of his vocation? What of mine? I think I was never a 'typical' vicar's wife but I found my niches, the areas where I could and wanted to contribute. I worked hard and found great fulfilment. I liked being needed, to be useful. Now what? My role has been taken from me – yes, perhaps status has something to do with it too, thought I am not proud of that. I think I did like to be special, a bit on a pedestal, to be needed even if most of it was because I was 'his wife' rather than me. There is a gaping empty space and loss of purpose where that role used to be. Much greater than I'd have anticipated.

Shall I stay in the same church? The people are wonderful, but can I bear to be there Sunday by Sunday, my heart breaking because he's not there? It's all so familiar and yet so different. All the words and hymns and prayers take on new significance and I can't control my emotions. God why? Where? What for? What am I supposed to be doing with my life? What do You want of me? What is Your purpose?

And where is God? I can't communicate with him or pray. I am afraid of losing my faith. Has all this time in my life, in church, in prayer, everything we've done 'religiously' simply been an illusion? Not true? From my new home I begin slipping into the early Communion Service at the nearest church. Sunday by Sunday anonymously, quietly, and so I have been hanging on by my fingertips. And waiting. Waiting for God. (Or is he waiting for me?) I've been in the wilderness before and found my way back.

And then there's been the devastating burden of responsibility. Responsibility for maintaining a home, of *having* to earn enough money to keep us. The worry of bills, of property. Wanting to curl up, give up, hide in the womb of my bed each morning and not face another day. But I have to. I have to work. The job scene is precarious now. The recession. Part-time social workers will be the first to go. Casual journalist work is becoming harder to find. The Church is in financial difficulties – will it go on helping me? Everything is so uncertain, so perilous.

And greatest of all, the responsibility for my children. For the decisions to be made – the day-to-day decisions and the life-changing decisions. How much to involve their father? How to work out how to parent together? Or separately? How to *be* a single parent.

Gradually as time goes by I manage to look a bit further into the future but it's frightening – the emptiness. So mostly I don't look. I keep the shutters down – at first I began to be able to look ahead hour by hour, then day by day, week by week . . . and it then became possible to plan a holiday . . . but I still shrink from thinking about long-term plans. Alone? Probably. I don't want to be alone. Sharing is one of the best things in life. But I don't want the hurt and all of that again. I would like to wake up in bed tomorrow morning with the 'right' person. I want a friend, a confidante and, yes a lover.

Reflections written a few days later:

I have been very near the cliff edge – still am at times. So how has despair, desolation, depression and yes, madness, been kept at bay? The first essential is not to try and look too far ahead, not beyond tomorrow; do the practical things I have to do in order for me and the children to *exist*.

Then there have been the props and distractions of radio, TV and books, and sometimes sleeping pills, to help me through the long wakeful silent hours of the nights especially. There have been friends who cared and loving support from my family. The telephone has been a lifeline.

Getting a job has been important. Going *out* to work. Out of the home. Braving the outside world. Social work. And this leads into the need to be needed, the purpose for living. I no longer have a husband who needs me; a parish that needs me; homeless men and women on the door step needing tea and sandwiches. The children of course need me and that is my reason for being, my motivation for getting up in the morning, for doing anything. But they will grow up and away. I need to be needed (not at first, at first I wanted only to be carried). Social work is demanding. However I may be feeling I can't let someone else down, there are people far worse off than me. That has been really important. I have been able to lose myself, shake off my self pity and absorb myself in other's needs for periods of time each week and feel valued. And it's been good – and hard – to have to meet and mix with colleagues. To find new ways of relating, how much to hide or share of my past (I have actually said very little and even that has been good – as time passes, there *are* other things to talk about, other than me and my troubles!) I have pushed the boundaries, opened the doors a bit further and a bit further. There is a lonely old housebound neighbour I 'take care of' – two actually. Then there's been my local church and vicar which have made no intrusive demands on me, but have just been there for me Sunday by Sunday.

There *are* ways to turn potential consuming self-pity and bitterness inside out and upside down. To learn to *live* again, not merely to exist. Brave face. I am not there yet and the despair, desolation, depression and yes, madness still crowd in. But not quite so constantly.

12

❧

QUESTIONS

This Christian faith business is not for the squeamish.

JONATHAN ANDREW

In his spirited defence of the family, Ferdinand Mount (1982) puts his finger on a profound truth about the relationship between Christianity and the family: the hostility between the two has at a profound level gone back two thousand years.

> It is not and never has been the Church's restrictions on sexuality which have constituted the basic threat which Christianity poses to the family. It is the carefree attitudes of the Sermon on the Mount . . . The Sermon on the Mount is a wonderful, intoxicating sermon, but it is a sermon for bachelors. (p. 28)

Indeed yes – Mount sees only too clearly that the cutting edge of the Christian imperative is incompatible with the modern privatized, materialistic family whose disintegration is so bewailed by both Church and State. Mount rightly points the finger at Christianity as the most subversive of influences and the family's greatest threat. This book has been an attempt to rescue family relatedness in all its many forms from the idolatry of 'the family' in all its seductive guises. It is an attempt to re-focus our concern on the deep longings for *relationship* which is, I believe, the agenda which unites, at a fundamental level, our humanity both created and redeemed.

One of Britain's largest computer dating services regularly advertises the fact that 96 per cent of its applicants are seeking 'one relationship for a lifetime of loving commitment'. The fact that fewer people are choosing marriage and that more marriages are breaking down does not in any way alter the longing, the deep yearning for

211

committed, faithful loving relationships. And yet the fulfilment of this yearning is now sought within a variety of forms and structures. As in the natural order, this variety is precious and life-giving, enabling adaptation to changing circumstances to occur. We are faced therefore with a fundamental question. How can we clarify the *essence* of this deep human yearning, accept it, value it, rejoice in it and encourage it within all the various forms and structures that it is now being expressed? And an equally fundamental question. How can we be cleansed of our idolatry of 'the family' which is the enemy of both this burgeoning variety and of the good news of the Gospel itself?

Michael Mann (1981) has commented that 'pluralism, in so far as it denotes a wide range of individual beliefs, does not necessarily mean that this variety can not lead to a consensus of agreed essential values' (p. 3).

What then might these agreed essential values be? What is of the essence as distinct from the form? I suggest that for most people, these essential values are well summarized in Paul's three theological virtues, whether people would articulate them quite like that or not. Faithfulness – a crucial core human need. To have faith – in oneself, in others, in life, in the world, in some benign Presence that holds and knows and is concerned for the world – all of that kind of faithfulness is of the essence of being rooted, being mature and being able to cope with being-in-the-world. To be full of faith, to hold faith, to have faith in another and to invest faith in a relationship is something that is *essential* to the fulfilment of our deepest needs. I need to belong to a family and I need to belong to a Family and both have, as we noted in chapter 1, crucial significance for my experience of life and the living of it. The values at the centre of this belonging are first of all faith, that makes such belonging possible. For some, this faith will be much more difficult to hold, if early life experiences have taught that relationships have not in fact been faithful or faith-filled.

The second is hope, the hope that, in a multiplicity of different ways and through a variety of different faithful relationships, such commitment of the self to others can be discovered and experienced. The third is love, the recognition and acceptance of authentic love, springing up in what may seem wholly unlikely places. Relationships that are rooted in faithful, hopeful love hold the possibility of meeting individual, interpersonal and societal needs.

The longing for faithfulness, hope and love, expressed in committed relationships, is a longing for the essential values that bind us together as human beings, across cultures and generations, across all our individual differences and across all the differences of family pattern and form. These are the values which most human beings want most of the time for themselves and for others and which they are motivated to seek more freely now in a whole variety of different family structures.

How can we, the Church, 'rejoice and be glad in it'? How can we support this search for faithful committed love in marriage, in community, amongst couples and family groups of every sort and kind? How can we at the same time help those for whom faithful committed relationships are elusive or lost – the men who are confused and uncertain of their role and identity; the abused and abandoned child; the battered and demoralized woman; the homeless poor; the alienated rich; those who bear the burden of a 'discreditable identity'; those who are discriminated against? How can we discern accurately and appropriately the different systems *level* which is the locus of difficulty? How can we have clarity of vision and firmness of purpose to intervene at the right level to bring about change?

These are some of the broad questions we need to answer. They are already being addressed in many different ways by committed Christians, working to bring about change as counsellors, community workers, campaigners, politicians and carers of all kinds. But there is still the need, I believe, to connect more closely with the nub of some of these difficulties and to realize our Christian concern for family life in a more specific and relevant way. Specifically I believe we need:

1. A concerted effort to promote what is of the *essence* of strong, committed, faithful, loving relationships independent of the form in which they are presented.
2. A commitment to eradicate in ourselves our sexism, racism and homophobia by undertaking anti-racist training and by exploring our gender prejudices in mixed and single-sex groups.

3. To improve our knowledge about and technical expertise in helping couples *prepare for* their new relationships and helping couples and families who are experiencing *difficulties in* their relationships. The Church's commitment needs to be the *long-term* support of families.

4. To make marriage a real choice, viewed as one choice amongst others, for creating family life.

5. To eradicate from the wedding service the bride's option to promise to obey her husband and her option to be given away by her father.

6. To welcome those who bring children for baptism, irrespective of the family structure in which their parents have chosen to live.

7. To create new rituals to help families negotiate the various transitions in their life cycle as creatively as possible – for example, entering a cohabiting union or a gay partnership, or leaving a marriage or other committed relationship, and dissolving the promises or vows that have been made and making use of the sacrament of reconciliation.

8. To promote better teaching about God's inclusive concern for all his people through a wholeness of ministry, and an inclusiveness of language and symbolism in our liturgy.

9. To campaign for more government support for counselling services for couples and families to help them work through relationship problems; to gain more government support for conciliation services to help people to separate constructively; and to persuade government to give the highest priority towards more family-friendly policies in the spheres of improved child care provision, dependants' leave from work for women and men and equal opportunities for women in the market place.

10. To witness more meaningfully to bringing about a society that closes the gap between rich and poor and which recognizes the central part played by poverty in the difficulties experienced by families, and to witness to the divisive effect of legislation, such as the Asylum Bill, designed to split families.

11. To cease propagating a model of the Church as 'family', based on the privatized, domestic retreat that has become our idolatry, and to promote instead a model of the Church as a family

that is inclusive and open, whose membership is derived from adoption and grace and whose task is the establishing of the kingdom.

12. To forge in our teaching a continuity over time between the family's experience of its history, its present and its future beyond death in ways which can be made relevant and meaningful to the family as it negotiates the death of its members.

In summary, we need I believe to adopt an approach of openness and welcome towards everyone who presents their infinitely varied patterns of family life to us. This requires of us an inner conversion of attitude and spirit whereby we set aside our defensive legalism and fear, and engage with 'what is' rather than what we think 'ought to be'. It means a continuous effort to foster the spiritual disciplines of charity, faithfulness and hope, that we may perceive in the relationships of others the unique possibilities for them, which, with God's grace, will lead them to abundant life.

BIBLIOGRAPHY

Ackerman, N. W., *Treating the Troubled Family* (New York, Basic Books, 1966)

Adams, D., 'Treatment Models of Men Who Batter: A Pro-Feminist Analysis' in Yllok and Bograd, M. (eds), *Feminist Perspectives on Wife Abuse* (California, Sage, 1988)

Ahmed, S., Cheetham, J. and Small, J., *Social Work with Black Children and their families* (London, Batsford, 1986)

Ahrons, C. R., 'Redefining the Divorced Family: A Conceptual Framework' in *Social Work* (Nov. 1980)

Alibhai-Brown, Y. and Montague, A., *The Colour of Love* (London, Virago, 1992)

Anderson, R. S. and Guernsey, D. B., *On Being Family – a Social Theology of the Family* (Michigan, Eerdmans, 1985)

Andrew, J., Speech given to the Southwark Diocesan Synod, March 1992

Aponte, H., 'Training the Person of the Therapist in Structural Family Therapy' in *Journal of Marital and Family Therapy*, vol 18 (1992), pp. 268–81

Armson, John, 'The Clergy and Sexuality' in *Contact*, vol 107 (1992), pp. 19–24

Association for Marriage Enrichment, *Focus on Couples* (London, Westminster Pastoral Foundation, 1983)

Avis, J. M., 'Where are all the Family Therapists? Abuse and Violence with Families and Family Therapy's Response' in *Journal of Marital and Family Therapy*, vol. 18 (1992), pp. 225–32

Baker, P., *Beyond Contradiction* (Bristol, Paul Baker Memorial Trust, 1992)

Balakrishnan, T. R. et al., 'A hazard model analysis of the co-variates of marriage dissolution in Canada' in *Demography*, vol 24 (1987), pp. 395–406

Barkla, D., 'Couple Therapy: The Agencies Approach' in Hooper and Dryden., op. cit.

Barrett, M. and McIntosh, M., *The Anti-Social Family* (London, Verso, 1982)

Barth, K., *Church Dogmatics* (G. W. Bromiley and T. F. Torrance (eds), Edinburgh, T. & T. Clark, 1969)

Barton, S., 'Towards a Theology of the Family' in *Crucible* (Jan-March 1993), pp. 4–13

Bateson, G., *Steps to an Ecology of Mind* (New York, Paladine, 1972)

—— *Mind and Nature*, (London, Flamingo, Wildwood House, 1979)

Bennun, I., 'Working with the Individual from the Couple' in Hooper and Dryden, op. cit.

Bennett, N. G. et al., 'Commitment and the Modern Union: Assessing the Link between Premarital Cohabitation and Subsequent Marital Stability' in *American Sociological Review,* vol. 53 (1988), pp. 127–38

Berger, B. and Berger, P., *The War over the Family* (London, Hutchinson, 1983)

Bernard, J., *The Future of Marriage* (New York, Bantam, 1972)

Bishops, Statement by the House of, *Issues in Human Sexuality* (London, Church House Publishing, 1991)

Black Sisters, Southall, *Against the Grain: A Celebration of Survival and Struggle* (Nottingham, Russell Press, 1990)

Bogle, J. (ed), *Families for Tomorrow* (Gracewing Books, 1991)

Borrowdale, A., *Distorted Images,* (London, SPCK, 1991)

Boscolo and Bertrando, P., 'The Reflexive Loop of Past, Present and Future in Systemic Therapy and Consultation' in *Family Process,* vol 31 (1992), pp. 119–30

Bowen, M., *Family Therapy in Clinical Practice* (New York, Aronson, 1978)

Bowlby, J., *Attachment and Loss,* vol 1 (London, Hogarth Press, 1969)

—— *Attachment and Loss,* vol 2 (London, Hogarth Press, 1973)

—— *Attachment and Loss,* vol 3 (London, Hogarth Press, 1980)

Bradt, J. and Moynihan, C., *Systems Therapy* (Washington, published by the authors, 1971)

Broderick, C. B., *The Therapeutic Triangle* (Beverly Hills, Sage, 1983)

Brodsky, A. M., 'A Decade of Feminist Influence on Psychotherapy' in *Psychology of Women Quarterly,* vol 4 (1980)

Bronfenbrenner, U., *The Ecology of Human Development: Experiments by Nature and Design* (Cambridge, Mass., Harvard University Press, 1979)

Brown, F. H., 'The Postdivorce Family' in Carter and McGoldrick, op. cit.

Brown, P., *The Body and Society* (London, Faber & Faber, 1989)

Bryan, B., Dadzie, S., and Scafe, S., *The Heart of the Race* (London, Virago, 1985)

Bumpas, L. L. and Sweet, J. A., 'Commitment and the modern union: assessing the link between pre-marital cohabitation and subsequent marital stability' in *American Sociological Review,* vol 53 (1989), pp. 127–38

Burgoyne, J. and Clarke, D., 'From Father to Step-Father' in McKee and O'Brien, op. cit.

Bussert, J., *Battered Women* (Lutheran Church in America, 1986)

Byng-Hall, J., 'Symptom-Bearer as Marital Distance Regulator – Clinical Implications' in *Family Process,* vol 19 (1980), pp. 355–65

—— 'Re-editing Family Mythology during Family Therapy' in *Journal of Family Therapy,* vol 1 (1979), pp. 2–14

Cade, W., 'The Potency of Impotence' in *Australian Journal of Family Therapy,* vol 4 (1982), pp. 23–6

Capra, F., *The Turning Point: Science, Society and the Rising Culture* (London, Wildwood House, 1982)

Carr, W., *Brief Encounters* (London, SPCK, 1985)

Carter, B. and McGoldrick, M. (eds), *The Changing Family Life Cycle* (2nd edn, Boston, Allyn and Bacon, 1989)

Casey, J., *The History of the Family* (Oxford, Blackwell, 1989)

Cherlin, A., 'Work Life and Marital Disillusion' in G. Levinger and O. Moles (eds), *Divorce and Separation: Context, Causes and Consequences* (New York, Basic Books, 1979)

Cherlin, A., 'Remarriage as an Incomplete Institution' in *American Journal of Sociology*, vol 84 (1978), pp. 634–50

Chodorow, N., *The Reproduction of Mothering* (California, University of California Press, 1978)

Clulow, C., *Marital Therapy: An Insider's View* (Aberdeen, Aberdeen University Press, 1985)

Coleman, D., *Ethnic intermarriage in Great Britain* (Population Trends, Office of Population Consensuses and Surveys, 1985)

Collard, J. and Mansfield, P., 'The Couple: A Sociological Perspective' in Hooper and Dryden, op. cit.

Cooper, D., *The Death of the Family* (Harmondsworth, Penguin, 1972)

Creighton, S. J. and Noyes, E., *Child Abuse Trends in England and Wales 1983–1987* (London, NSPCC, 1989)

Demaris, A. and Vaninadha, R., 'Premarital Cohabitation and Subsequent Marital Stability in the United States' in *Journal of Marriage and the Family*, vol 54 (1992)

Dicks, H. V., *Marital Tensions* (London, Routledge & Kegan Paul, 1967)

Dominian, J. et. al., *Marital Breakdown and the Health of the Nation* (London, One plus One, 1991a)

Dominian, J., *Passionate and Compassionate Love* (London, Darton, Longman & Todd, 1991b)

Dominelli, L., *Anti-racist Social Work* (London, Macmillan/BASW, 1988)

Dormor, D. J., *The Relationship Revolution* (London, One plus One, 1992)

Dowell, S., *They too shall be one* (London, Collins, 1990)

—— 'Keeping Faith with Fidelity' in *Contact*, vol 107 (1992), pp. 9–13

Dowell, S. and Hurcombe, L., *Dispossessed Daughters of Eve* (London, SCM, 1981)

Elliot, F. R., *The Family: Change or Continuity?* (London, Macmillan, 1986)

Emery, F. E., *Systems Thinking*, vols 1 and 2, (Harmondsworth, Penguin, 1969 and 1981)

Engels, F., 'The Origin and History of the Family, Private Property and the State' (1884) in Marx, K. and Engels, F., *Selected Works* (Moscow, Progress Publishers, 1970), vol 3, p. 233

Erikson, E., *Childhood and Society* (Harmondsworth, Penguin, 1950)

[Family Policy Studies Centre], Fact Sheet 1: *The Family Today* (Family Policy Studies Centre, 1991)

[——] Fact Sheet 3: *One Parent Families* (Family Policy Studies Centre, 1990)

[——] Fact Sheet 4: *Family Finances* (Family Policy Studies Centre, 1991)

Ferri, E., *Growing Up in a One Parent Family* (Slough, NFER Publishing Co., 1976)

Finkelhor, D., *Child Sexual Abuse* (New York, Free Press, 1984)

Fiorenza, E. S., *In Memory of Her* (London, SCM, 1983)

Firestone, S., *The Dialectic of Sex* (New York, Bantam Books, 1970)

Flandrin, J. L., *Families in Former Times* (Cambridge, Cambridge University Press, 1979)

Fletcher, R., *The Family and Marriage in Britain* (third edn) (Harmondsworth, Penguin, 1973)

Freud, S., 'A Case of Paranoia: Schreber' (1911) in *Case Histories*, vol 9, Pelican Freud Library (Penguin Books, 1977)

Friedman, E. H., *Generation to Generation: Family Process Church and Synagogue* (New York, The Guildford Press, 1985)

—— 'Systems and Ceremonies: A Family View of Rites of Passage' in Carter and McGoldrick (1989), op. cit.

Furlong, M., *Divorce – One Woman's View* (London, The Mothers' Union, 1981)

Furlong, M. (ed), *Mirror to the Church* (London, SPCK, 1988)

Gill, O. and Jackson, B., *Adoption and Race: Black, Asian and Mixed Race Children in White Families* (London, Batsford, 1983)

Gittings, D., *The Family in Question: Changing Households and Familiar Ideologies* (London, Macmillan, 1985)

Glaser, D. and Frosh, S., *Child Sexual Abuse* (London, Macmillan, 1988)

Goldenberg, H. and Goldenberg, I., *Counseling Today's Families* (California, Brooke/Cole, 1990)

Golder, V., 'Feminism and Family Therapy' in *Family Process*, vol 24 (1985)

Goode, W. J., 'A Sociological Perspective on Marital Dissolution' in Anderson, M. (ed), *Sociology of the Family* (Harmondsworth, Penguin Books, 1971, 2nd edn. 1982)

Grainger, R., *Staging Posts: Rites of Passage for Contemporary Christians* (Brauton, Merlin Books, 1987)

Green, R., *Only Connect* (London, Darton, Longman & Todd, 1987)

Guirguis, W., 'Sex Therapy with Couples' in Hooper and Dryden, op. cit.

Gurman, A. and Kniskern, D., 'Commentary: Individual Marital Therapy – have reports of your death been somewhat exaggerated?' in *Family Process*, vol 25 (1986), pp. 51–62

Haimes, E. and Timms, N., *Adoption, Identity and Social Policy* (Aldershot, Gower, 1985)

Hare-Mustin, R., 'A Feminist Approach to Family Therapy' in *Family Process*, vol 17 (1978)

Harries, R., *Is there a Gospel for the Rich?* (London, Mowbray, 1992)

Hart, N., *When Marriage Ends: A Study in Status Passage* (London, Tavistock, 1976)

Haskey, J., 'Pre-Marital Cohabitation and the Probability of Subsequent Divorce' in *Population Trends*, vol 68 (1992), pp. 10–19

Hebblethwaite, M., *Motherhood and God* (London, Chapman, 1984)

Hipgrave, T., 'Lone Fatherhood: A Problematic Status' in McKee and O'Brian, op. cit.

Hite, S., *Women in Love* (Harmondsworth, Penguin, 1988)

HMSO, *Households Below Average: A Statistical Analysis 1979–1988/9* (London, HMSO, 1992)

Hoem, B. and Hoem, J. M., 'The disruption of marital and non-marital unions in contemporary Sweden' in J. Trussell et al., *Demographic applications of event-history analysis* (Oxford, Clarendon Press, 1992), pp. 1–93

Hoffman, L., *Foundations of Family Therapy* (New York, Basic Books, 1981)

—— 'The Family Life Cycle and Discontinuous Change' in Carter and McGoldrick, op. cit.

Holloway, R. (ed), *Who needs Feminism? Men Respond to Sexism in the Church* (London, SPCK, 1992)

Hooper, D. and Dryden, W. (eds), *Couple Therapy* (Milton Keynes, Open University Press, 1991)

Hooper, D. and Dryden, W., 'Why Couple Therapy?' in Hooper and Dryden, op. cit.

Imber-Black, E., 'Idiosyncratic Life Cycle Transitions and Therapeutic Ritual' in Carter and McGoldrick op. cit.

Jenkins, G., *Cohabitation: A Biblical Perspective* (Bramcote, Nottingham, Grove Books, 1992)

John, J., *Permanent, Faithful, Stable – Christian Same-Sex Partnerships* (London, Affirming Catholicism, 1993)

Johnson, N. (ed), *Marital Violence* (London, Routledge and Kegan Paul, 1985)

Junker, B. H., *Fieldwork: An Introduction to the Social Sciences* (Chicago, University of Chicago Press, 1972)

Kaslow, F. W. and Sculman, N., 'The Family Life of Psychotherapists – Clinical Implications' in *Journal of Marriage and the Family*, vol 3 (1987), pp. 79–96

Kell, C., 'The Internal Dynamics of the Extra-Marital Relationship: A Counselling Perspective' in *Journal of Sexual and Marital Therapy*, vol. 7 (1992), pp. 157–72

Kiernan, K. and Wicks, M., *Family Change and Future Policy* (London, Family Policy Study Centre, 1990)

Kobrin, F. J. and Waite, L. J., 'Effects of Childhood Family Structure on the Transition to Marriage' in *Journal of Marriage and the Family*, vol. 4 (1984), pp. 807–16

Laing, R. D., *The Politics of the Family and other essays* (London, Tavistock, 1971)

—— *Wisdom, Madness and Folly – The Making of a Psychiatrist* (London, Macmillan, 1985)

Lambeth, London Borough of, Report by Social Services Committee (1981)

Laszlo, E., *Introduction to Systems Philosophy* (New York, Gordon Preach, 1972)

Laslett, P., *The World we have lost* (2nd edn, London, Methuen, 1971)

—— *Household and Family in Past-Time* (Cambridge, Cambridge University Press, 1972)

Leech, K., *Struggle in Babylon* (London, Sheldon Press, 1988)

McAdoo, H. P. (ed), *Black Families* (London, Sage, 1981)

McGoldrick, M., 'Ethnicity and the Family Life-Cycle' in Carter and McGoldrick, op. cit.

McGoldrick, M and Gerson, R., 'Genograms and the Family Life Cycle' in Carter and McGoldrick, op. cit.

McGoldrick, M. and Carter, B., 'Forming a Remarriage Family' in Carter and McGoldrick, op. cit.

McKee, L. and O'Brian, M., *The Father Figure* (London, Tavistock, 1982)

McWhirter, W. P. and Mattison, M. A., *The Male Couple: How Relationships Develop* (Inglewood Cliffs NJ, Prentice-Hall, 1984)

Macklin, E. D., 'Non Marital Heterosexual Cohabitation: An Overview' in Macklin, E. D. and Rueben, R. H. (eds), *Contemporary Family and Alternative Lifestyles* (Beverly Hills, Sage, 1983)

Maitland, S., *A Map of the New Country*, (London, Routledge & Kegan Paul, 1982)

Mann, M., *Changing Standards in Society: A Position Paper* (Windsor, St George's House, 1981)

Marris, P., *Loss and Change* (London, Routledge & Kegan Paul, 1974)

Mead, M., *Blackberry Winter* (New York, William Morrow, 1972)

Meth, R. L., 'Marriage and Family Therapists Working with Family Violence: Strained Bedfellows or Compatible Partners?' in *Journal of Marital and Family Therapy*, vol 18 (1992), pp. 257–61

Miller, J. B., *Toward a New Psychology of Women* (Harmondsworth, Penguin, 1976)

Millett, K., *Sexual Politics* (New York, Doubleday, 1970)

Minuchin, S., *Families and Family Therapy* (London, Tavistock, 1974)

Minuchin, S. and Fishman, H. C., *Family Therapy Techniques* (London, Harvard University Press, 1981)

Moberly, E., *Psychogenesis* (London, Routledge & Kegan Paul, 1983)

Moltmann-Wendel, E., *The Women around Jesus* (London, SCM, 1980)

Moltmann-Wendel, E. and Moltmann, J. *His God and Hers* (London, SCM, 1991)

Moraga, C. and Anzaldma, G. (eds), *Writings by Radical Women of Colour* (London, Persephone Press, 1981)

Morley, J., *All Desires Known* (London, WIT/MOW, 1988)

Mount, F., *The Subversive Family* (London, Jonathan Cape, 1982)

Newstatter, A., *Hyenas in Petticoats: A look at 20 years of Feminism* (Harmondsworth, Penguin, 1990)

Oakley, A., *Subject Women* (London, Collins, 1981)

Oddie, M., 'Conciliation and Marital and Divorce Counselling' in Thelma Fisher (ed), *Family Conciliation Within the UK* (Bristol, Jordon and Sons, 1990)

Office of Population and Census Surveys (1992)

Osborne, K., 'Women in Families: Feminist Therapy and Family Systems' in *Journal of Family Therapy*, vol 5 (1983)

Paolino, T. and McGrady, B., *Marriage and Marital Therapy* (New York, Brunner/Mazel, 1978)

Parkinson, L., *Conciliation in Separation and Divorce: Finding Common Ground* (London, Croom Helm, 1986)

—— *Separation, Divorce and Families* (London, Macmillan, 1987)

—— 'Comprehensive Mediation' in Thelma Fisher (ed), *Family Conciliation within the UK* (Bristol, Jordon & Sons, 1990)

—— 'The Split Couple: Conciliation and Mediation Approaches' in Hooper and Dryden op. cit.

Peck, J. S. and Manocherin, J. R., 'Divorce in the Changing Family Life Cycle' in Carter and McGoldrick, op. cit.

Phoenix, A., *Young Mothers?* (Cambridge, Polity Press, 1991)

Phoenix, A., Woollett, A. and Lloyd, E., *Motherhood: Meanings, Practices and Ideologies* (London, Sage, 1992)

Phypers, D., *Christian Marriage in Crisis* (Bromley, Kent, Marc Europe, 1985)

Pincus, L., 'The Nature of Marital Interaction' in Pincus et al., *The Marital Relationship as a focus for casework* (London, Tavistock Institute of Human Relations, 1971)

Plummer, K., 'Men in Love: Observations on Male Homosexual Couples' in Corbin, M. (ed), *The Couple* (Harmondsworth, Penguin, 1978)

Poster, M., *Critical Theory of the Family* (London, Pluto Press, 1978)

Pothan, P., *Unpackaging the Family* (Nottingham, Grove Books, 1992)

Pratt, E. A., *Living in Sin?* (Southsea, Hants, 1992)

Rapoport, R. N. and R., 'British Families in Transition' in Rapoport, R. N., Fogarty, M. P. and Rapoport, R. (eds), *Families in Britain* (London, Routledge & Kegan Paul, 1982)

Raynor, L., *The Adopted Child comes of Age* (London, George Allen and Unwin, 1980)

RELATE *Beyond the Couple: Annual Review 1991–2*

Rich, A., *Of Woman Born: Motherhood as Experience and Institution* (London, Virago, 1977)

Riddle, D. and Sang, B., 'Psychotherapy with Lesbians' in *Journal of Social Issues*, vol 34 (1978), pp. 84–100

Roll, J., *Family Fortunes: Parents' Incomes in the 1980s* (London, Family Policy Study Centre, 1988)

—— *What is a Family?* (London, Family Policy Study Centre, 1991)

Rochlin, R., 'Sexual Orientation of the Therapist and Therapeutic Effectiveness with Gay Clients' in *Journal of Homosexuality*, vol 7 (1981–2), pp. 21–9

Ruether, R. R., *Sexism and God-Talk* (London, SCM, 1983)

Rushton, R., 'The Gospel and Culture' (Unpublished lectures given to clergy in the Bristol Diocese, 1992)

Rycroft, C. *Psychoanalysis and Beyond* (London, Hogarth Press, 1985)

Sachs, J., The Reith Lectures (BBC, 1991)

Schaffer, H. R., 'Child Psychology: The Future' in *Journal of Child Psychology and Psychiatry*, vol 27 1986, pp. 761–90

Schatzman, M., *Soul Murder: Persecution in the Family* (London, Allen Lane, The Penguin Press, 1973)

Schoen, R., 'First Unions and the Stability of First Marriages' in *Journal of Marriage and the Family*, vol 65 (1992), pp. 281–4

Scott, J., 'Women and the Family' in Jowell, R. et al. (eds), *British Social Attitudes: the Seventh Report* (Basingstoke, Gower, 1990)

Segal, L., 'The Most Important Thing of All – Rethinking the Family' in Segal, L., *What is to be done about the family?* (Harmondsworth, Penguin, 1983)

Selby, P., *Be Longing* (London, SPCK, 1991)

Sheehy, G., *Passages* (New York, Bantam, 1977)

Simon, R. M., 'Family Life Cycle Issues in the Therapy System' in Carter and McGoldrick, op. cit.

Simons, S., 'Couple Therapy with Lesbians' in Hooper and Dryden, op. cit.

Skolnick, A., *The Intimate Environment: Exploring Marriage and the Family* (Boston, Little Brown, 1978)

Skynner, A. C. R., *One Flesh Separate Persons* (London, Constable, 1976)

Social Services Policy Forum, *Who Owns Welfare?* (London, NISW, 1992)

Spong, J. S., *Living in Sin?* (New York, Harper/Collins, 1990)

Stanley, L. and Wise, S., *Breaking Out: Feminist Consciousness and Feminist Research* (London, Routledge & Kegan Paul, 1983)

Stuart, E., *Daring to speak love's name* (London, Hamilton, 1992)

Tanner, D. M., *The Lesbian Couple* (Lexington Mass., Lexington Books, 1978)

Tatham, P., *The Makings of Maleness* (London, Karnac Books, 1992)

Teachman, J. and Polonko, K., 'Cohabitation and Marital Stability in the United States' in *Social Forces*, vol 69 (1990), pp. 207–20

Thomas, L., *The Lives of a Cell* (New York, Bantam, 1975)

Thomson, E. and Colella, V., 'Cohabitational Marital Stability: Quality or Commitment?' in *Journal of Marriage and the Family*, vol 54 (1992), pp. 259–67

Thornes, B. and Collard, J., *Who Divorces?* (London, Routledge & Kegan Paul, 1979)

Thornton, A., 'Influence of the Marital History of Parents on the Marital and Cohabitational Experiences of Children' in *American Sociological Review*, vol 96 (1991), pp. 868–94

Tilby, A., 'In Celebration of Sex' in *Contact*, vol 107 (1992), pp. 14–18

Toman, W. T., *Family Constellation* (2nd edn, New York, Springer, 1969)

Thomson, C. and Colella, V., 'Cohabitation and Marital Stability' in *Journal of Marriage and the family*, vol 54 (1992), pp. 259–67

Townsend, P., '*The Poor and the Poorer*', (University of Bristol, Statistical Monitoring Unit, Dept. of Social Policy and Social Planning, in *The Guardian*, 28 March 1991)

Trussell, J. et al., 'Union dissolution in Sweden' in J. Trussell et al., *Demographic applications of event-history analysis* (Oxford, Clarendon Press, 1992)

Tyler, P. A., 'Assortative Mating and Human Variation' in *Scientific Progress*, vol 72 (1988), pp. 451–66

Vaughan, P., *The Monogamy Myth* (London, Grafton, 1989)

Vetere, A. and Gale, A., *Ecological Studies of Family Life* (Chichester, Wiley, 1987)

Visher, E. B. and Visher, J., *Step Families: A Guide to Working with Step-Parents and Step-Children* (Brunner/Mazel, 1979)

Waldergrave, C., *Just Therapy* (Dulwich Centre Newsletter, No. 1., 1990)

Wallerstein, J. S. and Kelly, J. R., *Surviving the Break up* (London, Grant McIntyre, 1980)

Walrond-Skinner, S., *Family Therapy: The Treatment of Natural Systems* (London, Routledge & Kegan Paul, 1976)

—— *Family Matters: The Pastoral Care of Personal Relationships* (London, SPCK, 1988)

—— 'Creative Forms of Family Life' in Furlong (1988), op. cit.

Walrond-Skinner, S. and Watson, D., *Ethical Issues in Family Therapy* (London, Routledge & Kegan Paul, 1987)

Watson, R., 'Premarital Cohabitation vs. Traditional Courtship and Subsequent Marital Adjustment' in *Family Relations*, vol 36 (1987), pp. 193–7

Watzlawick P. et al., *Pragmatics of Human Communication* (New York, W. W. Norton, 1968)

Watzlawick, P., Weakland, J. and Fisch, R., *Principles of Problem Formation Problem Resolution* (New York, W. W. Norton, 1974)

Webster, A., 'Revolutionising Christian Sexual Ethics: A Feminist Perspective' in *Contact*, vol 107 (1992), pp. 25–9

Weeks, G. (ed), *Promoting Change through Paradoxical Therapy* (Illinois, Dow Jones-Erwin, 1984)

Weeks, J., *Sexuality and its Discontents* (London, Routledge & Kegan Paul, 1985)

West, A., 'Sex and Salvation: A Christian Feminist Study of 1 Cor. 6:12—7:39' in *Modern Churchman*, vol 29 (1987), no 3, pp. 17–24

White, D. and Woollett, A., *Families – A Context for Development* (London, The Falmer Press, 1992)

White, J., *Dynamics of Family Development* (New York, Guildford Press, 1991)

White, J. M., 'Premarital Cohabitation and Marital Stability in Canada' in *Journal of Marriage and the Family*, vol 49 (1987), pp. 641–7

Whybrew, L. E., *Minister, Wife and Church: Unlocking the Triangles* (Washington, The Alban Institute, 1984)

Wicks, M., *Families in the Future* (Study Commission on the Family, 1983)

Wilden, Antony, *System and Structure* (London, Tavistock, 1972)

Worsley, P., *Introducing Sociology* (2nd edn, Harmondsworth, Penguin, 1977)

Wyn, M., *Family Policy* (London, Michael Joseph, 1972)

Other Publications:

Faith in the City (London, Church House Publishing, 1985)

Living Faith in the City (London, Church House Publishing, 1990)

All passages from the Bible quoted in this book are taken from the *Good News Bible*.